Advance praise for
Constitutional Illusions and Anchoring Truths

"Hadley Arkes's *Constitutional Illusions and Anchoring Truths* clearly illustrates the value, famously emphasized by John Stuart Mill, of attending to important, carefully considered – if also unconventional, unsettling, or contrarian – arguments. Professor Arkes remains one of the law's most gifted and rewarding prose stylists."

– R. George Wright, Indiana University School of Law, Indianapolis

"Hadley Arkes is a well-known scholar, a superb stylist, and perpetual gadfly disturbing the peace of scholars on both the right and the left. *Constitutional Illusions and Anchoring Truths* continues his project of elaborating a 'natural law' approach to jurisprudence, which argues that implicit in widely accepted forms of legal reasoning is a commitment to certain principles of reason that transcend the text itself. He develops his argument through discussions of ex post facto laws, the Eleventh Amendment, substantive due process, prior restraint, and the Bob Jones case, and nothing indicates Arkes's skill as a writer and thinker better than his ability to find novel and fascinating perspectives on cases talked about endlessly by others. Constantly thought-provoking, chock-full of original insights, and elegantly written, this book is a powerful reminder to everyone that written law cannot be interpreted without reference to the fundamental moral understandings within which it is embedded."

– Christopher Wolfe, Marquette University

"In his extraordinary book, Arkes's powerful intellect, wit, encyclopedic knowledge, and grace are all on full display as he takes us through a number of landmark cases that we thought we knew – cases whose meaning, we thought, was firmly settled – only to have him show us that we do not know them as we thought we did. He shows us what a difference it makes if we read these cases with more attentiveness to their reasoning and a clearer sense of the logical properties of their propositions. In short, he shows us by his example how we, too, can be freed from the tyranny of understanding landmark cases through the eyes of others."

– Ralph Rossum, Claremont McKenna College

Constitutional Illusions and Anchoring Truths

This book stands against the current of judgments long settled in the schools of law in regard to classic cases such as *Lochner v. New York, Near v. Minnesota*, the Pentagon Papers case, and *Bob Jones University v. United States.* Professor Hadley Arkes takes as his subject concepts long regarded as familiar, settled principles in our law – "prior restraints," ex post facto laws – and he shows that there is actually a mystery about them, that their meaning is not as settled or clear as we have supposed. Those mysteries have often given rise to illusions or at least a series of puzzles in our law. They have at times acted as a lens through which we view the landscape of the law. We often see what the lens has made us used to seeing, instead of seeing what is actually there. Arkes tries to show, in this text, that the logic of the natural law provides the key to this chain of puzzles.

Hadley Arkes is Edward Ney Professor of American Institutions and Jurisprudence in the Department of Political Science at Amherst College. He is the author of six books, most notably *First Things* (1986), *Beyond the Constitution* (1990), and *Natural Rights and the Right to Choose* (Cambridge University Press, 2002). His articles have appeared in professional journals as well as the *Wall Street Journal*, the *Weekly Standard*, *National Review*, and *First Things*, a journal that took its name from his book of that title.

Constitutional Illusions and Anchoring Truths

The Touchstone of the Natural Law

Hadley Arkes

CAMBRIDGE
UNIVERSITY PRESS

CAMBRIDGE UNIVERSITY PRESS
Cambridge, New York, Melbourne, Madrid, Cape Town, Singapore,
São Paulo, Delhi, Dubai, Tokyo, Mexico City

Cambridge University Press
32 Avenue of the Americas, New York, NY 10013-2473, USA

www.cambridge.org
Information on this title: www.cambridge.org/9780521732086

First published 2010
Reprinted 2010

A catalog record for this publication is available from the British Library.

Library of Congress Cataloging in Publication Data

Arkes, Hadley.
Constitutional illusions and anchoring truths : the touchstone of the natural
law / Hadley Arkes.
   p.   cm.
Includes bibliographical references and index.
ISBN 978-0-521-51817-8 (hardback) – ISBN 978-0-521-73208-6 (pbk.)
1. Constitutional law – United States.   2. Natural law.   I. Title.
KF4550.A77   2010
340′.112 – dc22   2009028972

ISBN 978-0-521-51817-8 Hardback
ISBN 978-0-521-73208-6 Paperback

For Michael Petrino '68 and Michael Petrino '03,
Jay Beech '67 and Scott Beech '99,
Doug Neff '70 and John Neff '09
Kevin Conway '80 and Jack '10 and Ryan '12

From the professor blessed by their presence in class,
   And by their counsel in later years

Contents

Acknowledgments

At different stages in the work that brought forth these essays I was sustained by grants provided by the Lynne and Harry Bradley Foundation in Milwaukee, Wisconsin, and by the Earhart Foundation in Ann Arbor, Michigan. But there are certain things I would not want overlooked in a sweeping gesture of thanks. I must record a deep, enduring gratitude here to the late Michael Joyce (of the Bradley Foundation) and to David Kennedy and Ingrid Gregg, who have served as presidents of the Earhart Foundation. Mike, David, and Ingrid did not merely provide timely support for the work recorded here; they have been there for me in every season. It may be hard to convey, but it was palpably present: the buoying effect of the confidence that David and Ingrid were quick to affirm, and steady in sustaining, for virtually all of my projects. And now, as they set about the business of winding down the foundation, I wish them the best for the next phase of their lives, and for the projects yet to come.

But in recording words of gratitude, I would really be remiss if I did not say a special word for Lewis Bateman, my editor at Cambridge University Press. Few writers are blessed with the kind of devotion and savvy attentiveness that Lew has shown for my work. He reads my manuscripts against an understanding of the fuller body of my work; he grasps at once what I am doing, what I am saying – and where precisely the new pages fit in with the project I've been developing over thirty years. This book would not be presented to the public in its current form and finish without his guidance and his unflagging support.

Introduction

The Anchoring Common Sense and the Puzzles of the Law

It might have been struck off in Verona. Or at least, that was the first inference likely to spring to mind, for the statute sounded as though it had been drafted in response to Romeo and Juliet, that it had been framed in contemplation of a city riven by small wars, with factions and families set off against one another. It smacked, that is, of a place "where civil blood makes civil hands unclean." And indeed, it had come from a city in Italy in the late Renaissance – in the fifteenth century – but it was from Bologna, and it decreed "that whoever drew blood in the streets should be punished with the utmost severity." Blackstone had noted the case in his *Commentaries on the Laws of England*, and he reported the judgment, reached after a long debate, that the statute was "not to extend to the surgeon, who opened the vein of a person that fell down in the street with a fit."[1] That the question should arise at all is a kind of testament to the enduring credulity of human beings – or the powerful need many people have to follow the rigid letter of the law rather than seek counsel in their own judgment, not guided by anything set down in the law.

For many people that diffidence may reflect a proper doubt about their own resources of judgment when left unguided or uninstructed. But the case was cited by Blackstone, and it was drawn in turn from Samuel Pufendorf's classic study of the law of nations. The example was cited in both of these venerable sources precisely because it was understood at once that the law made no sense when it was applied to the doctor using his arts to save a human life. The case was used, that is, by the classic commentators on the

---

[1] William Blackstone, *Commentaries on the Laws of England* (Oxford: Clarendon Press, 1765), Bk. I, p. 60. I am using here the edition published by the University of Chicago Press in 1979, with a copy of the original plates and preserving the same pagination.

law, to make a point that runs counter to the doctrines of postmodernism, or to the dressed up versions of moral relativism that put themselves forward in our own time under the title of "theories of law." The classic commentators understood that the positive law, the law that was "posited," or written down in statutes, could not exhaust the definition of justice. It could not possibly take account of all of the facts and circumstances that could make a difference for a moral judgment, a judgment on the rightness or wrongness, the justice or injustice, of the situation at hand. The classic commentators knew that there were serious limits to the law, but they also assumed that neither the law nor its practitioners would be witless. The law sprang from deeper principles of justice or moral understanding; and when the law itself, in its narrow focus, seemed to confront a case beyond its terms, or a situation beyond the imagining of its drafters, those deeper principles of the law might still supply guidance. And so, Blackstone offered the example of a law, passed by Parliament, assigning to a certain man the authority "to try all causes, that arise within his manor of Dale":

> [Y]et, if a cause should arise in which he himself is a party, the act is construed not to extend to that; because it is unreasonable that any man should determine his own quarrel.[2]

Blackstone would commonly refer to "the laws of reason and nature" as he sought to explain the grounds of judgment. We know, of course, that there are some tangled philosophic problems behind those innocent terms, "reason and nature." We know that people could invoke "nature" while not being entirely clear as to whether they were offering generalizations about the way that most men, most of the time, tend to behave, or whether they were offering "first principles" or axioms, which have the quality of "necessary truths."[3] But in either event, there was a certain confidence that there were things in the domain of moral judgment that were accessible to our reason. Propositions about right and wrong were not merely matters of the most personal and subjective taste. Certain things in this domain were indeed true, which is to say, objectively true, true for others as well as ourselves. And at the very least, a lifetime of reflection on the conditions of justice or the principles of right was not thought to impair judges in the exercise of that judgment. That they were only human, that they were given to mistakes and corruption, merely confirmed the setting and conditions of the law. That state

[2] *Ibid.*, at 91.
[3] That critical difference is taken up in my book *First Things* (Princeton: Princeton University Press, 1986), Ch. 4.

of affairs did not call into question the very capacity of human beings to grasp the difference between a plausible and an implausible argument, between a reasonable and a corrupted judgment.

I was delighted, though I shouldn't say surprised, to find that the example of Bologna was cited by one of my favorite jurists of the nineteenth century, the redoubtable Stephen J. Field. The case was *United States v. Kirby* (1868), and it involved an act of Congress, from 1825, directed against persons who "shall knowingly and willfully obstruct or retard the passage of the mail, or of any driver or carrier, or of any horse or carriage carrying the same."[4] Kirby, who was prosecuted under the act, was a sheriff in Kentucky. He had been charged with the duty of executing a warrant for the arrest of one, Farris, who had been charged with murder. Farris happened to be a carrier of mail, and on the day of the arrest he was on a steamboat with the mail. Kirby had called to his aid a small posse of men, and together they entered the steamboat with the purpose of arresting Farris. As it was noted later, in the report of the Supreme Court, Kirby and the posse "entered the steamboat Buell to make the arrest, and only used such force as was necessary to accomplish this end; and . . . they acted without any intent or purpose to obstruct or retard the mail, or the passage of the steamer." When Kirby's act was set, though, against a literal rendering of the statute – a rendering, that is, detached from any sense of the moral purpose of the statute – Kirby could be prosecuted for "obstruct[ing] or retard[ing] the mail."

But Justice Field, writing for the Court, found it incomprehensible that Kirby could be charged with any intention of "knowingly and willfully" obstructing the mails. His purpose was not to do anything with the mail, but to make a lawful arrest. The arrest might indeed have caused a certain inter-ference with the mails, but people of ordinary sense could ordinarily make distinctions between interferences that were "justified" or "unjustified." As Field remarked, then,

> All laws should receive a sensible construction. General terms should be so limited in their application as not to lead to injustice, oppression, or an absurd consequence. It will always, therefore, be presumed that the legisla-ture intended exceptions to its language, which would avoid results of this character. The reason of the law in such cases should prevail over its letter.[5]

This bizarre reading of the law might be dismissed, of course, by some com-mentators as a throwback to an earlier, less sophisticated time. But they would

---

[4] 74 U.S. 482.
[5] *Ibid.*, at 486–87.

be making a notable mistake, for they would discount the way in which the same fallacies show a remarkable staying power among jurists, especially those who are "winging it" in their moral and jural reasoning. The most notable example cropped up in the spring of 2003, as Justice O'Connor wrote for her colleagues in addressing, again, the problem of burning crosses, this time in the case of *Virginia v. Black.*[6] O'Connor recognized that a burning cross was established, quite clearly, in our experience, as a gesture of assault. We might say, from another angle, that the meaning of this symbol was rather firmly established in our "ordinary language," or the way in which people commonly understand the meaning of words and symbols. In the case at hand, arising from Virginia, youngsters had burned a cross in the backyard of a black family newly moved into Virginia Beach, and in a companion case, a cross was burned at an outdoor meeting of the Ku Klux Klan in Carroll County. A statute in Virginia barred the burning of crosses with "an intent to intimidate a person or group of persons." The Court showed its willingness to break away from an earlier decision on the burning of crosses, and acknowledge more readily now that this gesture of assault could be restricted under the First Amendment even though it was a species of symbolic expression.

But in a curious turn, the Court professed to be more willing to sustain convictions in these cases because the statute did not seek to ban speech directed at only certain favored classes of victims. That had been the concern animating Justice Scalia, eleven years earlier, when he wrote for the Court in striking down an ordinance in St. Paul, Minnesota, forbidding the burning of crosses.[7] Faced then with another case, in 2003, the judges found ingredients in the case that meshed with Scalia's earlier opinion. As Justice O'Connor noted, the burning of crosses had been used in the past against Catholics and Jews, as well as blacks; and the statute did not tie the act of intimidation to any particular group of victims. Still, over the last fifty years, the burning of crosses has been understood rather plainly as a symbol of assault against black people. Nevertheless, the Court decided to strike down the conviction of Barry Black, leading the meeting of the Ku Klux Klan, because the Supreme Court of Virginia had interpreted the statute with this rule of construction: that "the act of burning a cross alone, with no evidence of intent to intimidate, will nonetheless suffice for arrest and prosecution." As Justice Scalia pointed out in dissent, the instruction offered to a jury did not bar evidence that would overcome the presumption, and permit the defendants to show that they had

---

[6] 538 U.S. 343 (2003).
[7] *R.A.V. v. St. Paul*, 505 U.S. 377, and see 380, 396 (1992).

not intended any act of intimidation. Yet, even Scalia was disposed to send the cases back to get a clearer reading of the intent of the people burning crosses. What made the issue more complicated for Justice O'Connor was the sense that not every act of burning a cross necessarily marked an intent to assault or intimidate. As O'Connor observed, "Cross burnings have appeared in movies such as Mississippi Burning, and in plays such as the stage adaptation of Sir Walter Scott's The Lady of the Lake."

But with that move of seeming open-mindedness to the world, the Justice detached herself from the moral reasoning that must ever be a part of the common sense that is incorporated in statutes – as in the case of Bologna in the fifteenth century. In the classic case of *Chaplinsky v. New Hampshire* (1942),[8] Justice Murphy described that category of insulting or "fighting words" – "those which by their very utterance inflict injury or incite to an immediate breach of the peace."[9] They were words or symbols, once again, clearly fixed in our language, at any given time, words such as "nigger," "kike," "wop" (and, not so clearly, words like "meter maid" or "telemarketer"). Even people unbedecked with college degrees, people who made their livings, say, in driving trucks or digging ditches, show the most acute sense of when they are being insulted or even subtly disparaged. And yet, at the same time, people commonly understood what linguistics also taught: context was utterly necessary to meaning. Justice Murphy caught that sense of things when he referred to words spoken "without a disarming smile." A person of ordinary wit would understand the difference between people cavorting in Nazi uniforms at the annual satire of the Harvard Lampoon, as compared with a bunch of scruffy characters parading with Nazi banners and uniforms in a Jewish neighborhood in Skokie, Illinois. In the same way, people could grasp, at once, the difference between a hostile mob and the crowd that welcomed home the Boston Red Sox after they had won the World Series. When a statute bars the burning of crosses, targeted at classes of persons, no one with a modicum of wit could suppose that the statute was doing anything but condemning and forbidding. What it figured to forbid were wrongful acts, acts animated by the intention of assaulting or intimidating. And no one could have supposed for a moment that the statute meant to forbid, say, the burning of crosses in a theatrical production or a film such as "Mississippi Burning."

In other words, the legislators were not acting in a random way, without moral common sense – and neither, as it turned out, had the assailants. Mark Russell once told the story of a family of Unitarians who moved into

---

[8] 315 U.S. 568.
[9] *Ibid.*, at 571–72.

a southern town. In the middle of the night some bigots burned a large question mark on their lawn. Something like that might have taken place if the young men in Virginia Beach had chosen, say, to paint swastikas on the house of the black family. There would have been an act of defacing property, but the assailants might have been counted as too witless to know what they were doing in carrying out acts of intimidation. The assailants in Virginia did not suffer that distraction or confusion, and they did not choose at random from the symbols available to them in our language. They chose a burning cross, planting it in the yard of a black family, and that joining of moves should have been sufficient to mark the understanding of what they were plainly doing. The Supreme Court in Virginia had not slipped then into carelessness when it offered as a presumptive rule that "the act of burning a cross alone, with no evidence of intent to intimidate, will nonetheless suffice for arrest and prosecution" – with the defendants free, of course, to rebut that presumption. And unless justices of the Supreme Court were consumed with theories so refined that they apply only to a closed system of their own, there should have been no need to send the cases back for clarification in a lower court. The meaning of the act should have been plain enough to be judged by people of ordinary sense, who find themselves every day making discriminations among the acts that are threatening or harmless, justified or unjustified.

And so, in a scene quite familiar, a person arrives home from work and discovers that the street containing his house has been blocked off, and his entrance barred. It makes the most notable and elementary difference as to whether it was barred, say, by the fire department, because firefighters are putting out a blaze; or whether it was barred through the obstruction of a gang, closing off the street to its enemies. In common parlance, we can distinguish between cases in which the access is temporarily barred for a purpose that was *justified* or *unjustified*. The Constitution does not seek to bar all searches and seizures, but only searches that are unreasonable or unjustified. As I sought to show then in another place, the task of judgment, in our constitutional law, persistently moves us away from the text, or from a gross description of the act, and it moves us to the commonsense understanding of the principles that guide these judgments: the principles that help us in making those distinctions between the things that are justified or unjustified.

As we make that move to the ground of our judgments, we find ourselves moving back to those deeper principles that informed and guided the judgment of the Founders as they went about the task of framing the

Constitution. I argued sometime back, in a book called *Beyond the Cons-titution*,[10] that there was a need to appeal beyond the text of the Constitution to those "first principles," those principles antecedent to the Constitution, if we were to apply the Constitution sensibly to the cases that arise in our law. As I sought to argue, that kind of move requires a certain practice, or a kind of reflection that is distinctly philosophic. It involves a certain style of principled reasoning, a style that was cultivated quite handsomely by the jurists in the Founding generation, and even by jurists in Abraham Lincoln's generation, even though many of them did not have the advantages of formal schooling.

In the course of making that argument, I offered as a dramatic case in point the original argument over the Bill of Rights. It seems to have slipped from the memory of most of our people – indeed, if it was ever lodged in that memory – that there was quite a serious debate about the Bill of Rights at the time of the Founding. The reservations about a Bill of Rights did not spring from people who were hostile to rights, but quite the reverse. There was a serious concern, held by some of the most thoughtful among the framers, that the Bill of Rights would have the effect of narrowing, or truncating, the rights that were protected under the Constitution. And it would have that effect mainly because it would misinstruct the American people about the ground of their rights. It has become quite common in our own time to hear people speak of "those rights we have *through* the First Amendment." But the understanding contained in that passage reveals precisely the problem. When we speak of those rights we have "through the First Amendment," does that not rather imply that the Amendment was the source of those rights? In the absence of the First Amendment, would we not have had those rights?

The Bill of Rights ran the risk of shaping the understanding of citizens and lawyers to this fallacy: that our rights did not spring from nature, from the things that marked our character as human beings, but that they arose merely from the law that was "posited" or written down. The rights mentioned in the Bill of Rights would be thought to have then the standing of rights, or their claim to solemnity, precisely because they had been written down, or stipulated in an inventory of "rights." The assumption would engage itself slowly, but steadily, that the things written down were far more important as rights than the things left unmentioned. In this subtle shift we find the essential move from natural rights to positive rights, from rights grounded in the nature of human beings as "moral agents," to the sense rather of rights that have standing as rights because we have decided, as a people, to confer

[10] (Princeton: Princeton University Press, 1990).

them on one another. In the age of a relativism so portable and facile, so deeply absorbed that it is rarely even noticed, many people by now have made the shift to the latter understanding without being aware that they had made any shift at all. Much less are they aware that they had made a decisive moral break from the premises of the American Founders.

In recovering this sense of the problem, I was trying to make the case for recovering at the same time the understanding of that Founding generation, for those lawyers and political men revealed furnishings of mind quite strikingly different from those of our own day. Consider the contrast: on the one hand a group of lawyers who have memorized a list of rights, set down in the first eight amendments to the Constitution; on the other hand, a generation of lawyers who had cultivated the art of tracing their judgments back to first principles and anchoring truths. There is no need for me here to renew the argument over the Bill of Rights; but there is ever a need to restore the remarkable capacity of that first generation of jurists to trace judgments back to first principles. My purpose in this book is to draw again on that perspective, cultivated long ago, for the sake of casting new light on parts of our Constitution that have remained in a curious shadow. These clauses, or doctrines, in the Constitution have become obscure to us, not because they are hidden and unfamiliar. They have become obscure, rather, because they have been placed beyond our sight, or beyond the kind of sight that looks closely, in a probing way, as though it were looking for the first time. These parts of our constitutional law have become hidden to us, even before our eyes, because they have been closed off to our inspection by understandings too quickly and complacently settled. But if we looked upon these clauses or doctrines with a fresh eye, or if we treated them as puzzles, we would find that they bear a certain mystery that beckons us in. If we respond to that beckoning, we would find, I think, that we would be drawn back to the root, to the philosophic ground of our understanding, before we could finally unlock the puzzles here, in the parts of the Constitution that we have thought, in the past, most firmly and serenely settled.

To take one notable example, the question arose during the Constitutional Convention in Philadelphia as to whether the framers should descend to the exercise of specifying particular kinds of rights, such as the right not to suffer the imposition of laws made "ex post facto." Roughly speaking, those were laws made after the fact, imposing penalties or enlarging them. And with this kind of a move, the law would make punishable something that had not been considered wrongful before the passage of the law. Or at least that was, by and large, the sense of the problem with "ex post facto laws." And yet, when the proposal was made to mention ex post facto laws explicitly, in the body of the Constitution, both Oliver Ellsworth and James Wilson entered some rather refined reservations. It was not that they doubted in the least the wrong of ex post facto laws. It was rather that the wrong was so obvious, and so widely known, that it was almost embarrassing to set it down as though the framers were proclaiming news.[11]

If there was any principle of constitutional government that had, for the Founders, a necessary force and a crisp definition, it was the principle that barred ex post facto laws. And yet, as I will try to show, there is a certain puzzle about the meaning of "ex post facto" laws, which emerges as soon as we look more closely into the subject. We come to discover, for example, that there are many instances, in our experience, of laws applying *retrospectively.* The fact that they administer surprises, and catch people unaware, has not been regarded as a decisive count against them. Consider – as we will later – that unlucky fellow, the first man to be sued because he had given herpes to his partner in sex. There had been no statutes or laws on the subject. No court had found people liable in the past for affecting others with the virus. And yet, courts came to the judgment *that he should have known.* What exactly he should have known and how he should have known it – those things I'll consider in due course in the opening chapter. I would also underscore the point that the law had placed these burdens of "knowing," not on people trained in the law, or people in high office, but on ordinary folk, of no special distinction, who were simply functioning in the world. Still, there are stories to tell in the ranks of the celebrities as well. During the 1980s, some rather important people, in offices of state, were embarrassed by certain laws, bristling with moral consequence, which were enacted and enforced *after the fact.* It is curious that even the engagement of celebrities did not seem to draw much attention to the fact that they had become the targets of ex post facto laws. The matter seemed to go strangely unnoticed by the world of law – but on that, more later.

I would suggest, then, that we treat the matter as the puzzle it is, and open ourselves to the mystery contained in the problem. For when we do, we find that the strands or the paths of reflection will lead us back to a philosophic root that runs even deeper. In the course of following out those paths, we may also illuminate something more about the conditions of constitutional government and that creature who is destined, by nature, to live in a *polis*, an association governed by law. To deepen the problem, I'd suggest that some of the same points of fascination can be found by treating, as problematic, other

---

[11] *The Records of the Federal Convention of 1787*, ed. Max Farrand (rev. ed. 1937) (New Haven: Yale University Press, 1966), Vol. 2, p. 376 [August 22].

notions that have been long settled. One such famous notion, passing from concepts into legend, has been the notion of "prior restraints" on publication. That term achieved a remarkable standing only in 1931, in the classic case of *Near v. Minnesota*. But by the time we reached the Pentagon Papers case in 1971, it was clear that the term had a near iconic standing. In that sweep of development, all too uncritical, something of moral substance was lost. I propose to take another, critical look at those cases, with the willingness to argue that the decisions in those cases might actually have been wrong; that there really could not be a plausible principle of constitutional law that rules out, categorically, all species of restraints in advance of publication. In that respect, I find myself running against the dominant lines of interpretation, which have hardened now into orthodoxies in the schools of law.

And just to make that point even clearer, I take the occasion, in one chapter, to offer, not an apology, but a defense of *Lochner v. New York* (1905). That case seems to inspire an even-handed condemnation, from the political Right as well as the Left. Yet, if we could detach ourselves from the slogans built up over the years, and look at the case again, it would become apparent, I think, that the cast of argument in *Lochner*, with Justice Rufus Peckham's opinion, marks the cast of our law today. For Justice Hugo Black and the judges of the New Deal, it became important to reject *Lochner* and discredit its principles. But after *Griswold v. Connecticut* in 1965, the Court brought forth a new jurisprudence, grounded in notions of "privacy" and personal autonomy, and that new doctrine would soon encompass a "right to abortion." Justice Black was a notable dissenter in the Griswold case, and it should have been apparent to anyone with the slenderest acquaintance with the law that the decisions on privacy and abortion had to rest on the most thoroughgoing rejection of the liberal jurisprudence of the New Deal. That is not to say that the jurisprudence of Rufus Peckham and the Old Court would have brought forth a "right to abortion." But it does suggest that any serious defense of rights will find its way back to the logic of natural rights, and there the understanding of Peckham and the Old Court would provide a more coherent fit. In fact, if we look again, and look anew – if we look with a willingness actually to read Peckham's opinions – we would find, in Peckham and his so-called conservative colleagues, a far more expansive view of personal freedom than the view we associate with the liberal judges of the New Deal. And if the question of the case arose for us in another form – say, in restricting the hours of work for assistant professors, or for people spending long hours over keyboards – the response of the judges is virtually certain to follow the lines of Peckham's understanding in *Lochner*. Peckham and *Lochner* are remarkably closer to us than most commentators seem willing to acknowledge, for as I will try to show, the understanding of the law in *Lochner* provides the template, or cast, of the law in our own day. It is the law we would choose again for ourselves whenever we are given the occasion to choose.

It is not my purpose to entertain with paradox, but it is part of my design to entertain by drawing the reader to a series of genuine puzzles that spring from our constitutional law. They are puzzles that have drawn my own deep interest over the years, and I decided finally to collect them, in a series of chapters that would offer the occasion to reflect on these cases in a more searching way, and pursue the threads that run through them. But the point that bears repeating is that the thread that runs through them, and connects everything, is the move back to first principles and the moral ground of the law. I would point out then that those threads, and the design, were there from the beginning, and it is mainly an accident that the first four essays seem to be shaped for quite different occasions. The first was a Bradley Lecture at the law school of Notre Dame in February 1999. The second was a lecture offered in Washington in April 2006 to launch the new Ralph McInerney Center, in honor of the legendary teacher, Thomist, novelist. The third was offered as a lecture at Princeton, in February 1997, as part of the celebration of the 250th anniversary of the university.

The lecture at Notre Dame offered me a chance to explore some of those understandings long thought settled in the law – notions such as "bills of attainder" and "ex post facto laws," laws casting blame and responsibility after the acts of wrongdoing had been committed. As I pursued the puzzle, the solution could be unlocked only with the understandings contained in the natural law. I could be counted, in my writings over the years, as a contributor to that project on the revival or restoration of natural law. John Finnis's book *Natural Law & Natural Rights* (1980) was an important marker here. My own version followed a different path, closer to the summons of my late teacher Leo Strauss in his *Natural Right and History* (1953). But my own work was far more precisely shaped by his devoted student Harry Jaffa in *Crisis of the House Divided* and the vast body of his writings. My book *First Things* (1986) offered another statement in this accumulating series of works, and yet it was not often noted as a work in natural law. For the advent of the McInerney Center, nothing seemed more apt than sounding anew the case for natural law. This launching of the Center offered then the occasion for me to try my own restatement of the issue. In the fall of 2008, I was invited to offer my latest refinement of this essay as a plenary address at the Maritain Society, meeting in Boston. The society is filled with colleagues who have made careers in the study of Thomas Aquinas, and it is fair to say that they are amply familiar with the literature on natural law. The reaction of this audience was buoying. Their response finally confirmed my sense that this essay should be part of a manuscript in which the key to a series of enduring puzzles in the law would be found in the natural law.

And so, while the occasions were various, along with the wines, I hope the reader will not be distracted by the sudden changes of scene, but notice, in these essays, a student of the law and politics pursuing the threads of the same set of concerns. I have brought together then a collection of puzzles I have found deeply engaging, but to switch the figure, the key that unlocks the various puzzles is to be found by returning to the axioms of the law, in the first principles of our moral judgment.

Part of my theme in these essays is to point up the fact that a Constitution, with settled understandings, and supposedly settled principles, may keep generating, for us, unsettling surprises. But that is in part the charm, and the deep magic, of real principles. With their abstract sweep, they can be detached from the instances of daily life that are more familiar to us, and suddenly cover cases we had never anticipated. And yet, more than that: They bring forth, in novel cases, implications that we had never seen lurking in them. That task of drawing them out may often be bracing, and yet it may also be jolting. It may be the source, as I say, of surprises that unsettle. I trust that the reader will see, from the outset, that my purpose is not to keep things unsettled, but to settle again, settle more surely – but with the awareness that the same questions, at another time, may be opened yet again. We may suddenly look at these doctrines of the law from another angle, as I seek to do here. Still, I hope the reader may find something either consoling or persuasive in the notion of settling judgments on a ground rendered ever firmer by "first principles," and yet preserving through it all a certain willingness to find puzzles lurking in cases and doctrines that were once thought to be comfortably settled. With that sense of the matter, I would beckon the reader in and consider, as I did at the law school at Notre Dame, the unsettling surprises that may still be served up by the most settled of constitutions.

One

On the Novelties of an Old Constitution: Settled Principles and Unsettling Surprises

There was a moment, in Evelyn Waugh's *Brideshead Revisited*, when the young, reflective, eccentric Lord Brideshead pondered aloud over the chapel attached to the family castle. Young Brideshead turned, in his thoughts, to the quality of the chapel as a work of architecture, and he took advantage of the presence of Charles Ryder, who was a student of art. "You are an artist, Ryder," he said, "what do you think of [the chapel] aesthetically.... Is it Good Art?"

"Well, I don't quite know what you mean," said Ryder. "I think it's quite a good example of its period. Probably in eighty years it will be greatly admired."

"But surely," said Brideshead, in the voice of Aristotle or Kant, "surely it can't be good twenty years ago, and good in eighty years, and not good now?"

Ryder spoke with the convictions of the modern historicist: He would not claim to speak about the things that are "good" or "bad" outside that epoch in which he lived and cast his judgments. Judgments of right and wrong, in aesthetics as well as politics, were always "relative," in this view, to the place and the time. He would not speak across historical epochs and pronounce on the goodness or badness of the buildings that were built in ancient Athens or in Paris at the turn of the century. He would not speak, that is, about any things that might be enduringly good. Brideshead seemed to grasp almost intuitively the logic that had to attach to the notion of "commending" a "good." It was a matter of moving beyond "personal feelings," to the grounds of reason that made a thing "good" for others as well as ourselves. It was a shift from notions of good that are entirely personal, subjective, and perhaps ephemeral, to notions of a good that are reasoned, impersonal, universal, and far more enduring.

In our own time, the notion of a "living Constitution" has been affected, in turn, by the "historicism" that pervades the world of letters. The Constitution is "adapted," as they say, to our own age. That can be done either by applying the principles of the Constitution to new cases or by suggesting that some of the provisions of the Constitution no longer fit the sensibilities of our time. Hence, the remarkable finding, on the part of Justices Thurgood Marshall and William Brennan, that capital punishment cannot be constitutional any longer, by the advanced views of our own generation, even though the Constitution contains several references to punishment for capital crimes. The Constitution also assigns, explicitly, to Congress the authority to alter the appellate jurisdiction of the federal courts. But when Congress showed signs of making use of that provision, on the matter of abortion, commentators came forth to suggest that this part of the Constitution had been repealed by the march of time. Professors of law offered the opinion, solemnly, that this part of the Constitution could no longer, decently, be used by the Congress even though it remained a part of the text.

But we might ask, in an echo of the young Lord Brideshead, how could the Constitution be good in one period and not good in another? If the principles of the Constitution prescribe what is right and bar what is wrong, why would they not enjoin or forbid the same things fifty years from now as well as today? They would enjoin the same things if those principles are true principles – if they name the things that are truly right or wrong. And so, if the Constitution condemns and forbids "bills of attainder" or ex post facto laws, would we not assume fifty years from now that the Constitution still meant to stamp these things as wrong and forbid them to us? We may discover that there is more of a mystery about these terms than we usually suppose – that they are not quite as clear, or as crisp in their edges, as we have been inclined to assume – and yet, we don't suffer a moment's doubt that whatever they are, bills of attainder or ex post facto laws were things that the Constitution meant to forbid.

These considerations may be elementary, and yet they may at times be elusive, and the temptation to evade these axioms may be seductive. They were especially seductive during the Depression, when legislators sought ever more inventive ways of canceling debts and disguising a rather brute, unromantic fact: that they were, in effect, relieving people of an obligation to return the money they had borrowed from others. The state of Minnesota found a social cause in saving farms from foreclosure and doing it through the device of declaring a moratorium on the foreclosure of mortgages. The sale of the property could be postponed, or there could be an extension in the period for the redemption of the mortgage.[1] This benevolent end was attained by removing, from the lender, the rights he possessed under the original contract for the loan. It barred him, that is, from reclaiming money that was his; money that he had been free to invest in other ways, with more profit and less hazard. What was morally problematic in this arrangement was a point that could be obscured by the high-minded rhetoric. Cicero had crystallized the moral problem long ago, in *De Officiis* (Of Duties): What is the meaning, he asked, of an "abolition of debts, except that you buy a farm with my money; that you have the farm, and I have not my money?"[2]

But a Court that did not wish to appear unfeeling, or too rigid to notice the Depression, was willing to bend, or find some angle from which to view the statute in a more defensible light. On the face of things, the statute looked to be a rather plain violation of that stricture, in Article I, Section 10, that states should pass no laws "impairing the Obligation of Contracts." Still, a majority of the Court was prepared to believe that this command, in the Constitution, could not be so unequivocal, or so indifferent to circumstances. The judges thought, in fine, that the Constitution could bear a certain degree of tinkering, or a *slight* impairment of the obligation of a contract, for the sake of a public benefit. Chief Justice Hughes invoked that memorable passage from John Marshall in *McCulloch v. Maryland*: "We must never forget that it is a *constitution* we are expounding." That Constitution was "intended to endure for ages to come, and consequently, to be adapted to the various crises of human affairs."[3] This famous line of Marshall's would be enduringly invoked, in the years to come, by the proponents of a "living Constitution" – a Constitution so adaptable to its times that the literal provisions of the Constitution could be turned into their contrarieties for the sake of accommodating the politics of the day.

In this manner did Chief Justice Hughes make a nullity of the Contracts Clause through "adaptation": When the honoring of contracts could affect many people adversely, then the Contracts clause could be in a state of tension with "public needs." The Court would then seek "to prevent the perversion of the clause through its use as an instrument to throttle the capacity of the States to protect their fundamental interests." And that new moral understanding would be incorporated in the very notion of the contracts that the

---

[1] See *Home Building & Loan Assoc. v. Blaisdell*, 290 U.S. 398, at 416 (1934).
[2] Cicero, *De Officiis* (Cambridge: Harvard University Press, Loeb edition, 1975), p. 261.
[3] 4 Wheat. 326, at 407 and 415 (1819), cited in *Home Building & Loan Assoc. v. Blaisdell*, *supra*, note 1, at 443. Italics in the original.

Constitution was meant to protect. For then "the reservation of the reason-able exercise of the protective power of the State is read into all contracts."[4] But as Chief Justice Marshall had explained long ago, in *Ogden v. Saunders*, this kind of construction would make a nullity of the very notion of an "obli-gation of contract." For built into every contract now was the possibility that the obligation of the contract could be suspended or dissolved at any moment by the intervention of the legislature. In that event, no contract would be made with the sense that there was an obligation attached to its terms. What-ever an agreement might be called under these new terms, it would certainly not contain the ingredients that defined a "contract." To put it another way, there would no longer be the kinds of "contracts" that the Constitution was meant to protect. In this manner, the provision in the Constitution would be emptied of its meaning in the course of interpreting or "adapting" the document.

Justice George Sutherland could write then, in dissent, with an appeal to rudimentary truths, and he would sound very much like the young Lord Brideshead, in wondering how a thing could be good in one generation and not good at another time: "A provision of the Constitution, it is hardly necessary to say, does not admit of two distinctly opposite interpretations. It does not mean one thing at one time and an entirely different thing at another time."[5] We may quibble over the question of what constitutes an impairment of the obligation of contracts, but there was little question that the Constitution meant to foreclose any tinkering that had, as its purpose, some clever method of undoing that obligation. And so, as Sutherland observed,

> If the contract impairment clause, when framed and adopted, meant that the terms of a contract for the payment of money could not be altered *in vitum* by a state statute enacted for the relief of hardly pressed debtors to the end and with the effect of postponing payment or enforcement during and because of an economic or financial emergency, it is but to state the obvious to say that it means the same now.[6]

It was feckless then, to suggest, with the Chief Justice, that the principle in the Contracts Clause had to be read, with prudence, against the background of an emergency in the country. That clause in the Constitution had been inspired by a time of stress that had been turned into an emergency or a crisis

[4] *Ibid.*, at 443–44.
[5] *Ibid.*, at 448–49.
[6] *Ibid.*, at 449.

precisely because of legislation like the legislation in Minnesota – legislation that sought to deal with hard times by canceling obligations. That legislation had made things notably worse by making it even more hazardous for money to be lent. The consequence had been a withdrawal of credit from anyone but the most creditworthy, and even then, as Sutherland noted, the loans would carry a high premium, with discounts approaching 50 percent. That is, in the most hazardous of times, loans would be made at an interest of almost 100 percent. The provision in the Constitution was meant to forestall these kinds of emergencies by striking at their moral root. Sutherland was on eminently sound ground, then, when he turned back the claim of his colleagues that the Contract Clause had to be accommodated to the emergency of the Depression: "A candid consideration of the history and circumstances which led [to the Contracts Clause] will demonstrate conclusively that it was framed and adopted with the specific and studied purpose of preventing legislation designed to relieve debtors *especially* in time of financial distress."[7]

There was a while, in Washington, when a theater in Georgetown, at midnight every Saturday, would hold a showing of that cult classic, *The Rocky Horror Picture Show*. It has struck me of late that if the management were still holding to this practice, it might revive the project one night, at midnight, by putting on the screen . . . the original text of the Constitution. For that document seems to foster, among the most seasoned inhabitants of Washington, D.C., some of the deepest tremors, moving to the edge of panic. Some members of the political class resident there were willing to bend themselves out of shape, not all that long ago, as they sought to contrive different schemes for the "censure" of the President, for the sake of avoiding an "impeachment" and trial of the President, as though this process, set forth in the Constitution, was simply too traumatic for this polity to bear. With the Democrats, of course, the problem was complicated as they sought to censure without really condemning. But as the various schemes touched on real penalties, they deepened the constitutional problem rather than evading it. For they threatened to have Congress back into the passage of a "Bill of Attainder." Every attempt, that is, to get around that project of applying the Constitution as it was written – every attempt of that kind seemed to push the proponents into schemes that violated, ever more deeply, the logic and principles of the Constitution.

The concern, in this case, for Bills of Attainder, was rooted in the very logic of the separation of powers, and by that I mean it was rooted in a logic

[7] *Ibid.*, at 453.

that was really bound up with the logic of morals itself. That connection may not be evident at once, and it may not become clear until we begin with the matter nearest at hand and work our way back to the deeper principles. To begin with the plainest things, any resolution of censure would have to name Mr. Clinton and pick him out for a stinging rebuke. As John Stuart Mill reminded us, we pronounce any act to be a wrong as we begin to move away from statements merely of "like" or "dislike" and show a willingness to punish someone for performing that act.[8] If Mr. Clinton were not sent to jail, he might be fined; and a substantial fine, drawing on his income or means of support, stands as a real penalty. But in that event, Congress would be inflicting a penalty on a particular person, by name. There would be no trial, no attempt to announce any laws that had been broken, no effort to weigh the evidence that might sustain the charges. With that kind of move, the Congress, as a legislative body, seems to act as prosecutor and judge, without the bother of a trial. And the earmark in all of this is the naming of names, the infliction of a penalty on a distinct person. That is the telling sign of a bill of attainder, or a bill of penalties as it would be known more accurately, for penalties less than capital punishment.

But what exactly is the problem of naming names? When I take up the question of Bills of Attainder with my own students, I usually take this angle into the problem: I usually recall the routine that Johnny Carson used to do of The Great Karnak. The Great Karnak would announce first the answer to the question, and then he would open up the envelope supplying the question. (And so the answer might be, "El Paso," and the question would be, "What does the quarterback call for after he has tried El Runno and El Kicko?") For this problem, however, I did a slight variant: I'll supply the answers in the form of names, and the question is whether people can describe the category, or the class, that the names would represent. The category might be fairly clear if the names were Arthur Miller and Joe DiMaggio. Category: Married to Marilyn Monroe. But what if the names were Frank Sinatra and Alexander Hamilton? The category was: born or dying in Hoboken.[9]

---

[8] See John Stuart Mill, *Utilitarianism* (Indianapolis: Bobbs-Merrill, 1957 [1861]), p. 61: "[W]e do not call anything wrong unless we mean to imply that a person ought to be punished in some way or other for doing it.... [T]hat we call any conduct wrong, or employ, instead some other term of dislike or disparagement, according as we think that the person ought, or ought not, to be punished for it."

[9] Hamilton was mortally wounded in a duel with Aaron Burr in Weehawken, New Jersey, and he was carried to Hoboken, before he could be brought finally to the home of a friend in Greenwich. See Harold C. Syrett and Jean G. Cooke, eds., *Interview in Weehawken* (Middleton: Weslyan University Press, 1960), p. 144.

The point is that even people tuned into the world may find it hard to see the list and understand at once the class, or the principle, of which the names are supposed to stand as instances or examples. And so now imagine that Congress passes a law saying, in part, that Mr. Robert Morss Lovett, Goodwin B. Watson, William E. Dodd, Jr., mentioned in this way by name, may not receive any compensation paid by the Treasury of the United States. The fact that they are named does not reveal to us the category, or the principle, of which they are offered as examples. As it happened, Lovett and his colleagues were suspected of disloyalty, but if Congress had made explicit the ground of its judgment, it would have exposed to legal challenge everything that was problematic in the ground on which it was acting.[10] If Congress says that we may inflict penalties on people who are *suspected* of disloyalty, the legislation is quickly open to the challenge that no wrongdoing has been proved, that no charges have been made, that no evidence has been presented and tested in a court. If Congress were stipulating criminal penalties, these kinds of defects would be telling and damning. But they would still be serious even if there were no criminal charges involved. It seems to be widely forgotten that the landmark cases on Bills of Attainder in our own law did not involve criminal penalties: They involved, for example, a priest who was barred from serving in his vocation (in *Cummings v. Missouri*),[11] or a lawyer who would have been barred from arguing before the Supreme Court of the United States (*Ex parte Garland*).[12] These cases involved a deprivation of livelihood, but also the sting of a reproach or condemnation, a calumny, pronounced by the law. That is what made it all the more curious when the civil libertarians acquiesced in the move to deprive one former president of the United States of control of his personal papers and tapes, and do that by name. Richard Nixon was affected in that way by a dispossession that was not applied to the papers of any president who had preceded him nor (at that time) to those of any president who would succeed him. Of course, the suggestion was made at the time that Mr. Nixon was in a class by himself. But the Congress would have encountered real awkwardness if it had undertaken the discipline of explaining the class of which Mr. Nixon was taken as the sole example. For Congress could not have created a disability for Mr. Nixon on the basis of the fact that he was the first president to resign his office. Congress could not make resignation a predicate of guilt without undercutting the very purpose

---

[10] The reference, of course, is to the circumstances that defined *U.S. v. Lovett*, 328 U.S. 303 (1946).

[11] *Cummings v. Missouri*, 71 U.S. 277 (1867).

[12] *Ex parte Garland*, 71 U.S. 333 (1867).

of that resignation: to avoid a trial in the Senate, culminating in a judgment of guilt.

But all of this is meant to point up again the critical difference between mentioning names and defining, in *impersonal* terms, the class of wrongdoers. Defining the class is virtually the same as defining the nature of the wrong. As Felix Frankfurter remarked, the decision was made in America to get legislatures eventually out of the business of acting in the style of courts.[13] A legislature should act as a legislature, and it does that by accepting the discipline of defining, in impersonal terms, the character of the wrong and the wrongdoers.

It may be said that a constitution seeks to translate, into a legal structure, or a structure of practical judgment, the principles that define the character of the polity. It may be said in a similar way that the separation of powers offers one way of conveying, in a structure of practical judgment, a property that is quite central to morality or moral judgment – namely, the so-called universalizability principle. That principle bids us to consider whether the maxim behind our acts is *fit to be installed* as a universal rule – or to put it more modestly, as a rule that would apply to all similar cases. This connection seems to come as a surprise, but John Locke caught the sense of this matter quite precisely in his *Second Treatise*:

> And because it may be too great temptation to human frailty, apt to grasp at power, for the same persons who have the power of making laws, to have also in their hands the power to execute them. . . . [I]n well-ordered commonwealths, where the good of the whole is so considered as it ought, the legislative power is put into the hands of divers persons who, . . . have by themselves, or jointly with others, a power to make laws, which when they have done, being separated again, they are themselves subject to the law they have made; which is a new and near tie upon them to take care that they make them for the public good.[14]

To put it another way, the structure of the separation of powers works to impart this caution – and this mandate – to those who legislate: You had better be careful in the laws you frame because you will not be given the right to direct prosecutions under those laws. Once you have passed any bill into a law, that law will be put in hands other than your own to administer – and those could be unfriendly hands, the hands of people who count themselves as your political enemies. Therefore, as a matter of high prudence, you should

---

[13] See *Lovett, supra*, note 10, at 322.
[14] Locke, *Second Treatise on Civil Government*, Sec. 143.

be careful not to legislate for others what you would not be willing applied with its full force to yourself as well.

But that scheme of principle is subverted if the Congress finds a way of prodding the Executive along a certain path, toward a certain prosecution. And that scheme is subverted, also, through the willingness to draw the Congress into a new pattern of voting censure, or inflicting penalties, on presidents – or on anyone else in the country – by pronouncing the name of a person, and then annexing to that name a charge of wrongdoing. In the midst, then, of a crisis in our politics, the Constitution became the source of a certain illumination, which suddenly clarified something about the legal landscape. That revelation flashed upon people in a rather unsettling way. For it blocked off a path that might have dissolved their political problem – in this case, the problem of impeaching Mr. Clinton. Now, would we say that this had been an instance of "the living Constitution," the Constitution that suddenly bears for us on a novel problem, here and now, of our own day? Is it an example of an old Constitution showing its capacity to change, in reaching a case utterly new? We run the risk here of falling into the kind of fallacy that Professor Tribe was willing to absorb in an effort to twit Justice Scalia. In a critique of Scalia's lecture at Princeton several years ago,[15] Tribe noted that Scalia had voted to protect, under the First Amendment, the freedom to burn the American flag or burn crosses outside the homes of black families.[16] Was it not clear then, asked Tribe, that Scalia was not "freezing a fixed set of rights into the constitutional ice"; that he was willing to bring under the First Amendment liberties that would not have been protected in the eighteenth century, or for that matter, in the 1940s? Was that not in fact an exercise of adapting the provisions of the Constitution to the circumstances of our own day? Had Scalia not provided us then with living evidence of the Living Constitution?

And yet, what seems to have slipped, quite curiously, from Professor Tribe are the properties of a "principle." Once we grasp the principle by which the ball rolls down the inclined plane, we understand that the principle is utterly indifferent to the color of the plane and the ball, and whether they are made of aluminum or wood. It is precisely because a principle is abstract that it can be applied, over time, to a limitless number of *instances*. Once we understand what is wrong in principle with discriminations based on race, we need no new principle to explain the wrongness of barring people, on

---

[15] See Antonin Scalia, *A Matter of Interpretation* (Princeton: Princeton University Press, 1997), and for Tribe's commentary, pp. 65–94.

[16] *R.A.V v. St. Paul*, 505 U.S. 377 (1992).

the basis of race, from their access, say, to swimming pools, tennis courts, photocopy machines, marriage licenses. We would understand that these are all but instances in which the same principle is being manifested.[17]

If we understand, then, the principles behind the protection of "speech" or the ban on racial discrimination, then we would understand how those principles may be engaged in circumstances quite distant in time and quite varied in their technology, from quills to computers. In the case of the burning crosses and the burning flags, I happen to think myself that Scalia made a rare mistake here, that he read into the First Amendment a species of relativism – as though we lacked the standards for judging any longer the difference between "speech acts" that were on the one hand assaulting and, on the other, innocent, untouched by malice.[18] But whether we happen to coincide with his judgments there or not, it should be clear that Scalia did not need any novel principle in order to cover, with the First Amendment, the "expression" engaged in burning draft cards or burning crosses. There was no need for him to "update" the First Amendment. As Scalia understood it, the principle that protects speech under the Constitution means now what it has always meant, and the task of the judge now, as ever, is to apply the principles to the novel cases that arise in our daily lives.

But then is it not also possible that we may draw out of those principled implications that have heretofore gone unforeseen? Indeed, the moral life itself may involve an ongoing effort to draw out of our principles – to

---

[17] On this matter, see Arkes, *The Philosopher in the City* (Princeton: Princeton University Press, 1981), ch. 9; and my *First Things* (Princeton: Princeton University Press, 1986), pp. 344–45, on racial discrimination and "Zabar's v. Virginia."

[18] One of my own students expressed puzzlement over this point: Scalia had found no such lurking principle of relativism in the First Amendment when it came to protecting people who engaged in nude dancing or lewd entertainments. In *Barnes v. Glen Theatre*, he thought that the legislature could properly "enforce the traditional moral belief that people should not expose their private parts indiscriminately, regardless of whether those who see them are disedified." In that respect, there did not seem to be much question for him that the legislature could act, not merely for the sake of dealing with the "secondary effects" of lewdness, but for the sake simply of conveying a moral understanding – that certain acts were "contra bonos mores," or immoral. See 115 L Ed 2d 504, at 517 (Scalia, concurring). But in that event, my student was moved to wonder just why a local legislature might not find something comparably "immoral" in an attempt to terrorize black people through the burning of crosses, a gesture that was long understood, in our common usage, as a gesture of assault and threat. Under the traditional doctrine of "fighting words," it had been possible, after all, to recognize certain forms of expression that constituted assaults, and it was possible to restrain those modes of expression without interfering, in any way, with the freedom of people to make substantive arguments. For an extended treatment of this problem, see Arkes, *The Philosopher in the City*, chs. 2–3.

bring to a new level of awareness – the implications that had previously gone unnoticed. And it bears pointing out that none of this implies that there has been any change in the Constitution or its meaning, as though the Constitution had "changed with the times." If the implications are drawn rightly from the deep principles of the Constitution, then the novelty comes only with the recognition clicking in. But the logic, or the meaning, would have been contained in the Constitution all along. On this point, there is probably no more dramatic or telling example than the problem of the Fourteenth Amendment and miscegenation. Senator Lyman Trumbull, one of the managers of the Amendment, had assured his colleagues that there was nothing in the Amendment that would overturn the laws on miscegenation in the separate states. As Trumbull reasoned, those statutes would not violate the "Equal Protection of the Laws" because they bore equally on blacks as well as whites: They barred whites from marrying blacks as they barred blacks from marrying whites.[19] We would not take that view of the matter today, and not merely because "times have changed." It might be as apt to say that times have changed precisely because we have come to understand, in a more demanding, rigorous way, the principle that bars discriminations based on race.

We might have, for example, two couples, one black, one white, and they are free to marry. But another couple, made up of one black person and one white, might be barred from the same freedom to marry. The difference in treatment must pivot entirely on the race of the two persons forming the couple – which is to say that the law is creating a disability based entirely on race. To explain what is wrong with that, we would have to move more deeply into the principle, to explain what is wrong with drawing adverse moral inferences – judgments about the goodness or badness of people – solely on the basis of race, as though the moral conduct of any person was "determined" or controlled by race. As I have sought to explain at length in other places, that kind of an assumption would be at odds with the necessary assumption of freedom, or free will, that must be part of the very logic of "law" and moral judgment.[20] We do not hold people responsible for acts

---

[19] See, in this vein, the exchange among Senators Trumbull, Fessenden, and Johnson, during the debate over the Civil Rights Act of 1866, in *Congressional Globe*, 39th Cong., 1st Sess.; Vol. 36, part 1, p. 505; and the exchange between Trumbull and Sen. Davis, in *ibid.*, at 600. This understanding was also incorporated in some early cases, testing the laws on miscegenation under the Fourteenth Amendment. See *In re Hobbes*, 12 Fed. Cas. 262 (C.C.N.D. Ga., 1871), *State v. Gibson*, 36 Ind. 389 (1871), *State v. Hairston and Williams*, 63 N.C. 451 (1869), *Doc. Lonas v. State*, 50 Tenn. 287 (1871).

[20] See Arkes, *First Things*, pp. 92–99; and see below, ch. 2, pp. 75–77.

they were powerless to affect. If everyone were controlled in his conduct by his race, if no one were responsible for his own acts, then we could have no system of law, for we could not be justified in casting moral judgments on anyone.

But to make that move to the deeper principles behind the law is nothing less than a move of the natural law. That recognition may be rather unsettling to some exponents of "conservative jurisprudence," who seem to take a certain pleasure in deriding natural law, even as they persistently find themselves "doing" natural law. That is to say, they persistently find themselves falling back upon the "laws of reason" or the maxims that make up the very ground of the natural law, even as they profess that natural law cannot be done.[21] It seems to have fled the recognition, even of some rather accomplished lawyers, that the attempt to found a Constitution on certain first principles is itself a move distinctly of the natural law.

The problem might come out more clearly if we recalled for a moment the old question about the sources or origins of the law. John Locke suggested this chain of reasoning: We might say that the legislature is the source of the positive law, the law that is posited or enacted. But then what is the source of the legislature, or the authority to legislate? In our own country, the Constitution would establish that we have a legislature, of two houses, with the authority to enact laws. The source of the legislature then would be in the positive law of the Constitution, the Constitution that was drafted and ratified in a vote by the people. But then what was the ground of that original right, exercised by the people, to enact a Constitution? As Locke put it in his *Second Treatise*, "the constitution of the legislative being the original and supreme act of the society," it had to be "antecedent to all positive laws." The power to make the positive law is defined by the Constitution, but the Constitution itself cannot spring then from the positive law. It had to find its origins, as Locke said, in that understanding "antecedent to all positive laws," and that authority was "depending wholly on the people," on their natural right to be governed with their own consent.[22]

We have become, in this country, the children of this regime or this Constitution, and it may be hard to grasp the situation of the Founders, who understood a world of law, and principles of law, before they set about framing

---

[21] A notable case in point may be found in an exchange with my good friend Robert Bork. See Robert Bork, "Natural Law and the Constitution," *First Things* [the journal] (March 1992), pp. 16–20; Arkes, reply, *First Things* (May 1992), pp. 45–48.

[22] See Locke, *An Essay Concerning the True Original, Extent, and End of Civil Government*, Sec. 157.

a Constitution. Lawyers like Alexander Hamilton and John Marshall made their way, with a strainless grace and no small touch of elegance, as they traced their judgments back to the first principles of law. And so, in the *Federalist* No. 78, Alexander Hamilton noted the rule that guided the courts in dealing with statutes in conflict: The statute passed later is presumed to have superseded the law enacted earlier. The same rule does not come into play, of course, with the Constitution, for a Constitution framed earlier would have to be given a logical precedence over the statute that came later. Were that not the case, the Constitution would lose its function, or its logic, as a restraint on the legislative power. But these rules for the interpretation of statutes are nowhere mentioned in the Constitution. As Hamilton remarked, they were "not derived from any positive law, but from the nature and reason of the thing."[23]

Somewhat later, in the *Federalist* No. 81, he went on to point out that the notion of "parliamentary supremacy" in Britain had never been taken to mean that the legislature was empowered to overturn a verdict rendered in a court. The understanding seemed to be settled that the legislature might act instead to "prescribe a new rule for future cases." But here, too, this understanding was not expressed anywhere in the positive law of the Constitution. What made it valid, then, or authoritative, as an understanding bound up with the Constitution itself? As Hamilton explained, this understanding was simply anchored in "the general principles of law and reason."[24]

It is curious that these passages often come as a surprise even to conservative lawyers and jurists. And it seems to come as a further surprise that judges are "doing" natural law when they simply appeal, as Blackstone said, to the "law of nature and reason." The Founders saw nothing particularly strange, or insuperable, in the task of appealing to those laws of reason for the sake of filling in the assumptions that lay behind the law, or behind even the provisions of the Constitution. They saw themselves doing nothing arbitrary, for they thought there was a discipline of logic that made some judgments plausible and some notably implausible. That bracing clarity, or that sense of being anchored in the axioms of reason, is precisely the sense that came into play in that argument, at the very beginning, over the Bill of Rights. As I mentioned earlier, the reservations about the Bill of Rights did not spring from a fear or dubiety about rights. It arose, rather, from the concern that a Bill of Rights would have the effect of diminishing the body of rights protected under the Constitution, precisely because it would foster, among

---

[23] *The Federalist Papers* (New York: Random House, n.d.), p. 507.
[24] *Ibid.*, p. 526.

the American people, a serious misunderstanding about the very ground of their rights. There was the danger of conveying the notion that these rights were rights only of "positive law" – that they were rights only because they had been posited, set down, enacted in a Bill of Rights. That anticipation of things would be chillingly confirmed in experience, as people would commonly speak in later years, say, of those "rights we enjoy through the First Amendment" – as though, in the absence of that Amendment, we would not have those rights. The impression would soon take hold that the rights set down in the Constitution, or the Bill of Rights, were more important than the rights we had neglected to mention in the text. And as some of the Founders feared, there was a risk of suggesting, to people overly literal, that the rights set down were the only rights we had.

During the debate over the Bill of Rights in that first Congress, Theodore Sedgwick (of Connecticut) expressed his dubiety and asked, Why don't you specify my right to get up in the morning, my right to walk down the street, my right to wear a hat? His colleagues felt the sting of his wit without quite grasping his point. His concern was not for redundancy but for the state of mind that seemed to lose the distinction between principles and their instances. And so, as I've argued in another place, one could plausibly add to the provisions of the Constitution these other rights: my right not to be stopped in my automobile without cause; my right not to have blood removed from my arm after an auto accident, except for good reason, to establish my sobriety or intoxication; my right not to have my luggage inspected at an airport without a compelling need. We could go on in this way, proliferating our inventory of the kinds of instances in which we might be treated wrongly, but without getting clear on the principles that are truly pivotal or decisive. In any instance it is a matter of determining whether we have good reasons or plausible suspicions for searching, or seeking evidence – which is to say, we are always faced with the question of whether we are restricting freedom *with or without justification*. Everything must pivot then on our understanding of the principles of judgment, the principles that guide us in distinguishing between the things that are justified or unjustified. But the principles of justification, those standards of judgment, are nowhere adumbrated in the Constitution.

That sense of the matter, running deeper, explains the evident discomfort felt by some of the Federalists, even during the framing of the Constitution, as some members of the Constitutional Convention sought to advance the project of securing rights by setting down those bans on ex post facto laws and bills of attainder. But rather than finding assurance in these moves, some of the most thoughtful men among the framers were made quite uneasy, as they sensed in the air the spirit that would later be identified as "positivism." And so James Wilson and Oliver Ellsworth registered a certain dubiety when the proposal was brought forth, at the Convention, to prohibit "ex post facto" laws. Ellsworth remarked that any lawyer, or even any citizen, would know that "ex post facto laws were void in themselves." Wilson, too, was "against inserting anything in the Constitution as to ex post facto laws. It will bring reflexions on the Constitution – and proclaim that we are ignorant of the first principles of Legislation, or are constituting a Government which will be so."[25]

Wilson's concern was that this exercise in stipulating rights would embarrass the Founders in the eyes of the urbane. To mention one or two principles, and leave others unmentioned, ran the risk of suggesting that these were the only principles or maxims of the law that the Founders happened to know. Years later, in the landmark case of *Fletcher v. Peck*, the Court would strike down an act of the legislature rescinding the act of an earlier legislature, and find in that act the ingredients of an "ex post facto law." Chief Justice Marshall would take the case as an occasion for doing some extraordinary teaching and drawing a powerful lesson. Marshall and his colleagues concluded that the rescinding of a grant of lands had the effect of dispossessing ownership from buyers of the land who had no involvement in any act of corruption or wrongdoing. As for those owners, who came into possession of the land quite innocently, the act of the legislature constituted an impairing of the obligations of contract. That is to say, the wrong of the case, as construed by Marshall and his colleagues, could have been subsumed neatly under the Contracts Clause of the Constitution (Article 1, Section 10). But instead of doing it that way, Marshall did something far more elegant: He sought to show that the Contracts Clause could be drawn *deductively* from the principle on ex post facto laws. As Marshall put it,

> This rescinding act [in Georgia] would have the effect of an *ex post facto* law. It forfeits the estate of [the buyer] for a crime not committed by himself, but by those from whom he purchased. This cannot be effected in the form of an *ex post facto* law, or bill of attainder; why, then, is it allowable in the form of a law annulling the original grant?[26]

With that predicate in place, Marshall went on to do something, as I say, truly elegant: He remarked that Georgia was "part of a large empire; she is a member of the American union," and the Union had a Constitution that

---

[25] *The Records of the Federal Convention of 1787*, ed. Max Farrand (rev. ed. 1937) (New Haven: Yale University Press, 1966), Vol. 2, p. 376 [August 22].

[26] *Fletcher v. Peck*, 6 Cranch 87, 138–39 (1810) [italics in original].

was supreme over its separate parts. But as a result of the argument that Marshall had made here, Marshall could point out that the rescinding act passed by the legislature of Georgia "might well be doubted, were Georgia a single sovereign power."[27] That is, even if Georgia had not come under the Constitution and the restrictions of the Contracts Clause, the action of the legislature would still have been wrong. For the legislature had violated a principle that did not depend for its validity on the explicit provisions of the Constitution, or on the membership of Georgia in the American Union.

In a separate, concurring opinion, Justice Johnson wished to underscore the point that the holding in this case did not depend on the written words of the Constitution. "I do not hesitate to declare," he wrote, "that a state does not possess the power of revoking its own grants. But I do it on a general principle, on the reason and nature of things: a principle which will impose laws even on the Deity."[28] Even God was not morally free to violate the principle on ex post facto laws.

For the Founders, the principle on "ex post facto" laws was one of those deep principles of lawfulness that had a claim to be respected in all places, or incorporated in the basic law of any country that would claim to be a civilized country under the rule of law. And yet, if we would look closely, or come to the problem with a mind opened to the experience of the law and its puzzles, we would discover that ex post facto laws are not as clear or unmistakable in their definition as the Founders seemed to assume. There is – if we are open to it – an interesting mystery about ex post facto laws. If we follow the threads of that mystery, if we open ourselves to the puzzle, I think we would be led to recesses of our law that are even more intriguing – and revealing.

Any account of ex post facto laws in the work of the Supreme Court begins with Justice Samuel Chase's opinion in *Calder v. Bull I* (1798), setting down clearly the ingredients that define ex post facto laws – and at the same time marking the practical limits of the doctrine. And it was not long before experience began to render that definition a bit hazy at the edges. But Chase set forth the defining features rather emphatically. He had no doubt that certain retrospective laws could injure people by impairing rights and dispossessing people of their property. Still, he thought that this concern had been met, in the Constitution, by other provisions, namely, the clauses that barred making anything but gold or silver a tender in payment of debts, or barring any law that impaired the obligation of contracts. The concern behind ex post facto

---

[27] *Ibid.*, at 136.
[28] *Ibid.*, at 143.

laws, he thought, was notably different. It involved certain dramatic acts that often merged with Bills of Attainder – for example, the acts that ordered the execution of King Charles I in England or King Louis XVI in France. Not all retrospective acts were covered then by the clause on ex post facto laws, even though many more retrospective laws were wrongful. But that meaning of the provision on ex post facto laws was further confined by the recognition that not all retrospective laws were wrong. Certain laws conferred pardons or lightened the punishments for crimes after the fact, and Chase never thought those laws were called into question by the provision on ex post facto laws. Marking off those boundaries, he was persuaded that ex post facto laws could be defined in four ways, all involving criminal penalties. He condensed the description in this manner:

> 1st. Every law that makes an action done before the passing of the law, and which was innocent when done, criminal, and punishes such action. 2d. Every law that aggravates a crime, or makes it greater than it was, when committed. 3d. Every law that changes the punishment, and inflicts a greater punishment, than the law annexed to the crime, when committed. 4th. Every law that alters the legal rules of evidence, and receives less, or different, testimony, than the law required at the time of the commission of the offence, in order to convict the offender.[29]

But why would the meaning of the term be cabined in this way, to involve only retrospective acts with *criminal* penalties? The account usually offered is that criminal penalties are simply more serious, and they would seem to offer a more dramatic example of the wrongness of inflicting penalties on people for acts that had not been branded as crimes at the time they were committed. And yet, we know also that the distinction between criminal and civil penalties may not coincide with the difference between severe and lighter penalties. There may be criminal fines of $100, but a civil penalty may take the form of a knockout award for damages, in litigation over libel or tobacco or the liability for asbestos. The fines, in these cases, may put companies out of business, strip people of their assets and their livelihoods. As part of a civil penalty in a divorce and settlement, men and women could be denied custody of their children. Civil penalties are hardly, then, more trivial penalties. But the problem was revealed by Justice Iredell, in his concurring opinion in *Calder v. Bull*. As Iredell explained,

> Some of the most necessary and important acts of Legislation are . . . founded upon the principle, that private rights must yield to public exigenci[e]s.

[29] *Calder v. Bull*, 3 Dallas (3 U.S.) 386, at 390 (1798).

Highways are run through private grounds. Fortifications, Light-houses, and other public edifices, are necessarily sometimes built upon the soil owned by individuals. . . . Without the possession of this power the operations of Government would often be obstructed, and society itself would be endangered.[30]

If anything, Iredell might have understated his argument. For example, the federal government might decide to remove the deduction from taxes that has been provided over the years for the payments of interest in the purchase of private homes. In that event, a house, as an asset, could lose a substantial portion of its value. People who had purchased houses had probably counted on the presence of that deduction. But even if that deduction were preserved for them – even if it were removed only *prospectively*, to purchases of real estate from that point forward, *after* the passage of the law – the concerns of the owners would not be met. For the fact of the matter is that the purchase of the houses might not be as attractive to buyers in the future if they would not have the deduction from taxes, and so the investment in the real estate might have lost a hefty part of its value. The same story could be played out with almost any article or policy. The taxes may be raised on luxury autos, and a dealer holding a substantial inventory of Mercedes may find them unsalable. And so, if the principle on ex post facto laws was not confined to criminal cases, it would undercut not only the powers of taxation or the regulation of the economy but almost any kind of regulation a government may enact.

Yet, as Bernard Siegan managed to show, in his book on *Economic Liberties and the Constitution*,[31] the distinction between the criminal and the civil, on this subject, had not been taken for granted by the framers who had drafted the Constitution. There had been a concern, at the Convention, with attempts on the part of the states to interfere with the obligation of contracts, but Madison remarked that this concern had been met, for the most part, through the provision barring ex post facto laws.[32] That is, the assumption, left unchallenged, was that ex post facto laws were *not* confined to matters containing a criminal penalty. And not long after the Constitution went into effect, John Marshall offered an elegant reflection on the subject in *Fletcher v. Peck*. As we have seen, that case involved the rescinding of a grant of lands made by an earlier legislature, with the consequence of dispossessing innocent buyers of the properties they had purchased. In an exercise of jural teaching, Marshall went on to show that the offending law in Georgia was indeed an

---

[30] *Ibid.*
[31] (Chicago: University of Chicago Press, 1980).
[32] See *ibid.*, pp. 62–82, especially pp. 72–75.

ex post facto law, even though it did not impose criminal penalties. The law worked its punitive effect by depriving people of their assets, and that kind of arrangement, acquiesced in by the Court, could license mischiefs and injuries on a vast scale.[33]

Let us suppose, for example, that the city council of Boston, as part of a policy of rent control, passes a law saying that anyone who charges more than $500 for a studio apartment or an apartment with one bedroom can be sent to jail and fined. No one would doubt that a policy of that kind, sprung upon the owners of apartments, would constitute an ex post facto law. But let us say that the city council simply stipulates that the owners may not charge more than $500 per month for the apartment. Or suppose that the council defines a just and tenable rent at a substantially lower figure, well below the level needed by the owners to recover their costs and stay in business. The legislation may do nothing less than destroy the assets of the owners of the apartments, or carry out a transfer of income from the owners to their tenants. And yet, this kind of policy, which works with comparable, serious effects, would not ordinarily be considered an ex post facto law. The matter may come as a surprise to us precisely because we do not hear the language of constitutional challenge any longer when policies of this kind are proposed or resisted. Still, the most serious question must remain as to whether these policies, which have become familiar parts of the legal landscape, are not in fact incompatible with the deeper principles of law, which encompass the provision on ex post facto laws.[34]

Chief Justice Marshall complicated the mystery in a subtle way in *Ogden v. Saunders*, in 1824, when he remarked that "there is an essential difference in principle between laws which act on past, and those which act on future

---

[33] Marshall's colleague, William Johnson, went on to do a study of ex post facto laws in the statutes and judicial decisions in England, and he found the weight of authorities dominantly against the understanding set forth in *Calder v. Bull*, and strongly in support of the line taken by Marshall and himself in *Fletcher v. Peck*, that the principle on ex post facto laws would cover even civil penalties. And in our own time, that judgment was sustained by Professor Crosskey. See *ibid.*, pp. 69–70, 74–75, citing from W.W. Crosskey, "The True Meaning of the Constitutional Prohibition of Ex-Post-Facto Laws," 14 *U. of Chicago L. Rev.* 539 (1947), and "The Ex-Post-Facto and the Contracts Clauses in the Federal Convention: A Note on the Editorial Ingenuity of James Madison," 35 *U. of Chicago L. Rev.* 248 (1968).

[34] In an opinion still not really appreciated, Justice Sutherland managed to show the deep principles of lawfulness that would have to challenge these controls on wages and prices, and he never even raised the problem of ex post facto laws. See *Adkins v. Children's Hospital*, 261 U.S. 525, and see an extended treatment of this case, and Sutherland's reasoning, in my book, *The Return of George Sutherland* (Princeton: Princeton University Press, 1994), pp. 71–80.

contracts; that those of the first description can seldom be justified, while those of the last are proper subjects of ordinary legislative discretion."[35]

Most retrospective laws were ex post facto, but some apparently were not. To put it another way, some laws may bear retrospectively; they may impose substantial costs, as a form of penalty, and yet they may be valid. As I have said, then, we have the ingredients of a puzzle: The Founders were convinced, beyond the need for discussion, that the principle on ex post facto laws was one of those enduring principles of lawfulness that would give the law even to the Deity, as Justice Johnson had said. The framers doubted that the principle could be confined to laws bearing a criminal penalty, and yet they recognized that if the laws were not confined in that way, the principle could call into question virtually every regulation offered by the government in flexing its powers. Marshall thought that most retrospective laws were wrongful and yet some might be justified. But *if they were justified, they were evidently not ex post facto laws*, of the kind that the Constitution meant to forbid. And so, how do we know, when we see them, the ex post facto laws that the Founders thought any civilized people would reject?

As Marshall had pointed out, the Contracts Clause could be drawn deductively from the principle on ex post facto laws. Every law impairing of the obligation of contracts may be an instance of an ex post facto law; but we must ask: Is every act, impairing the obligation of a contract, truly wrong? Those of us who studied constitutional law in the early 1960s became aware of the situation of the Girard School in Philadelphia. That school had been founded as a private academy through a bequest of that Jeffersonian Democrat, Stephen Girard. Nothing in his Jeffersonian persuasion had alerted him to the least moral problem in his act of charity as he provided an education for *poor white orphan boys.* The problems would sharpen in later years, as the Girard School was incorporated into the public schools of Philadelphia. For the decision of the Supreme Court in 1954, in *Brown v. Board of Education,* made it utterly untenable for the public schools of Philadelphia to absorb the Girard bequest and at the same time honor the terms set down by the donor. A public school system could no longer manage, officially, a school confined exclusively to white children (or white males). After a challenge in the courts, the provisions in the bequest had to be superseded. But that is to say, the courts and the authorities had been obliged to impair, *after the fact,* the explicit obligation that attached to the contract, or bequest, left by Stephen Girard. I once imagined, as a parallel case, a situation in which a southerner with a kindly heart, wished to provide comfortable jobs for black

---

[35] *Ogden v. Saunders,* 6 Wheaton 213, at 334.

slaves as servants in a grand house. Imagine that the house was left as part of a donation to form a new college. But then the Thirteenth Amendment intervenes, and it becomes untenable to hold blacks, or anyone else, in slavery in the United States. The bequest would suddenly become untenable in the law – it could not be enforced any longer in the courts – because it would be in conflict now with the "basic law" underlying all of our laws. But if the judgment on racial segregation was firmly grounded in principle – if it arose, compellingly, as a logical and necessary part of our basic law – then we would have no choice but to impair, *after the fact*, the obligation contained in the bequest by Stephen Girard. For we would have no tenable ground on which to justify the enforcement of that bequest as "law."

That kind of case would lead us to return to that original account of ex post facto laws by Justice Chase in *Calder v. Bull*: An ex post facto law may make an innocent act *wrongful*, as opposed, he said, to an act that made an unlawful act lawful. But Chase seemed to rule out this possibility: that the law may act, after the fact, to declare, as wrongful, a truly wrongful act. And as it does that, it may impair a wrongful contract, or it may create a disability or a penalty. This was, I take it, what was done quite explicitly and self-consciously by the American Congress as late as 1978 when it voted to bar, from entry into the United States, anyone who might have been involved in war crimes arising out of the Nazi movement and the war in Europe in the period of 1933–45.[36] As people may still recall, one of the most visible figures snared in the sweep of that law was Mr. Kurt Waldheim, the former Secretary General of the United Nations and, by that time, President of Austria. It was an embarrassment, to say the least, that the head of a substantial country in Europe was barred from paying a state visit, or indeed any other kind of visit, to the United States. I take it as a telling omission that no one thought it sensible to mention at the time the concern for ex post facto laws as understood by the legal positivist: No one evidently wished to make a joke of himself by arguing, in the voice of Waldheim, "If I had only known – if I had only known that I could be barred from New York, and its fine restaurants, in the 1970s and 1980s, I would have behaved myself far better as an officer in the Balkans in the 1940s."

But then the same understanding that came into play here could have arisen quite as plausibly in that landmark case in the 1860s on ex post facto laws, *Ex parte Garland*. That case involved a lawyer, a member of the bar of the Supreme Court, who had joined the Confederacy and even risen to office as a senator in the Confederate government. After the war, he had received a pardon. But there was a question of whether the pardon could

---

[36] See 8 U.S.C.A. Sec. 1182; Pub. L 95–549 (1978).

restore his privilege of practicing law as a member of the bar of the Supreme Court. An act of Congress denied the bar of the Supreme Court – and the standing of an officer of the Court – to anyone who had borne arms against the United States, or to anyone who had exercised the functions of office in any "pretended government . . . within the United States, hostile or inimical thereto."[37] In an opinion ringing to this day, but ringing at times off tune, the legendary Justice Stephen Field struck down this act of Congress as an ex post facto law and a Bill of Attainder. And yet, what was involved here was not merely political passion, or "partisanship," as that notion is bandied about so cheaply these days. Those divisions brought forth in the Civil War ran to the deepest principles of the regime. They involved, as Lincoln said, nothing less than the fundamental right of a people finally to govern itself. And therefore, the attempt to undermine and destroy a free government had to be taken as profoundly serious by anyone who realized, as many of the soldiers stated in their letters home, that some people were willing to take from them and their families their right to have a government of their own choosing.[38] As Justice Miller noted, in his dissenting opinion in *Garland*, the matter of access to the bar involved the question of who would be fit to act as an officer of the court in upholding the system of justice. Miller crystallized the problem in this way:

> [A] person who . . . has voluntarily borne arms against the government of the United States while a citizen thereof, or who has voluntarily given aid, comfort, counsel, or encouragement to persons engaged in armed hostility to the government, has, by doing those things, forfeited his right to appear in her courts and take part in the administration of her laws.[39]

Lincoln had shown, in his First Inaugural Address, that the doctrine of secession was sprung from the same logic that entailed anarchy or despotism.[40] The case of men like Garland would be understood only in a vulgar way if it were described as a matter merely of betting wrong politically. We may expect a wide variation in the political reflexes of people who call themselves lawyers, but one thing a lawyer had to understand is that the willingness to take up arms against a government of free elections and open courts

---

[37] *Ex parte Garland*, 71 U.S. 333, at 376 (1967).

[38] See James M. McPherson, *What They Fought For, 1861–65* (New York: Anchor Books, 1994), pp. 29–30.

[39] *Ex parte Garland, supra*, note 37, at 393.

[40] See Lincoln, First Inaugural Address, in *The Collected Works of Abraham Lincoln*, ed. Roy P. Basler (Brunswick, N.J.: Rutgers University Press, 1953), Vol. 4, pp. 262–71, especially pp. 267–68.

could be understood as nothing other than an appeal to brute force. And nothing was more at odds with the notion of "the rule of law." It was hardly extravagant then to say that any man who did not understand that rudimentary point was not fit to practice law. And as Garland himself had already shown, he could surely not be depended on, as an officer of the Court, to preserve and defend a regime of law.

When we take matters back then to the root principles of the regime, when we simply insist again that these principles matter profoundly, then it is not so astonishing that there may be a serious purge of the bar, of the judiciary, and the higher posts in the military and civil service. It is not, after all, merely a surge of partisanship but a deadly serious matter: With acts of awful consequence, some people had made of themselves, in all literal strictness, enemies of a republican regime. It is curious that people tend now not to notice or remember that in our own recent history, the political leadership of this country did preside over a thoroughgoing purge of a civil service and judiciary. No, it was not the effort to expel Communists from the government in the 1950s but the program administered by the occupation authorities in Germany and referred to as "de-Nazification." And now, in the aftermath of the war in Iraq, the United States was faced with the strains of a similar purge, removing from the military, the judiciary, and the government the most committed members of the Baathist Party.

Yet, when we make the connection in that way, we recall that there was another regimen of review and retribution here, administered with law made *after the fact* and carrying penalties far more dire than the removal of people from their jobs. What I have in mind, of course, are the Nuremberg trials. It seems to have been a source of embarrassment, even on the part of people quite supportive of that process, that the law administered in that case was pronounced after the fact, after the Allied victory. And the penalties there ran beyond fines and forfeitures, to capital punishment. But Justice Robert Jackson, acting now as a prosecutor, brought to this project a passion that reflected the purest moral outrage. In one of life's curious turns, however, that passion happened to be in conflict with the jural doctrines that had recruited his deepest loyalties. As a lawyer and then jurist of the New Deal, Jackson had come to dismiss "natural law" as a doctrine empty of substance and reactionary in its political tendency. But the situation after the war seemed to require, of the jurist, nothing less than an appeal to the logic of natural law, since Jackson could not evidently base the prosecution on any positive law. Still, he could not, as a New Dealer, fly suddenly to natural law, and with a certain exertion of wit he managed to find a ground for the trials in positive law: He would base the process on the Kellogg-Briand Pact of the 1920s, the pact that bound its signatories to refrain from "aggressive" war.[41]

But of course, the question of aggression did not hinge on the matter of who crossed a frontier first. From the perspective of the positive law of the Third Reich, the Allied forces landing in Normandy in June 1944 were involved in a massive act of aggression. The question of aggression had to turn on the question of whether the military action was justified or unjustified, whether it was directed to a just or unjust end. Which is to say, the deliberation that we would require, in reaching a judgment on that matter, would be at one with the nature of the deliberation that we would have to carry through in any other act of moral judgment. And what I would suggest here is that the puzzle over ex post facto laws is simply cut from the same cloth, and the resolution of the puzzle moves along the same familiar lines.

Consider the problem cast simply in this way: We know that the notion of positive law is consistent with the understanding of natural law. We know that we need to move from the abstraction of the natural law to rules that bear on the circumstances at hand. At the same time, we know that it is the underlying natural law that renders the regulation of the positive law both intelligible and defensible as law. We know, for example, that there is nothing particularly compelling, in nature, about the regulation expressed in a sign on the highway, saying "55" – 55 miles per hour as the speed limit. But that regulation, we know, can be drawn from a deeper principle that tells us why it would be wrongful to hazard innocent lives on the highway by driving at a speed that would be reckless under the circumstances of a certain terrain. And when we are asked to explain and justify this notion of a restraint, enforced with the power of law, we naturally fall back upon that deeper principle.[42] That difference between the principle and the regulation, between the natural law and the positive law, may be the simple key to the problem. It might not be strange if a law were passed saying that people convicted in the past five years of reckless driving, or multiple acts of reckless

---

[41] Jackson's position can be found in his Report to President Truman on the Legal Basis for Trial of War Criminals; and wanting the original, there are sufficient citations in Jeffrey D. Hocket, "Justice Robert Jackson, the Supreme Court, and the Nuremberg Trial," in *The Supreme Court Review* (1990), pp. 257–99, at 266–68.

[42] Cf., in this respect, Kant, in *The Metaphysics of Morals*: "Among external laws, those to which an obligation can be recognized a priori by reason without external legislation are *natural laws*, whereas those that would neither obligate nor be laws without actual external legislation are called *positive laws*." *The Metaphysics of Morals*, trans. John Ladd (Indianapolis: Bobbs-Merrill, 1965; originally published in 1797), p. 26 [p. 224 in the standard edition of the Royal Prussian Academy].

driving, must have their licenses renewed with more demanding examination, at more frequent intervals. Yet, it would strike us as notably different if the same law were suddenly pronounced on anyone over the past several years who had exceeded a speed of 55 miles per hour. We cannot attach significance to the number without knowing the circumstances. And we cannot expect people to have anticipated, with precision, that the number "55" would mark something of grave significance.

To put it another way, *we cannot expect people to know, in advance, the precise regulations of the positive law;* but we can expect them to have understood those deeper principles of what we used to call "common sense," even without the law. And so, Citronelle Mobile, the oil company, had not anticipated the troubles it was buying for itself when it contracted to sell 128,000 barrels of oil to Gulf Oil in the 1970s. At that time price controls had been removed and Gulf Oil was willing to buy oil, on the market, at the uncontrolled price of $13 per barrel. There were clear signs, of course, that the Democratic Congress sustained a lively interest in restoring controls. Still, for most of September 1975 the controls were off, and companies that needed crude oil were showing a willingness to pay the market price. Even if Congress put the controls back on, Citronelle Mobile could not be faulted for assuming that the contracts entered into knowingly in the market would nevertheless be honored. Yet, even with its experience in politics and the market, the company did not foresee that Congress would not only restore the controls, but would also make them *retroactive.* Surely the company did not anticipate that Gulf Oil would have the chutzpah to sue Citronelle for violating the new law and insist that the contract be revised, with the price rolled back to the controlled price of only $5.40 per barrel! With a reduction of $7.60 a barrel, the difference came to just under a million dollars – hardly a trivial sum for just two contracts arranging for deliveries. Citronelle Mobile could have sold to anyone in that earlier period, including people who would not have taken advantage of the company. I think it could be argued then persuasively that there was no way Citronelle should have known, in advance, that the right price should be $5.40. Even with high foresight and caution, the executives of the company could not have been expected to anticipate that the company should absorb serious penalties, attended by charges of legal fault, because it could not divine, in advance, that Congress would settle on a figure of $5.40. It seemed more than sufficient to know that Gulf Oil had been willing to purchase oil at the price commanded in the market at the time. That figure of $5.40 could have the standing of "law" only in positive law. And yet, in a profession that has thoroughly absorbed the premises of legal positivism, a federal court saw nothing wrong in the arrangement.[43] But I think others of us could make a compelling case that this imposition of price controls was a serious example of an ex post facto law. It was precisely the kind of arrangement that Madison and his colleagues thought would be covered by the principle on ex post facto laws. And it involved only a "civil" penalty.

To restate the matter, we would not expect people to know, in advance, the precise regulations of the positive law. But we can expect them to have some glimmer, or grasp, of the principle behind the law so that they cannot affect to be surprised or shocked if the law, after the fact, treats a serious crime with a punishment more aptly scaled to the offense.

And yet when we say those things, we come close to replicating the case, several years back, in which the Supreme Court startled some lawyers by suggesting that certain alterations in penalties, ex post facto, might be justified. Jose Ramon Morales had killed his girlfriend in 1971 in a grisly way, amputated her right thumb, and slashed her face. He was sentenced to life in prison, but put in a halfway house in 1980 on the way to release. Lois Washbaugh, seventy-five years old, had taken an interest in prisoners, and when Morales was still in prison, she formed a romantic attachment to him. When he was released they were married. Just three months later she disappeared. Her severed hand was recovered, but never her body. Morales pleaded nolo contendere to the second murder. Under the laws of California, he was

---

[43] Judge Pittman, in the district court in Alabama, first sought to sidestep the question by invoking *Calder v. Bull* and insisting that ex post facto laws had to involve criminal penalties. But with that façade of surety he neatly overlooked, as we have seen, *Fletcher v. Peck*, along with *Cummings v. Maryland*, and *Ex parte Garland*, cases in which the Court had found the presence of ex post facto laws even with only civil penalties. The judge cast the problem then in this way: When there is retroactive legislation, we may ask whether the legislation is justified. To that extent, the judge got it partially right: We would ask of retroactive legislation what we would ask of any legislation – whether it is justified. But the deeper complication for retroactive legislation is whether the standard of judgment, imposed after the fact, involved those axioms of common sense which ordinary people can divine, or whether it involved a standard simply installed by fiat through the positive law. In any case, Judge Pittman dissolved any discipline of moral judgment in weighing justifications, when he reasoned in this way: A retroactive law, to be valid, must reflect an important public interest, and the willingness of Congress to enact the controls on prices indicates just how seriously Congress regarded the problem of energy as a matter of urgent public interest. But of course, the very act of legislating must imply the judgment that the subject of the law is regarded as important, for it is no trivial thing to restrict the freedom of people by imposing laws. With Judge Pittman's formula, the very enactment of the law would establish the grounds for its own justification. Or to put it another way, the very exercise of power was sufficient to establish its justification. Thus a snapshot on the state of jural minds even in the 1970s. See *Citronelle-Mobile Gathering Co. v. Gulf Oil Corp.*, 420 F. Supp. 162, 164–68, and especially 170.

sentenced to a term of fifteen years to life (believe it or not), with the possibility of parole beginning in 1990. But around the same time even the legislators in California began to have access to some minimal common sense. Under the laws earlier in force, prisoners could have an annual review of their suitability as prospects for parole. The legislature now changed the terms of review, not to remove parole but just to say that the reviews need not be held every year: They could be held now *once every three years* for a certain class of prisoners, those who had been convicted of "more than one offense which involves the taking of a life."[44]

Morales's lawyers challenged the new law as an ex post facto law on the claim that it indirectly enlarged the penalty by making it harder for Morales to gain a parole. Morales should have been grateful that he had not been drawn and quartered for his offenses, and yet the Ninth Circuit in California upheld his claim. But in a turn that has become familiar, the Ninth Circuit was overruled by the Supreme Court, this time with an opinion written by Justice Thomas. Still, there was a dissent by Justices Stevens and Souter. With sensibilities tuned to pains ever more refined, Stevens and Souter were willing to agree that there was a deepening of the penalty for Morales. But even more seriously, they thought the legislation was coming close to a Bill of Attainder by picking out a class of distinct persons. Yes, but the members of the class were not identified by their personal names; they were identified by the fact they had committed multiple murders. And did the case reveal the enduring concern about ex post facto laws? Had people not been put on proper notice in advance that they might be doing something wrong, something that the law was likely to punish? But surely, as a man already convicted for a homicide, Morales must have had a notice fully adequate that the law took a dim view of dismembering other people, even if they happened to be one's spouses. Or was it possible that he truly might have been given pause before killing and dismembering his second wife *if he had only known* that his annual reviews for parole would be shifted from one a year to one every three years?

To state the matter frankly in those terms, the terms that fit the conventional arguments over ex post facto laws, is to elicit a certain embarrassment at once among people with ordinary moral reflexes. Still, the dissenters had a point when they remarked that Justice Thomas and the majority sought to deal with the problem simply by arguing that the change was minuscule, that Morales could still be eligible for parole beginning in 1990.[45] What Thomas and the majority conspicuously did not do was explain that though the change was

---

[44] See *California Dept of Corrections v. Morales*, 514 U.S. 499, 501–504 (1995).
[45] *Ibid.*, at 504–5, 507–9.

made after the fact, it was a *thoroughly justified change*. And though it was the most modest of moves, the new arrangement bore a larger measure of justice because it came closer to treating a serious crime with the seriousness that it deserved.

There is an immanent risk, in the study of law, that cases arising in novel settings may begin to suggest novel principles at work. But if we put aside the special setting of the military, we would discover that the common law has worked routinely now to mete out penalties quite severe for wrongs that have never been spelled out in statutes. And in doing that work the common law persistently assigns to ordinary people a responsibility to deliberate about the principles of lawfulness even if they have not been trained in the law. We can only imagine the surprise, not too long ago, of the first man who was sued for giving herpes to his partner in sex. When that first action came in an ordinary case on torts, there had been, after all, no statutes on the subject. How would anyone, then, have had adequate warning? And yet, the law rather expected him "to know." To know what? If we reduced the matter to its root propositions, the disposition to hold him responsible probably rested on three things: If he knew that he had the virus, and if he knew how it was transmitted – if he knew then that his partner was in serious danger of contracting it from him – then it became reasonable to ask, What *justifiable* reason – what reason apart from his own pleasures or satisfaction – could he have had for not warning her?

I do not pretend here to encapsulate the law of torts on this matter. I offer merely my surmise on the elements, or ingredients, that would bear with a more evident relevance on the moral grounds of judgment. There is nothing particularly abstruse here, and indeed we may curiously overlook some rather extraordinary things that we seem willing to attribute routinely to people who are appealingly ordinary, with no pretensions to the arts of philosophy. We would not take it seriously for a moment if Jones, after stealing a squash racquet, professed not to have read the laws on theft, or if he asked whether those laws happen to mention squash racquets. We tend to hold Jones responsible for knowing that it is wrong to take what is not his, even if he has never read the statutes or heard anything of the common law. As for squash racquets, we apparently expect even the most unlettered among us to grasp this point: that once we understand the notion of theft, or a wrongful taking, we understand that the principle is virtually indifferent to the instances that fall under that principle. The objects purloined may be squash racquets or automobiles or computers. It really does not matter. But it may be sobering to step back and ponder for a moment just what proposition of philosophic reach we expect ordinary people to understand as a matter of course. Even if they cannot know all of the principles, we apparently impute to ordinary people – like the fellow with herpes – the capacity to flex their wit in deliberating seriously about the implications of what they know.

But once we have said that, have we not simply backed ourselves into Aristotle's point at the beginning of political philosophy? The polis is an emanation from human nature; it springs distinctly from our capacity to do more than emit sounds indicating pleasure or pain, but to reason over the things that are just and unjust, good and bad. Kant said, in that famous phrase, that the idea of law springs from the very notion of "a rational being as such."[46] And of course we know, anthropologically, that we are the only creatures suited for a polis because we are, as moral agents, the only creatures capable of generating law in the strictest sense. We are aware of our freedom to make a practical choice over a course of action, and we are the only creatures who are drawn then to reflect about the reasons that command our judgments as we weigh those choices. But as Aristotle also suggested, there is something divine about reason. It may simply be a function of our lofty station that we no longer recognize what is so lofty in it, and what momentous things, of philosophy and law, we expect ordinary men and women to understand.

Aristotle observed, in the *Posterior Analytics*, that "it is not possible to understand if we are not aware of the primitive, immediate principles." Before we can grasp a demonstration, certain axioms or truths need to be grasped in themselves, as the grounds of knowing. All animals, he said, have perception, but in some animals, he continued, "retention of the percept comes about, but in others it does not come about." Someone may see, or perceive, a figure of three sides, and from that perception, as Aristotle says, there may come a memory of the experience or the perception. "And from experience," he says, or "from the whole universal that has come to rest in the soul . . . there comes a principle of skill and understanding."[47] Some people may see a three-sided figure, and in time some will come to recognize it as a triangle, representative

---

[46] "[N]othing but the idea of law in itself, which admittedly is present only in a rational being . . . can constitute that preeminent good which we call moral." And, "Since moral laws have to hold for every rational being as such, we ought . . . to derive our principles from the general concept of a rational being as such, and on this basis to expound the whole of ethics." See Kant, *Groundwork of the Metaphysics of Morals*, trans. H. J. Paton (New York: Harper & Row, 1964), pp. 69, 79; in the standard edition of the Royal Prussian Academy, pp. 401, 412.

[47] Aristotle, Posterior Analytics, Bk. II, ch. 19, trans. Jonathan Barnes, in Barnes, ed., *The Complete Works of Aristotle* (Princeton: Princeton University Press, 1984).

of a class of many things bearing the same properties. As Daniel Robinson has put it, in a parallel commentary:

> Smith and Jones might both know that the triangle they perceive contains 180 degrees. Smith knows this because he has used a measuring device and has discovered that there are three 60-degree angles within a triangle. Jones, however, knows because he knows that *all* triangles circumscribe 180 degrees. What Smith knows is chiefly the gift of perception by which particulars enter the mind. What Jones knows is a kind of *scientific* knowledge (*episteme*) which acquires the capacity for abstract and deliberative rationality. Children and non-human animals, on Aristotle's account, can know what Smith knows but not what Jones knows.[48]

In the law, we seem to expect that everyone will know what Jones, roughly, or essentially, knows. We expect Jones to know, for example, the law of identity – that he is, today, the same person he was yesterday. And even though he may be convinced that he is now a different man from the one who was caught embezzling yesterday, we know that he knows the truth of the matter. Just as we know that he knows there is no effect without a cause, and that two contradictory things cannot both be true. But that is to say, law is made in contemplation of that creature who carries a metaphysic within himself, and it can be routinely administered, every day, only by that same creature. He may be prosaic, his sentences will not always be crackling – and to take a line again from Evelyn Waugh, his diaries may be much in need of editing. But the capacity to understand "the laws of nature and reason" he carries, ever, within himself. He is, as he is, never detached from the natural law.

[48] Daniel Robinson, in Robinson, ed., *The Mind* (Oxford: Oxford University Press, 1998), p. 62.

Two

The Natural Law – Again, Ever

A dear friend, who has done premier work in the neural sciences and several books on philosophical psychology, remarked that he wanted, as the epitaph on his gravestone, "He died without a theory." A former colleague of mine remarked that I had a "theory" of natural law. But I can join my friend in saying that I, too, have no "theory." To say that someone has a "theory" of natural law is to suggest that an observer, looking on, can see played out before him people seized with "theories" – that he may stand there, in a wholesome detachment, seeing theories of various sorts whizzing past. From that vantage point we are encouraged to make judgments about the theories, or fragments of theories, that are plausible or implausible, right or wrong, true or false. I said then: Just tell me the ground on which you are making *those* judgments about the theories that are plausible or implausible, true or false, and you would have been led back to the ground of what I understand as the natural law. For you would have been led back to the ground on which we have confidence in the things we can truly know about the properties of propositions, about the statements that are true and false, and finally, then, about the things that are morally right or wrong. You would be led back to what Blackstone called "the laws of reason and nature."

Many high-flown things have been said about natural law, including many high-flown mistakes by people rather accomplished in the law. And so Richard Posner, a legend in his own time as professor and federal judge, has suggested that "the survival of the fittest" may be taken as an example of "natural law," because it purports to describe a law of behavior that finds its source in the "nature" of human beings.[1] By this reasoning, infanticide and genocide seem

[1] See Richard Posner, *The Problems of Jurisprudence* (Cambridge: Harvard University Press, 1990), pp. 235–36, 238–39, 376, 396–405.

43

to be a persisting, intractable part of the human record, and so it seems plausible that they spring from something deeply planted in human nature. And yet, natural law has ever set itself against the killing of the innocent.

Spinoza identified natural law with laws of nature that governed the ways of each individual thing. And so, as he said, "[F]ishes are determined by nature to swim, the large ones to live off the smaller; therefore fishes are using this greatest natural right when they possess the water."[2] This may be called the Kern and Hammerstein theory of natural law: fish gotta swim/birds gotta fly. But as one commentator, the redoubtable Samuel Pufendorf, rightly put it, it was a mistake to confound these meanings of natural law, to confuse the laws of determinism with "laws" and "rights" in their moral significance.[3] It was especially inapt to attribute a moral intention, or a moral understanding, to "animals that are not endowed with reason." The fish may swim, but it would be hard to attribute to them the understanding that they were engaging their *rights* as they glided about.[4]

Over a hundred years earlier (in 1539), Francisco de Vitoria rejected a comparable argument, to the effect that the stars had a natural right to shine, and the sun to emit light. By that reasoning, as Vitoria had pointed out, we would be doing "an injustice against the sun" by closing the blinds and blocking the light.[5] And of course, in these arguments, Pufendorf and Vitoria had been preceded by Aquinas.[6]

These are all venerable confusions, but it is time we stopped falling into them, for they have been persistently countered, with compelling reasons. The expounders of natural law did not confuse natural law with regularities in nature, or with *generalizations* about the behavior of humans over time, drawn from the checkered history of our species. Immanuel Kant had warned about that temptation to draw principles of moral judgment from "the particular natural characteristics of humanity" or the "particular constitution of human nature."[7] The teachers of natural law began, rather, with an understanding of the things that were higher and lower in human nature. Which is to say, they had to begin with an understanding of what was in principle higher or lower.

---

[2] Spinoza, *Theological-Political Treatise*, ch. 16.

[3] Pufendorf, *The Elements of Universal Jurisprudence* (Oxford: Clarendon Press, 1931; originally published in English translation, 1672), p. xxxi.

[4] *Ibid.*, at p. 159.

[5] Francisco Vitoria, *Reflections in Moral Theology* (Washington: Carnegie Institution, 1917; originally published, 1696), p. 248; from a lecture delivered at the University of Salamanca in 1539.

[6] See the *Summa Theologica*, Q92, Art.2.

[7] Immanuel Kant, *Fundamental Principles of the Metaphysics of Morals* [1785], trans. Thomas K. Abbott (Indianapolis: Bobbs-Merrill, 1949), pp. 42 and 58.

On that point, they could take their bearings in part from Aristotle, on the things that made human beings decisively different from animals. Animals could emit sounds to indicate pleasure or pain, but human beings could "declare what is just and is unjust"; they could give reasons over matters of right and wrong.[8] In the culminating lines of his First Inaugural Address, Lincoln appealed to "the better angels of our nature." He could invoke the understanding of what was higher and lower in the nature of human beings.

With Aristotle and Lincoln we had an appeal to what could be called a "commonsense" understanding: We would begin with the kinds of things that were accessible to ordinary folk, without the need for any specialized, scientific vocabulary. That kind of perspective found its understanding of the "human" by separating human things from the things that were *subhuman* or *superhuman*. And there it would begin with the things nearest at hand, in the difference between men and animals.

What seems to come as a surprise to many accomplished lawyers, who affect dubiety over "natural law," is that the natural law may take its bearing from this very notion of the things that mark a distinctly human nature. Which is to say, what seems to have fled from the memories of the lawyers are the plainest things that Aristotle taught in that first book on politics and law. And lost in the same way is the recognition of how widely the reasoning of natural law has been absorbed in the common sense of ordinary people. That point was less obscure in a time when the language of moral reasoning was used by political men with the art of speaking to the multitude, or making themselves understood among a large, public audience. When Lincoln spoke of natural rights he spoke of the rights that arise distinctly from human nature, and he spoke in a manner that was instantly intelligible:

> Equal justice to the south, it is said, requires us to consent to the extending of slavery to new countries. That is to say, inasmuch as you do not object to my taking my hog to Nebraska, therefore I must not object to you taking your slave. Now, I admit this is perfectly logical, if there is no difference between hogs and negroes.[9]

Or, in the same speech, the famous Peoria Speech (October 1854), Lincoln noted that even people from the South had not understood black people to be really nothing more than horses or cattle. He noted that, in 1820, congressmen from the South had joined congressmen from the North almost

---

[8] See Aristotle, *The Politics*, 1252a–3a.
[9] Lincoln, Speech at Peoria (October 16, 1854), in *The Collected Works of Abraham Lincoln*, ed. Roy P. Blaser (Brunswick, N.J: Rutgers University Press, 1953), Vol. 2, p. 264.

unanimously in outlawing the African slave trade as a form of "piracy" and "annexing to [that crime] the punishment of death":

> Why did you do this? If you did not feel that it was wrong, why did you join in providing that men should be hung for it? The practice was no more than bringing wild negroes from Africa, to sell to such as would buy them. But you never thought of hanging men for catching and selling wild horses, wild buffaloes or wild bears.[10]

And then, in a passage as moving as it was analytically pointed, Lincoln observed that

> there are in the United States and territories, including the District of Columbia, 433,643 free blacks. At $500 per head they are worth over two hundred millions of dollars. How comes this vast amount of property to be running about without owners? We do not see free horses or free cattle running at large. How is this? All these free blacks are the descendants of slaves, or have been slaves themselves, and they would be slaves now, but for SOMETHING which has operated on their white owners, inducing them, at vast pecuniary sacrifices, to liberate them. What is that SOMETHING? Is there any mistaking it? In all these cases it is your sense of justice, and human sympathy, continually telling you, that the poor negro has some natural right to himself – that those who deny it, and make mere merchandise of him, deserve kickings, contempt and death.
>
> And now, why will you ask us to deny the humanity of the slave? and estimate him only as the equal of the hog? Why ask us to do what you will not do yourselves? Why ask us to do for nothing, what two hundred million of dollars could not induce you to do?[11]

Lincoln would deftly bring his listeners back to that original ground, the difference between men and animals. In the hands of Lincoln, that casting of the argument was critical to the point that the rights articulated in the Declaration of Independence had a *natural* foundation. They were not "rights" that were merely established or *posited* in any place by the people with the power to lay down rules, like the right to use the library in town or the squash courts at the club. They were rights that would arise for all human beings by nature, and they would remain the same in all places where that nature remained the same. Drawing on the same ancient understanding, John Locke would put the matter in this way:

> For men being all the workmanship of one . . . wise Maker . . . and being furnished with like faculties, sharing all in one community of nature, there

[10] *Ibid.*
[11] *Ibid.*, pp. 264–65.

cannot be supposed any such subordination among us that may authorize us to destroy one another, as if we were made for one another's uses, as the inferior ranks of creatures are for ours.[12]

And in his own work on the Social Contract, Jean-Jacques Rousseau could add:

> Since no man has natural authority over his fellows, and since Might can produce no Right, the only foundation left for legitimate authority in human societies is agreement.[13]

As the understanding ran then, no man was by nature the ruler of other men in the way that God was by nature the ruler of men and men were by nature the rulers of horses and cows. Therefore, in the second step, if we find a state of affairs in which some men are ruling over others, that situation could not have arisen from *nature*. It must have arisen from convention, agreement, or consent. To deny that understanding, said Jefferson, was to suggest that the "mass of mankind" had been "born with saddles on their backs," and that a favored few had been born "booted and spurred, ready to ride them legitimately, with the grace of God."[14]

Even in this age of "animal liberation" we do not find people signing labor contracts with their horses and cows, or seeking the "informed consent" of their household pets before they authorize surgery upon them. But we continue to think that beings who can give and understand reasons deserve to be ruled with a rendering of reasons, in a regime that elicits their consent. And yet, in our own day, these classic arguments, grounded in the plainest things we can know, have actually been derided and rejected by the orthodoxies now dominant on the American campuses. The fashionable doctrines of postmodernism and radical feminism have denied that we can know moral truths, let alone truths that hold across different countries and cultures. And at the foundation of everything, the exponents of these doctrines often deny that there is really a human nature. What we take to be human nature they regard as "social constructs" that vary from one place to another according to the vagaries of the local cultures. I have had the chance to address this problem in another place,[15] but it is worth noting yet again that the people who

---

[12] Locke, *Second Treatise on Civil Government* [1690], Bk. I, ch. 2, in *Social Contract*, ed. Sir Ernest Barker (London, Oxford University Press, 1960), pp. 5–6.

[13] *The Social Contract* [1762], Bk. I, ch. 4, in *ibid*, p. 173.

[14] Thomas Jefferson, letter to Roger Weightman (June 24, 1826), reprinted in *The Political Thought of American Statesmen*, ed. Morton G. Frisch and Richard G. Stevens (Itasca, Ill.: E. E. Peacock, 1973), p. 13.

[15] See my own *Natural Rights and the Right to Choose* (Cambridge: Cambridge University Press, 2002), pp. 18–19. It may be sobering to discover that even here, in the brash

take this line nevertheless keep casting moral judgments across cultures: They condemn genocide in Darfur, as they had condemned a regime of apartheid in the old South Africa, and they seem able to discern "wrongs" done to women. In fact, they seem to be able to recognize *women* when they see them, even in exotic and primitive places. And so, in the world of the postmodernists now on the campuses, there are human rights to be vindicated all over the globe, but strictly speaking there are no *humans*. For there is no human nature. And since there are no moral truths, there are no human "rights" that are truly *rightful*.

If we follow again Aristotle's understanding, the nature that is enduring becomes the source in turn of laws that spring enduringly from that nature. Aristotle would speak then about the law that is peculiar to any place or people and the kind of law that would be true in all places. And Cicero could write then in his *Republic* that "there will not be different laws at Rome and at Athens, or different laws now and in the future, but one eternal and unchangeable law will be valid for all nations and all times."[16] The late Heinrich Rommen drew upon recognitions of this kind when he remarked of the natural law that it was "an imperishable possession of the human mind."[17] It was an imperishable part of the things we could know, either because there was something permanent and enduring in the truths that it grasped, or something enduring in the nature of a creature that had a distinct access, through his reason, to those truths. It should occasion no surprise then that, in countless ways, those truths break through in the most ordinary cases. A visitor from London gets off a plane in New York, and we do not think we have to look at his passport, or take note of his citizenship, before we protect him from an unjustified assault in the street. But we seem to understand that the same man may not take himself over to the City College of New York and claim admission, or claim the same, subsidized rate of tuition that the people of New York are willing to make available to citizens of New York. The latter is a claim or right that arises in a particular place, out of a particular

world of modern relativism, there is nothing new. Skeptics in the ancient world had even more untethered things to say in denying the existence of objective moral truths. For a remarkable recollection of those ancient skeptics, see Ralph Cudworth, *A Treatise Concerning Eternal and Immutable Morality* (London, 1731), reprinted in a version edited by Sarah Hutton (Cambridge: Cambridge University Press, 1996), Bk. I.

[16] See Cicero, *The Republic*, III, xxii.

[17] Heinrich Rommen, *The Natural Law*, trans. Thomas R. Hanley (Indianapolis: Liberty Fund, 1998; published first in German in 1936 and in English in 1947), p. 190. It is notable that the original title in German was *Die Ewige Wiederkehr des Naturrechts* [The Perpetual Return of Natural Law].

association (like the right to use the squash courts at Amherst College). But the right to be protected against an unjustified assault is a right we would expect to be respected in all places by governments that purport to be decent and lawful governments.

During the recent, tumultuous demonstrations on immigration, we found many illegal aliens and their sympathizers carrying banners urging the conferral of citizenship even on those who came to this country illegally (in violation of the "positive laws"). What the demonstrators were arguing, I take it, was the rightfulness of conferring citizenship upon them quite apart from what the positive law had stipulated. They themselves were not citizens, but they wished to be, and they believed they had a *rightful claim* to be recognized as citizens. But again we may be surprised by the obvious: Since these people are not citizens, the "rights" they are invoking cannot spring from any rights they possess now *as citizens.* They must be invoking an understanding of right and wrong that stands quite apart from the positive law, the law that is "posited," set down, enacted in any place. The demonstrators were evidently invoking a standard of right and wrong that could be posed against the positive laws in judging the rightness or wrongness of those laws. In other words, they were appealing, in effect, to an understanding of natural right or natural law. And once again, they were doing it without any particular awareness that they were doing anything distinctly philosophic or juridical.

In the same way, we find that ordinary people show a commonsense understanding of the properties of a moral argument, even if they have not had a college education. And so, without making too much of it, people seem well aware of the difference between the things that are of the day, evanescent, and the things that are permanent, the things that are always. Or they grasp the difference between the things whose goodness is merely *contingent* upon their results, as opposed to things good or bad in themselves. Even people who have never been instructed in philosophy, and do not have the terms or the jargon, are aware of things whose goodness and badness is contingent on matters of degree and circumstance. They may readily grasp that the taking of an alcoholic drink is not always harmful; that it matters notably if it is taken in moderation, or taken in excess, without restraint. But we do not find the same people saying that "genocide, if taken in moderation, may be harmless or inoffensive." Ordinary people may have a keen sense of those things whose wrongness will not be effaced by matters of degree and circumstance. In that vein, we may find ourselves raising the question of whether racial discrimination – the willingness to assign benefits and disabilities to people solely on the basis of their race – is in principle wrong or merely contingently wrong, depending on its result from case to case. If it is in principle wrong, we would be led to conclude that it is wrong even if we do it just a bit of the time or, as the saying goes, that "we take race into account" at the margins of certain cases. Imagine saying that "it is wrong to kill on the basis of race, but perhaps legitimate to 'take race into account,' to let any decision on killing hinge on the matter of race." And so, if it is wrong in principle to make decisions on admission to universities hinge on race, then it would be quite as wrong to "take race into account" in making decisions in marginal cases. Just how we show that something is indeed in principle or categorically wrong in that way is a matter that may run well beyond the facility of the man on the street. And yet there is, without doubt, an awareness among ordinary people that there are certain things so wrong that their wrongness will not be diminished even if they are done only occasionally, in small doses.

It is one of the oddities of our recent experience that we can count on ordinary people to have the sense of these things, even as academics contrive theories to talk themselves out of these moral recognitions. But that may confirm the ancient truth that these are the kinds of things that we are simply constituted, in our nature, to understand. That lingering truth may account for the willingness of that eminent jurist Antonin Scalia to be open to the possibility of natural law, even as he has been rather scathing in rejecting natural law as a plausible scheme for judging in our own law.[18] One gathers that, for Scalia, the telling mark against natural law is that it inspires too ample a variety of theories and interpretations. But as we have to come to see in other domains, the mere presence of disagreement cannot be taken itself as proof that there are no truths to discern. Still, even a generation of Founders who were quite clear about natural right and natural justice could find certain advantages in a written Constitution. Many of them thought, with Scalia, that a written Constitution, published and confirmed over the years, would make it far easier for the public and for lawyers to become clear on the meaning of the "fundamental law."

But as I have tried to show, with a certain persistence in my own writing, none of this dispenses with the need and the utility of natural law reasoning. At almost every practical turn, as we try to apply the Constitution to the cases that come before us, we find the need to move beyond the text of the

---

[18] Justice Scalia has offered, of course, the clearest account of his jurisprudence in the opinions he has written over twenty years on the Supreme Court. But see also his notable lecture at Princeton in 1996, published as *A Matter of Interpretation: Federal Courts and the Law* (Princeton: Princeton University Press, 1997). He offers there, in a distinctly separate statement, a crisp, sharp exposition of his perspective on the law and the discipline of judges.

Constitution to those premises, or principles, that were antecedent to the text.[19] They were the first principles of "lawfulness," so fundamental that few people thought it necessary even to state them. (One of them, as we have seen, was the principle that barred "ex post facto laws.") But in their axiomatic quality, they touched the first principles in logic or the "laws of reason." James Wilson, one of the truly premier figures among the Founders and the members of the first Supreme Court, put it most aptly when he observed that, as we sought the ground of the law, we were brought to nothing less than the "principles of mind" or to the grounds on which we can claim truly to *know* anything.[20] The first generation of jurists made these moves with little strain. And yet, it seems to come as a surprise to many jurists and lawyers today that they are relying on these axioms of reason when they are "doing" law, or that these axioms of reason are indeed at the foundation of what the Founders understood as the "laws of reason and nature."

Among our current jurists, Justice Scalia has invoked those grounding truths with the most telling effect, even while professing his deep skepticism or wariness about natural law. As we shall see in a moment, Scalia, too, has had to make appeals to these canons of reason. That may be but another way of confirming that even the presence of a written Constitution does not relieve us of the need to deliberate in this manner, with a discipline of reason that was there, after all, to guide the framers even as they set about the task of drafting a constitution. And surely we have had ample experience by now to know that we have encountered some of the deepest disagreement over the meaning of terms in the most familiar passages in the Constitution – for example, laws "Impairing the Obligation of Contracts," or violating the Due Process of Law, or abridging the Equal Protection of the Law. We have seen judges fully willing to insist that a Constitution that refers at several points to Capital

---

[19] See my own book *Beyond the Constitution* (Princeton: Princeton University Press, 1990).

[20] See Wilson in *Chisholm v. Georgia* (1793), 2 U.S. 419, at 453–54: Before Wilson would invoke the authority of any case at law or any writer on matters legal, he would invoke the authority of "Dr. [Thomas] Reid, in his excellent enquiry into the human mind, on the principles of *common sense*, speaking of the sceptical and illiberal philosophy, which under bold, but false pretentions to liberality, prevailed in many parts of Europe before he wrote." But even more fully on this point, see Wilson's lectures on what could be called the "epistemology" of constitutional government – his lectures "The Philosophy of Evidence" and "Of Man, As a Member of Society," in *The Works of James Wilson* (Cambridge: Harvard University Press, 1967), ed. Robert Green McCloskey, Vol 1, pp. 370–98 and 197–226, respectively. But see also the new edition of Wilson's writings, including the lectures on jurisprudence, published in 2007 by the Liberty Fund: Kermit L. Hall and Mark David Hall (eds.), *Collected Works of James Wilson*, Vol. 2, pp. 792–826 (on the philosophy of evidence) and Vol. 1, pp. 621–44 (on man as "a member of society").

Offenses somehow, in its truer meaning, precludes capital punishment. On the other hand, as we shall see, some of the precepts or principles of natural law are so firmly in place, so bound up with the axioms of our reasoning, that there is no serious dispute about them. Nor is there any sense that they are "hazy," vague, incapable of being grasped and applied in the most practical way. In fact, these axioms are so woven in with our understanding that we may no longer even be aware of them as first principles.

In that vein, one of the first things we understand about the domain of moral judgment is that we cast judgments only on those acts that take place in the domain of freedom, where people are free to choose one course of action over another. As Thomas Reid observed, then, one of the first principles of moral reasoning is a proposition I have recast in this way: that we don't hold people blameworthy and responsible for acts they were powerless to affect.[21] If Smith is thrown out the window and on the way down lands on Jones, we don't hold him responsible for an assault. If Smith was born after the crime was committed we take that as powerful evidence of his innocence. If Smith was acting under hypnosis, so that his acts were directed by someone else, and sprung from no reasons or motives of his own, we take those facts as diminishing or dissolving his fault. If Smith met some clinical test of insanity, if it could be shown that he was not really in control of himself, that too would argue against his guilt. All of these are but instances informed by the same principle. As it turns out, there are no contingencies or circumstances in which that underlying principle will fail to be true. And yet from that proposition may spring, as I say, things like the insanity defense or the wrong of people suffering discrimination over something like their race, which is beyond their control.[22]

But of course "race" is not entirely beyond one's control: there are many black people of light skin who "passed" for white, and in this age of many mixed racial marriages, we find offspring who have choices in the racial definition they offer of themselves. The wrong of racial discrimination reaches a slightly different variant with the same ground of principle. For the issue is bound up with the enduring question of "determinism" as the radical denial

---

[21] Reid cast the matter in this way: that "what is done from unavoidable necessity . . . cannot be the object either of blame or moral approbation." Reid, *Essays on the Active Powers of the Human Mind* (Cambridge: MIT Press, 1969 [1788]), p. 361.

[22] For the fuller exposition of this account of the domain of freedom as a necessary condition of moral judgment, see Arkes, *First Things* (Princeton: Princeton University Press, 1986), pp. 88, 92–93, 97.

of "freedom." I have argued this matter at length in other places,[23] and it may be enough here to offer this more compressed account. Behind the will or passion to discriminate on the basis of race is a species of "determinism": the notion that race exerts a kind of deterministic control over the character and moral conduct of persons. Under this persuasion people may slide into the assumption that if they know someone's race, they can draw some plausible moral inferences about him: whether he is, on balance, a good or bad man; whether his presence in the firm or the neighborhood would improve the business or the community, or whether that presence would have a degrading effect. To know someone's race, then, on these premises, is to know something about that person that would mark him, with a high probability, as being fit or unfit for any place, more or less deserving of hiring and promotion. In short we would have the clearest ground for assigning benefits and disabilities to people on the basis, decisively, of their race.

But if this sense of things were true – that we are "determined" or controlled in our conduct by our race – then none of us could plausibly bear responsibility for our own acts. It might be said, in this respect, that the willingness to discriminate on the basis of race denies that moral autonomy, or freedom, that is the very premise of our standing as "moral agents." If we were not in control of our own acts, we would never deserve punishment at the hands of the law – and neither would we ever deserve praise. And so in all strictness it could be said that if this notion of "racial determinism" were not wrong, then nothing literally could ever be "wrong," for there would be no plausible standards of right and wrong to which persons might be held accountable. The whole language and logic of moral judgment, and of legal judgment, would be stripped of its meaning. These words "right" and "wrong" would be reduced to the oddity of words without meaning or function. They might imply a vague approval or disapproval, but not strictly a ground for casting judgments of right and wrong on other people.

When understood in this way, the wrongness of racial discrimination is anchored in the very logic of law and moral judgment. The wrong then is not merely "contingent" on circumstances, or on its effects in any case, but is *categorical*: There are no circumstances under which it fails to be wrong. That sense of the matter would stand in sharp contrast to the way in which the case against racial segregation was made in the federal courts, in that celebrated pattern of litigation carried through from the 1930s to the 1950s, with

---

[23] See *Ibid.*, and Arkes, *The Philosopher in the City* (Princeton: Princeton University Press, 1981), chs. 2 and 3, on "Civility and the Restriction of Speech," and on the matter of "determinism," pp. 46–48 and *passim*.

Brown v. Board of Education. And so the argument was heard that discrimination in colleges and law schools would be wrong because black students would be deprived of the acquaintances and "contacts" that would enlarge their horizons and the prospect for their careers.[24] Or with the *Brown* case, the argument was made that the separation of children on the basis of race would impair the motivation of black children to learn and, with that, their performance in school.[25] Never mind that there were cases of all-black high schools, with motivated pupils, families, and teachers, that went on to produce many black people for professional life.[26] And never mind, too, that these conjectures were inherently probabilistic: In the nature of things, one could not know for sure that, by bringing together people of different races, the mixture would beget affection, conversation, and friendships carried over into business. These were all predictions quite hostage to the results. And the radical defects in this mode of argument would make themselves manifest as soon as one posed the question in this way: If we separate students on the basis of race and their reading scores *go up*, would that mean that the racial segregation had ceased to be wrong? Or are we inclined to say, rather, that the segregation is wrong *in principle*? I once offered the example of the redoubtable Cecil Partee, the legendary black ward committeeman in Chicago. In Partee's account, he had graduated from the University of Arkansas in 1938 near the top of his class, and he applied to the law school. But Arkansas would not permit blacks to attend the law school of the public university. The state offered instead a voucher that would permit Partee to pursue his studies in law schools outside the state. And so, barred by law from the law school of the University of Arkansas, Partee was compelled to choose instead between the law schools of the University of Chicago and Northwestern. As Partee later put it, "I laughed all the way to Chicago."[27] Cecil Partee did not suffer a material harm as a result of the policy of segregation in Arkansas; but he was "wronged." He was treated according to the maxims of an unjust principle.

To take the matter from yet another angle, a sober reckoning of violent crime in New York or other cities would point to a clear "demographic"

---

[24] See, for example, *McLaurin v. Oklahoma State Regents,* 339 U.S. 637 (1950), and *Missouri ex. rel Gaines v. Canada,* 305 U.S. 337 (1938).

[25] See *Brown v. Board of Education,* 347 U.S. 483, at 494–95.

[26] See Thomas Sowell, "Black Excellence: The Case of Dunbar High School," *The Public Interest* (Spring 1974), pp. 3–21.

[27] Quoted in the interview with Partee conducted by my late, beloved professor, Milton Rakove; see Rakove, *We Don't Want Nobody Nobody Sent* (Bloomington: University of Indiana Press, 1979), p. 156.

cohort, quite likely to produce assaults well beyond the levels shown by other groups. Young black and Hispanic males, between fourteen and twenty-five, are far more likely to commit violent, armed assaults than white male accountants or female lawyers in their forties and fifties. If it were a matter strictly of playing the odds, or being governed by the probabilities, it would be entirely conceivable at least to cast an argument on utilitarian grounds for a certain preventive detention, or perhaps "closer official governance," of young males in this category. Balancing risks against gains, it is certainly arguable that the community would be a net gainer in the lives saved and the families preserved against the loss of productive members. And yet no one would come even close to offering such a proposal for discussion, let alone a serious plan to act upon. When we recoil from a scheme of that kind, the aversion can be explained only by the recognition that a policy of that sort would catch, in its sweep, many innocent people. They may be poor, but they may have no disposition to make their way in life by hurting others. But that is to say, when we hold back from that scheme, we seem to recognize that the features of ethnicity or race, mingled with poverty, do not control or "determine" character. We back into the recognition that we are imputing, even to ordinary folk, a certain capacity to hold themselves back from the ethic that may be dominant in their neighborhood or among their racial group, and reach their own judgments about the things that are right or wrong. To put it another way – without royalties to Immanuel Kant – we are recognizing a certain *moral autonomy* that must be characteristic of human beings. And it must be indeed the predicate of that freedom we impute to moral agents.

It is another of those curiosities of our own day that the notion of "moral autonomy" has been taken by liberals as the anchoring ground for new rights of sexual liberation. And at the same time, those extravagant claims have stirred a recoil among conservatives. In both instances, the notion of autonomy is gravely misunderstood. We may coherently impute a certain moral autonomy only to moral agents – those creatures who are capable of deliberating about the grounds of their well-being, and giving reasons. But it is in the nature of moral agents also that they have an understanding of right and wrong. They could grasp then, as Aquinas and Lincoln recognized, that there cannot be a "right to do a wrong." They could grasp, in other words, the things they can have no right to do or to claim in the name of their "autonomy." To invoke "autonomy" is not to invoke a license for a freedom emancipated from moral restraint, in private or in public. But when we fill in the portrait of that creature bearing this moral autonomy, we are describing again that creature described by Aristotle, standing somewhere between the beasts and the gods. It is the only animal fitted for political life and law because it is the only creature who can frame propositions, grasp the nature of an obligation, and respect a law beyond himself; a law that runs counter to his own inclinations or interests. When viewed through the lens of the American Founders, these are the creatures encompassed by that proposition, as Lincoln called it, "all men created equal." The political Left in our own day reproaches the American Founders for their putative failure to respect that principle. In that argument, the Founders have been indicted for the accommodations they made with the evil of slavery. But as we have seen, the embarrassment for writers on the Left is that they deny that there is a "nature" that provides the ground for these claims of equality and rights. They take a moral high ground in relation to the Founders, and yet they deny that there are moral truths that reason can know. And so, while they elevate "equality" as a principle, they deny that principle, or any other moral principle, the standing of a truth.

The confusion suffered here by the Left may be bound up with certain confusions suffered by many other people on what it means to regard "all men are created equal" as a self-evident or necessary truth. A "self-evident" truth is not one of those things "evident" to every "self" happening along the street. It was closer to what Aquinas described as a truth that had to be grasped *per se nota*, as something true in itself. Aquinas remarked that it was one of those "evident" principles of what he called "speculative reason," a truth that is "the same for all, but . . . not equally known to all. Thus it is true for all that the three angles of a triangle are together equal to two right angles, although it is not known to all."[28] If a person could not grasp the law of contradiction – that two contradictory propositions both could not be true – there would be no way of explaining it to him. For virtually anything we said could be contradicted, and if he thought that everything said was equally plausible – if he could entertain at the same time propositions that were at war with one another – there was nothing he could ever literally come to "know." If we sought to stage a controlled experiment – say, with a ball rolling down an inclined plane – we might test one plane with a slight angle set against a plane with a steeper angle. We could measure then what effect the steepness of the angle had on the acceleration of the ball. But we would need to understand at once that we were dealing with two different angles – that we have angle A, we might say, set against non-A. If we did not know the "law of contradiction," we could hardly understand the significance of comparing two or more distinct angles. We would have to know that A does

---

[28] *Summa Theologica*, Q94, Art 4.

not equal non-A if the experiment is to make sense. If we did not know the "principle of identity," we might not grasp the importance of the things held constant during the experiments, retaining their identity through changes in positioning. In other words, someone would have to understand these first principles before he could understand an experiment. And if he professed not to understand, say, the law of contradiction, then *there would be no way to convey the point to him in the form of an experiment.*

That the American Founders understood this matter of truths that had to be grasped *per se nota* was nowhere confirmed with more eloquence or clarity than by Alexander Hamilton in his opening paragraph for the *Federalist* No. 31. I have had the occasion to quote this passage before, but it is never out of season to quote it, for it still offers the most compelling example of what that generation of lawyers and Founders understood about the nature of axioms. This is the way Hamilton set up the problem in the *Federalist* No. 31:

> In disquisitions of every kind there are certain primary truths, or first princi-
> ples, upon which all subsequent reasonings must depend. These contain an
> internal evidence which, antecedent to all reflection or combination, com-
> mands the assent of the mind.... Of this nature are the maxims in geometry
> that the whole is greater than its parts; that things equal to the same are
> equal to one another; that two straight lines cannot enclose a space; and
> that all right angles are equal to each other. Of the same nature are these
> other maxims in ethics and politics, that there cannot be an effect without
> a cause; that the means ought to be proportioned to the end; that every
> power ought to be commensurate with its object; that there ought to be no
> limitation of a power destined to effect a purpose which is itself incapable of
> limitation.[29]

Hamilton, in this passage, clearly grasped the properties of a "first principle." The question persistently arises as to what kind of a proposition, exactly, was "all men are created equal" if that proposition really had the standing of a first principle. Some people have regarded it as an *inductive* proposition – that it is drawn as a generalization from experience, in taking account of the differences between men and animals, differences accessible to people of common sense. But as Thomas Reid pointed out, an inductive proposition claims to offer nothing more than a generalization drawn from experience, and therefore it cannot rise above a statement of probability.[30] If "all men

---

[29] Hamilton, *Federalist* No. 31, in *The Federalist Papers* (New York: Random House, n.d.), p. 188.

[30] See Reid, *Essays on the Intellectual Powers of Man* (Cambridge: MIT Press, 1969 [origi-nally published, 1814–15]), p. 654.

are created equal" were really an inductive proposition, it would have to be recast as "Most men are created equal, most of the time."

In my childhood, in the early days of television, there was a program called *Candid Camera,* and in one of the early episodes the producers set up a microphone in a mailbox. The mailbox then would engage the people dropping in letters. The mailbox would say something like, "Is it still raining?" And what was astonishing was just how many people, without skipping a beat, would answer and fall into a conversation with the mailbox. It occurred to me recently that we could put the question: If most of us don't talk to mailboxes, do we make that judgment *inductively* or *deductively?* That is, if we are asked why we don't speak to the mailboxes, are we inclined to say, "They usually don't talk to me"? That is, do we induce what strikes us as a general rule, likely to be true, as we draw the lessons from experience in the past? Or is it that we grasp something about the nature of mailboxes, and we have no expectation of carrying on conversations with mailboxes, household appliances, or other inanimate objects?

As Reid taught, a "first principle" had to state a "necessary" proposition, and "propositions of this kind, from their nature, are incapable of proof by induction." They could not be demonstrated by experiments because experiments depend on experience, and "experience," he said, "informs us only what is, or has been, not of what must be":

> Though it should be found by experience in a thousand cases, that the area of a plane triangle is equal to the rectangle under the altitude and half the base, this would not prove that it must be so in all cases, and cannot be otherwise.... [31]

The hard fact was that one could not "experience" a necessary proposition. Experience could tell us only of the things experienced, and we have no experience of the future. At the most, we might say that, in certain cases, the future is likely to be similar to the past and yield similar outcomes. That the advent of major league baseball in any city will foster many new jobs and lift the level of prosperity may be a high probability indeed. Still, that relation of cause and effect would not be true of necessity. But that it is "wrong to hold people blameworthy or responsible for acts they are powerless to affect" would in fact be true under all conditions and circumstances, now and in the future. A necessary proposition would hold true at all times, in all cases. When Lincoln said that the American republic began, not with the Constitution, but with that "proposition" that "all men are created equal,"

---

[31] *Ibid.*

he seemed to regard that proposition as conveying the principle that defined the character of the regime. From that proposition, everything else radiated. That proposition, he said, marked "an abstract truth applicable to all men and all times." The notion of government by consent, or as Lincoln put it, "the doctrine of self-government," was, as he said, "absolutely and eternally right."[32] And with that, he left us the clearest sense that this principle, the founding principle of the regime, was nothing less than a first principle, with nothing merely contingent or probabilistic about it.

In the same way that ordinary people reveal a philosophic sense without being quite aware of it, some of my best friends among lawyers tend to back into these first principles even while professing that they cannot reliably know them. One judge I know insists that we should not be legislating on matters of moral consequence in the absence of a consensus – to which his friends respond by asking, "Do you claim to have arrived at *that* proposition or rule on the basis of a consensus? Have you taken a survey and established that this rule you announce has elicited the widespread, or even unanimous, agreement of the public? If so, we have to report that we didn't receive *our* ballots. And if we had, you would not have had any consensus to report."

But of course this judge had not taken a survey before he announced this proposition, which he evidently regarded as a cardinal point in jurisprudence. To take those lines from Hamilton, he had apparently regarded this proposition as one of those truths "which antecedent to all reflection or combination commands the assent of the mind." Which is to say, he took it as nothing less than a first principle, from which we could draw a substantial body of judgments in the law. But a principle of that kind could not depend on a consensus or the taking of a vote. And if we can know at least one proposition of that kind, whose claim to our respect does not depend in the least on a consensus or the vote of a majority, we may reasonably expect to know one or two others.

What undoes this offhand gesture toward a first principle on the part of the jurist is that it backs into self-contradiction. It runs afoul of the laws of reason. The nearest variant on this mistake is probably the most familiar refrain, on the political Right as well as the Left, among those who express dubiety about natural law. It usually runs in this way: "If there were moral truths that held universally, they would be acknowledged in all places. The fact that they are not – that we find instead a widespread disagreement over the things that are right and wrong – stands as prima facie evidence that those 'universal moral truths' do not exist." As I have pointed out in another place, that argument

---

[32] Lincoln, Speech at Peoria, *supra*, note 9, p. 265.

really reduces to this proposition: that the absence of consensus or agreement indicates the absence of truth. Now of course I would have to register my own disagreement with *that proposition*, and on its own terms that should be enough to establish its falsity.

There are no tricks, and this is not a game with words. It is a matter of people simply falling into what the philosophers call a self-refuting proposition. What is odd is to see how many people experienced in law still regard that proposition with evident seriousness, and that some judges are willing to take it as a foundational point in their jurisprudence. There is surely no more telling example on that head than that proposition offered earnestly by Justice Harry Blackmun:

> When those trained in the respective disciplines of medicine, philosophy, and theology are unable to arrive at any consensus [on the question of when human life begins], the judiciary, in this point in the development of man's knowledge, is not in a position to speculate as to the answer.[33]

Actually, there was no want of consensus in the textbooks on embryology and obstetric gynecology on this matter of when human life began. That point was amply established by the Senate Committee on the Judiciary in 1981, when it surveyed all of the leading textbooks in the field.[34] Obviously, Blackmun had undertaken no survey to gauge the absence of a consensus; he was simply stating what he took to be a truism. But if he had been alert to the property of propositions he might have recognized that he too had simply backed into a self-refuting proposition. Again, what seems to come as a surprise for lawyers and judges, whether conservative or liberal, is that natural law is bound up with the laws of reason, or the canons of logic. One of the most gifted lawyers this country has produced, a man who made his way into the profession by "reading at law," gave us the simplest example of natural law reasoning. And in the spirit of natural law, it could be grasped readily even by people without training in law. In a fragment he had written for himself, Abraham Lincoln imagined himself in a conversation with the

---

[33] *Roe v. Wade*, 410 U.S. 113 at 159 (1973).

[34] Report from the Senate Committee on the Judiciary, drawn from Hearings before the Subcommittee on the Separation of Powers Committee on the Judiciary, U.S. Senate; 97th Cong., 1st Sess., on S. 158 ("a bill to provide that Human Life shall be deemed to exist from conception"), April–June, 1981. The findings of the Committee on the Judiciary were amply confirmed recently in a comparable survey of the most recent books and revised editions of the books cited by the Committee. See Ryan Anderson, "The Beginning of Life: An Update of the Medical Texts," Witherspoon Center (Princeton), May 2006.

owner of black slaves, raising the question of how he could justify making a slave of black people:

> You say A. is white, and B. is black. It is *color*, then: the lighter having the right to enslave the darker? Take care. By this rule, you are to be slave to the first man you meet, with a fairer skin than your own.
>
> You do not mean *color* exactly? – You mean the whites are *intellectually* the superiors of the blacks, and therefore have the right to enslave them? Take care again. By this rule, you are to be slave to the first man you meet, with an intellect superior to your own.
>
> But, say you, it is a question of interest; and, if you can make it your *interest*, you have the right to enslave another. Very well. And if he can make it his interest, he has the right to enslave you.[35]

Lincoln offered, in the most concentrated form, a model of principled reasoning: There was nothing one could cite to disqualify the black man as a human being, and the bearer of rights, that would not apply to many whites as well. There was an apt lesson to be drawn in pointing out that nowhere, in this chain of reasoning, was there an appeal to faith or revelation. Lincoln's argument could be understood across the divisions of religion or race or class – it could be understood by Catholics or Baptists, by geologists or carpenters, and even by people unburdened with a college education. It could be understood then by ordinary people, using the wit of rational creatures, and in my own experience no one, hearing the argument, has failed to grasp it. For the natural law to function as law, it has to be accessible, fairly commonly, to those creatures of reason who walk among us.

As Aquinas observed, the divine law we know through revelation, but the natural law we know through that reason that is natural to human beings, accessible to ordinary people as creatures of reason. That understanding was carried down over the years to the American Founders through other sources confirming that teaching. James Wilson often cited the formidable Jean-Jacques Burlamaqui in his classic work *The Principles of Natural and Politic Law* (1748), and Burlamaqui thought it critical to get clear on why natural law could not be dependent on revelation. No doubt, he wrote, "God was at liberty . . . to create or not create man," and to impart to him quite a different nature. But "having determined to form a rational and social being, he could not prescribe any thing unsuitable to such a creature." In fact, Burlamaqui

---

[35] *The Works of Abraham Lincoln, supra,* note 9, pp. 222–23.

suggested that the notion of law and its principles would be subverted if they were thought to depend on "the arbitrary will of God":

> For, if these laws were not a necessary consequence of the nature, consti-
> tution, and state of man, it would be impossible for us to have a certain
> knowledge of them, except by a very clear revelation, or by some other
> formal promulgation on the part of God. But . . . the law of nature is, and
> ought to be, known by the mere light of reason.[36]

Long before Burlamaqui and the teachers of international law, the same point was made by "the judicious Hooker," as Locke called him. Richard Hooker, in his *Laws on Eccesiastical Polity*, explained the elementary point that the natural law would be known through that reason that is distinctive to human beings:

> Law rational therefore, which men commonly use to call the law of nature,
> meaning thereby the law which human nature knoweth itself in reason
> universally bound unto, which also for that cause may be termed most fitly
> the law of reason.[37]

But long before Hooker were the Church fathers – *vide* St. John Chrysostom: "We use not only Scripture but also reason in arguing against the pagans." And of course, running back to the beginning of the Church, St. Paul in Romans: "When the gentiles, which have not the law, do by nature the things contained in the law, [they] are a law unto themselves" (Romans 2: 14). On the central place of reason, then, in natural law, there is a convergence of teaching emanating from both Jerusalem and Athens, with the moderns as well as the ancients. In fact, as John Paul II and his successor have argued in our own day, the tradition of philosophy coming down from the Greeks has been, as John Paul II said, "the hedge and protective wall around the vineyard" of the Church. For the discipline of philosophy has been critical in helping to discriminate between readings of revelation that were plausible or spurious. John Paul II thought that it was the considerable service of the "fathers of philosophy to bring to light the link between reason and religion":

> As they broadened their view to include universal principles, they no longer
> rested content with the ancient myths, but wanted to provide a rational
> foundation for their belief in the divinity. . . . Superstitions were recognized

---

[36] J.-J. Burlamaqui, *The Principles of Natural and Politic Law* (1748), Part 2, ch. 5.

[37] Hooker, *Of the Laws on Ecclesiastical Polity* (Cambridge: Cambridge University Press, 1989; originally published in parts, in 1593 and 1597, with the latter sections not being published until 1648 and 1661), p. 82.

for what they were and religion was, at least in part, purified by rational analysis.[38]

The tie to philosophy, even for religion, marked the unity of knowledge, and it provided the anchoring point of conviction that there could be no real division between religion and science. As John Paul II observed, "[T]he two modes of knowledge lead to truth in all its fullness. The unity of truth is a fundamental premise of human reasoning, *as the principle of non-contradiction makes clear*" [my italics]:

> Revelation renders this unity certain, showing that the God of creation is also the God of salvation history. It is the one and the same God who establishes and guarantees the intelligibility and reasonableness of the natural order of things upon which scientists confidently depend.... [39]

I would not want to claim that John Paul II was coinciding with Immanuel Kant in all critical respects; but I would point out that the Holy Father saw no strain in finding the ground of moral reasoning, as Kant did, in the laws of reason, anchored in the law of contradiction. It should not have come as news to writers in our own day, and yet it seems to come as a kind of revelation to discover that "natural law" does not depend on religious beliefs, ever evading the test of reason. Quite to the contrary, natural law has ever been bound up with "the laws of reason," and the laws of reason find their own touchstone, or their anchoring ground, in the law of contradiction.

By the time we have taken these simple steps, tracing back the tradition, we will have backed into Immanuel Kant's recognition: that what we mean by the "moral laws" is nothing more than those laws of reason themselves. They are the *laws of reason*, the canons of logic, that command our judgment in the *domain of freedom*. For it is only in the domain of freedom that a practical judgment becomes possible. It is only when we have the freedom to choose that we are drawn outward to the standards that govern our choice between the things that are good or bad, right or wrong, just or unjust. Kant used that curious expression "the laws of freedom" to mean the "moral laws." At first glance that might sound like an oxymoron, for if there are laws governing us we would not be free exactly to do as we wished. But the point rather was that the "moral world," with the casting of moral judgments, makes sense only in that domain in which people are *free* to choose one course of action over another. The "laws of freedom" are those "laws of reason" that command

[38] John Paul II, *Faith and Reason* [Fides et Ratio], sec. 36.
[39] *Ibid.*, sec. 34.

our judgment in the domain of freedom. We do not impute wrongs to the movement of rocks in a landslide; we do not say it would be morally *wrong* if Smith, falling out of a window, fell down upon Jones. The "laws of freedom" would refer then to those "laws of reason" that command and guide our acts in the domain of freedom. But they are "laws" only if they have about them the quality of necessity. And they can have that quality only if they find their ground indeed in the "laws of reason" strictly understood – in propositions we cannot deny without falling into contradiction.

Still, one might ask, How are they "laws" like the "laws of physics"? After all, we cannot repeal the "laws of gravity." And those strike us more forcibly as laws: laws that cannot depend on our will or intentions, laws that we are obliged to respect because they are forces of nature. In contrast, people are every day violating the law of contradiction; they often find ways of being inconsistent, especially on things that matter to them. The "laws of reason," anchored by the "law of contradiction," would be a different species of "law." And what makes them a species of "law" is that they have the force of being inescapably true. The ceiling does not fall in when we do things that are contradictory. The law of contradiction claims the standing of law because it has the sovereign attribute of being not only true, but true of necessity. It commands our respect then as creatures of reason in the domain of freedom. These are creatures who have reasons for their acts, and beyond that, creatures who may be concerned to describe, in their own acts, a principled course of conduct.

As Aristotle reminded us, we would not assume that all human beings, at all ages or stages of maturity, would have that concern as a matter of high rank in their lives. For those people, as he said, life may consist of a series of disconnected emotional episodes, so that the decision taken yesterday bears no relation to the decision taken today.[40] Yet, even ordinary people, not especially reflective, will show that concern in one degree or another; and even if they do not, the main point is not dislodged. To the extent that we

---

[40] See Aristotle, *Nicomachean Ethics*, Bk. I, ch. 3:

> Every man is a good judge of what he understands: in special subjects the specialist, over the whole field of knowledge the man of general culture. This is the reason why political science is not a proper study for the young. The young man is not versed in the practical business of life from which politics draws its premises and its data. He is, besides, swayed by his feelings, with the result that he will make no headway and derive no benefit from a study the end of which is not knowing but doing. It makes no difference whether the immaturity is in age or in character. The defect is not due to lack of years but to living the kind of life which is a succession of unrelated emotional experiences. To one who is like that, knowledge is as unprofitable as it is to the morally unstable. On the other hand, for those whose desires and actions have a rational basis, a knowledge of these principles of morals must be of great advantage.

would govern our acts by principles of judgment that are true, the standards that are grounded in this way, in propositions that must be true of necessity, have an unsurpassed claim on us. To the extent that we are governed and guided by them, they offer the grounds on which we can give a compelling account of our own acts. And if our acts find their ground in the "laws of reason," in propositions that are true of necessity, *those reasons will hold in all places.* They will hold, that is, in all places where human creatures can be found and the laws of reason are intact. Hence the understanding summarized in such a compressed way in the Categorical Imperative: Act only on that maxim fit to be installed as a universal rule.

The subject of this sentence is the unexpressed "You," a person in the domain of freedom who faces a choice over different courses of conduct. To extent that you allow yourself to be governed by "the laws of reason," by propositions that must be true of necessity, your acts are guided by a proposition "fit to be installed as a universal law." If a proposition is true of necessity, then as we say, "perforce" it must be true in all places. It must be universal in its reach or application.

Let me recap quickly and offer an example. We know that we are dealing with a proposition true of necessity when we confront a proposition that cannot be denied without falling into contradiction. The skeptic who denies that we are in the domain of freedom manifests his own freedom to stand apart and refuse his assent to our claim that freedom, as a practical matter, does exist. To the extent that he insists that we are "wrong" or mistaken to assert the existence of freedom – or assert the truth of anything – he does not merely register his feelings or his personal aversion. He is telling us that we are *wrong*, that we are mistaken. But that move must imply that he has access to standards of reason, accessible to us as they are to him – standards of judgment that would tell us that we are wrong. He has merely found another way of confirming his own access to the "laws of reason." With these moves he not only backs into self-contradiction; he also confirms the Kantian proof of what we mean by "the laws of freedom" or moral laws: (i) that in some parts of our lives at least we are in the domain of freedom, with the freedom to choose our own course of conduct, and (ii) that we have access to the "laws of reason" in gauging whether the maxims, or reasons, underlying our acts are true or false, right or wrong.

But if all of that is the case, then we would confirm in the same way that proposition I mentioned earlier, as the first implication springing from the logic of morals: namely, that moral judgments cast upon others make sense only if we can assume that people were free to form their own acts;

that we may not hold people blameworthy or responsible for acts they were powerless to affect. With but a short step, we may add the implication that springs up for racial discrimination: that we cannot credit the notion that race essentially controls or "determines" the moral character of any person. For under those conditions, no one would be responsible for his own acts, and no one could possibly merit either praise or blame, rewards or punishments. With those elementary points in place, consider one application of the Kantian understanding:

Let us suppose that we have two owners of restaurants in that liberal town called Amherst, Massachusetts, a college town, peopled richly with persons of the most advanced liberal reflexes. The two owners decide to arrange their establishments on the rule that there shall be no discrimination on the basis of race in admitting customers to their places of business. But we know that people may act in the same way even when their conduct springs from reasons or maxims that are strikingly different. Restaurant Owner A is working on the maxim that "it is good to accord the rules of one's business with the local ethos or the 'culture' of that community in which the business is located. It would be thoroughly bad for business in liberal Massachusetts if the word got out that the proprietors of this restaurant were racist, that they were willing to find certain customers undesirable solely on the basis of their race."

In contrast, Restaurant Owner B works on this maxim: "It would be incoherent to assume that race determines moral character, and that I could draw any interesting inferences about my potential customers based upon their race. It might be reasonable to discriminate, say, on the basis of a dress code, but it would be utterly indefensible to mark my customers worthy or unworthy solely on the basis of their race."

But then, in the usual license of a thought-experiment, let us imagine that both owners are somehow transported to South Africa during the regime of apartheid. Restaurant Owner A holds to his maxim as one that is eminently portable, but he is now in a different place, with a different ethos, and so the result is that he now flips in his operating rule. All around him people make the most important discriminations based on race, and he will not offend the local culture; he will adopt its racial principles as his own. With Restaurant Owner B there is the same willingness to stick with the same maxim, because it has not been affected by the shift in locale. He still understands that it would be not only wrong, but incoherent, to indulge the assumption that people are controlled or determined in their conduct by their race. The difference, however, is that Owner B's maxim is grounded in a law of reason, a proposition that is true of necessity. We need not be overly romantic and suppose that

Owner B is utterly indifferent to "results." It may matter profoundly to him that he might not be able to stay in business, and make a living, if he adheres to the maxim that claimed his respect, and governed his acts, when he was in Amherst, Massachusetts. He is bound to understand all of that. It is just that, in all honesty, he still finds that the principle he recognized earlier has not been diminished at all in its validity merely because he has moved from Massachusetts to South Africa. If he would be governed by a moral principle that is true and commands his allegiance, he simply reports that he can do no other. Lincoln once remarked on the young man aspiring to be a lawyer that "if in your own judgment you cannot be an honest lawyer, resolve to be honest without being a lawyer. Choose some other occupation, rather than one in the choosing of which you do, in advance, consent to be a knave."[41] Advice aptly and soberly offered to lawyers would not become wildly utopian when addressed to the owners of restaurants.

But what we have then, with Owner B, is the case of an actor in the domain of freedom who accorded his conduct with a maxim fit to be installed as a universal rule. The maxim was as valid in South Africa as in Amherst, and the validity of that maxim was utterly unaffected by the prospect that the results could be dire, that he could fall out of that business. And that is what we may tenably mean by that language, often appearing grandiloquent, that something categorically wrong retains its standing as a wrong even if the results are unhappy and even ruinous.

If that construction is intelligible, then we could see more readily what Kant meant when he said that everything that has standing as a moral principle has that standing as it is drawn as a logical implication from this core: an actor in the domain of freedom, seeking to accord his acts with a maxim grounded in the laws of reason. And so as Kant said, "[W]e ought . . . to derive our principles from the general concept of a rational being as such, and on this basis to expound the whole of ethics."[42] The body of principles we draw in that way may be quite economical or parsimonious. We are not asking, "What do most people around here *regard* as good or bad, right or wrong?" We would be lifting the bar – which is to say, we would be far more demanding and cautious before we invoke the language of "morality" and impose those judgments as law. But what comes as surprising in another degree is just how

---

[41] "Fragment: Notes for a Law Lecture [July 1850?], in *The Collected Works of Abraham Lincoln, supra*, note 9, p. 82.

[42] Kant, *Groundwork of the Metaphysics of Morals* [1785], trans. H. J. Paton (New York: Harper and Row, 1964), p. 79; p. 412 of the standard edition of the Royal Prussian Academy [hereafter, RPA ed.].

much, in our public discourse, or in our moral judgments, may be drawn as implications from this limited, precise sense of the "logic of morals" itself.

In fact, I think we would find that most of our judgments would fall into a class of propositions that are understood readily, even instantly, by ordinary people, even if they have no awareness that they are seeing merely instances of the same, simple principle at work. And what I have in mind are those recognitions, grasped by virtually everyone, of the attributes or conditions that have "no moral significance" and cannot supply the ground then of any adverse moral judgments. To put it another way, the point is so obvious that we may be startled even to hear it raised as a question. If we were told, for example, that a person was tall or short, thin or heavy, that he had dark hair or light hair, would we think that any of these points had given us the ground for any inferences on whether we were dealing with a person who was brilliant or dim, admirable or corrupt, someone who deserved praise or blame? We grasp these points readily, but if there was a need to explain the ground of the understanding, it would lie once again in the problem of "determinism": We know that none of these features – height, weight, color of hair – "determines" in any way the moral character of any person, and therefore none of them would supply a ground for any inferences as to whether this person deserved to be celebrated or shunned, rewarded or punished.

Traced to its core, this is how we would explain what we mean when we say that these features are utterly wanting in moral significance. But they are but part of a larger scheme that actually does find expression in our law, for the same underlying principle would finally explain why it would be unwarranted to draw adverse inferences about people who are suffering from various disabilities. People quite brilliant may be afflicted with stuttering, or with diabetes, with poor eyesight and tremors. Their maladies may act as barriers to many activities – the stutterer may not work well as an actor or as an announcer on the BBC; the nurse afflicted with poor eyesight may be disqualified to participate in serious surgery. But their disabilities would not bar them from many other occupations, and that sense of things would stand behind the laws that now bar certain discriminations based on "disabilities." In the infamous case of Baby Doe on Long Island in the 1980s, the child was afflicted at birth with spina bifida and Down's syndrome.[43] The parents, in league with the doctors, refused to provide medical care to this newborn, with the sense that she had, with these afflictions, a life not worth living.

---

[43] See the discussion of this case in my book *Beyond the Constitution, supra,* note 19, pp. 232–45. The case was *Bowen v. American Hospital Association,* 476 U.S. 610 (1986).

The case became difficult to disentangle as the Reagan administration was perpetually stymied in the effort to gain access to the records of the hospital and to determine the ground on which the medical care had been withheld from this newborn. If the situation had been inoperable, the administration would not have been seeking to press people into futile surgery. But if the withholding of care turned on a moral judgment – that people afflicted with Down's syndrome or spina bifida had lives "not worth living," lives that could be "terminated" without the need to render a justification – then that was a case that came within the moral understanding that barred discriminations based on "disability." The "discriminations" in these cases involved nothing less than a willingness to end the life of a person on the premise that a person with these afflictions did not really deserve to live.

In comparable cases, we've seen patients who were quadriplegic seek a "right" to end their lives on the claim that their lives were devoid of "dignity and purpose." In one notable case, of Elizabeth Bouvia in Los Angeles, a court sustained her "right" to end her life on the reasons she tendered – but at the same time commended her for being "brave and feisty." Not only that, the court awarded her lawyers' fees for propelling through the court, through the force of her own will and advocacy, a holding that could advance the public interest. The judges were willing to credit her account that her life was fixed now in "uselessness," and "her existence meaningless."[44] And yet, even without control of her limbs, she had argued and pressed a case receiving high praise from the court. The combination virtually refuted the claims. Even a quadriplegic, dependent on the care of others at every turn, had the means of acting upon her world, and the people around her, with the most pronounced moral effect.

In the cases that keep arising over a "right to die," the courts are persistently being asked to confirm the rightness, the moral justification, for ending the life of a patient because he may be afflicted with AIDS, or with cancer, and perhaps even with deafness. Deafness could be the most disabling of conditions for a conductor in an orchestra, and there are surely people who will claim that, for them, a life without music is a life not worth living. But to leap then to a moral conclusion – that a person afflicted with deafness has no

---

[44] See Judge Beach in *Bouvia v. Superior Court*, 225 Cal.Rptr. 297 (Cal.App 2 Dist. 1986), at 304, 305 (1986). The award of lawyers' fees came a year later. In the expression of her despair, Ms. Bouvia had professed her want of interest in taking in food. But after her success in pressing her lawsuit, her appetite for litigation seemed unappeasable. She won her suit for lawyers' fees in *Bouvia v. County of Los Angeles* (1987), 195 Cal.App.3d 1075, and see especially 1085–86.

means of living a life of moral consequence – is to make an extravagant and deeply incoherent move.

A man may have the means of taking his own life, but something else needs to be said in order to establish that it is "rightful" to end any life, even one's own, on the basis of "reasons" that are irretrievably false and indefensible. And of course it is only when premises of that kind are put in place – that it is somehow rightful to end the life, say, of a patient with AIDS – that the ground is laid for relatives or even strangers to assist in the ending of that life. For if Jones has a "right" to end his life, why should he be deprived of that right when he is incapable of acting himself to end it? Why should he not be free to authorize someone else to act as an agent in vindicating his right? If he happens to be an orphan, or one without relatives or friends, why should an administrator in a hospital not be able to stand in the place of missing relatives and act as an agent in helping this man act out his "right"?

My purpose here, though, is not to probe the deeper argument that is engaged in the matter of suicide, assisted or unassisted. I am only pointing out that what is engaged in these cases is a problem that runs to the same root in principle, on the matter of "determinism." That point, quite primary and simple, shows itself in instances spread widely in our law and public life. But to put this point into place is to provide the ground for some lessons that may be received as fairly astounding among lawyers and judges who have been the most dismissive of natural law as an enterprise too ethereal, too hazy, to provide any practical import for the law.

We may take again as an example the judgment on deafness and disabilities – the wrong of drawing adverse inferences about any person, or even ending a life, on the basis of deafness. It makes the most profound difference to know that this judgment is anchored in the laws of reason themselves. It is bound up with the rejection of determinism in all of its varieties. But if we come to understand the matter in that way – if we understand just why it would be deeply indefensible to punish people on account of their height, their weight, their deafness, their afflictions – we would understand that this moral reflex of ours does not represent merely some local custom, or *some peculiarity of this tribe of Americans.* We may ask then, Where in the world would it be wrong to withhold medical treatment from a newborn – or for that matter, from any other person – because he is afflicted with Down's syndrome or deafness? Would it not be as wrong in Lichtenstein, the Ivory Coast, or New Jersey? I leave aside here the usual array of lifeboat problems in which the deaf person may be expendable because he is the least able to keep watch and be alert to noises at sea. I focus entirely on the matter of withdrawing medical care because one has drawn an adverse inference about the moral worth of a person based on his deafness or Down's syndrome. And the answer I would earnestly offer is that this act of withdrawing care, on those grounds, would be wrong anywhere, everywhere, where the laws of reason are intact, and where creatures of reason bother to consider whether they truly have reasons to justify their acts.

I would submit then to a candid world – and to some of my friends among the judges – that there is nothing here the least opaque, foggy, imprecise; nothing that depends on the manipulation of words or a rarefied vocabulary. What is offered here is grounded in the first premises of moral judgment, and in things that are readily grasped by ordinary people even without an education in philosophy. And the judgment that is offered here would be concrete, precise, not the least hazy – and universal in its reach.

This matter of assisted suicide offers the thread of connection back to one of my favorite jurists, who has expressed often his dubiety about natural law, even as he has expressed also his reverence for the moral tradition from which natural law has sprung.

I have in mind that estimable man of the law Antonin Scalia. And I would bring this exploration of natural law to its last phase here by recalling that forceful dissenting opinion he wrote in January 2006 in *Gonzales v. Oregon*, on the problem of assisted suicide in Oregon.[45] In that case, a bare majority on the Court came down on the side of permitting the state of Oregon a certain latitude, under the scheme of federalism, in allowing doctors to prescribe drugs, in certain supposedly "terminal" cases, to hasten the death of the patient. By now the news has diffused widely in the land that the diagnosis of a "terminal condition," with the patient having six months to live, has been notoriously, or happily, unreliable. The law in Oregon contained all kinds of measures designed to confine the decision, but we are all wise now to the fact that those so-called safeguards, so precise in their construction, virtually dissolve in practice. They dissolve in the face of a determination on the part of some patients and their relatives to end their lives, with the complaisance of certain doctors in making themselves instruments of that policy. No matter the paper barriers cast up to provide assurances here; at the end of the day the policy results in doctors willing to make themselves agents in administering death.

In order to sustain this arrangement, the Supreme Court itself had to get past some considerable barriers of the federal law, not the least of which was

---

[45] 163 L. Ed. 2d 748 (2006).

that the Court itself, only several months earlier, had confirmed that the control of drugs, or the regulation of "controlled substances," was preeminently a matter of federal jurisdiction.[46] That jurisdiction by the federal government also seemed to repel, quite clearly, any attempt of the various states to install their own regime for the regulation of drugs.

In the case from Oregon, even the judges in the majority had to recognize that they needed to come up with a refined explanation to show why the exclusive federal control of drugs suddenly yields to this permission for the states on assisted suicide. The argument offered by Justice Kennedy was that it was not clear, under the statutes, that the Attorney General had the authority to make a judgment about the proper and improper uses of drugs – which is to say, the proper or improper ends of medicine.[47] The judges complained also that this was a decision that the Attorney General took without bothering to consult the Secretary of Health, Education and Welfare or anyone with any recognized medical competence.[48]

But these points were met by Justice Scalia, in dissent, in a withering rebuttal. It was not clear why the Secretary of Health and Human Services should be armed with an authority to pronounce on the legal or illegal use of drugs, and put himself in place of the chief "law officer" of the federal government.[49] But even more critically, the judgment on assisted suicide was not a medical or scientific judgment. It was a *moral judgment* on the rightness or wrongness, the justification or the want of justification, for assisted suicide.[50] Science, by its own profession, does not claim to reach to the knowledge of moral things, to pronounce on the truth or falsity of moral propositions. If it has become clear now that the regulation of drugs is distinctly, and solely, under the authority of the federal government, then *perforce*, as a matter of necessity,

---

[46] See *Gonzales v. Raich*, 545 U.S. 1 (June 2005, just six months before *Gonzales v. Oregon*).

[47] *Gonzales v. Oregon*, 163 L. Ed. 2d 748 (2006), at 768–75, especially 768–70.

[48] *Ibid.*, at 772–75, especially 775.

[49] *Ibid.*, at 791–92.

[50] As Scalia put it,

> It is...perfectly consistent with an intelligent "design of the statute" to give the Nation's chief law enforcement official, not its chief health official, broad discretion over the substantive standards that govern registration and deregistration. That is *especially* true where the contested "scientific and medical" judgment at issue has to do with the legitimacy of physician-assisted suicide, which ultimately rests, not on "science" or "medicine," but on a naked value judgment. It no more depends upon a "quintessentially medical judgment," ... than does the legitimacy of polygamy or eugenic infanticide. And it requires no particular *medical* training to undertake the objective inquiry into how the continuing traditions of Western medicine have consistently treated this subject.

> *Ibid.*, at 792.

it must fall to an officer of high standing in the federal government to pronounce on the meaning of federal law. That person figures to be the Attorney General, which means that he has to pronounce on the question, standing at the head of all questions, and bound up with the authority to engage in *licensing*: namely, the question of just what is a legitimate or illegitimate purpose for these drugs. In addressing that question, the Attorney General, John Ashcroft, did not invoke any sentiments merely personal: His staff recalled, in a memo, the understanding of medical ethics running back to Hippocrates. Justice Scalia summed up the memo:

> [V]irtually every medical authority from Hippocrates to the current American Medical Association (AMA) confirms that assisting suicide has seldom or never been viewed as a form of "prevention, cure, or alleviation of disease," and (even more so) that assisting suicide is not a "legitimate" branch of that "science and art." See OLC Memo, App. to Pet. for Cert. 113a-130a. Indeed, the AMA has determined that "physician-assisted suicide is fundamentally incompatible with the physician's role as a healer."[51]

In his opinion for the majority, Justice Kennedy was compelled to acknowledge this traditional teaching, settled over two thousand years. But in a curious move, so reflective of the stylish relativism that now prevails among the judges, Kennedy reduced this traditional understanding to – as he put it – "one reasonable understanding of medical practice."[52] In this construal, the Attorney General, by his own order, was stamping as criminal those people who simply had another reasonable view of what could be called "medical practice." And by construing the case in this way, the judges gently conferred, on the scheme of assisted suicide, a new standing as *immanently plausible and therefore legitimate in the eyes of the law.*

Justice Scalia was struck by the same move to reduce the traditional teaching to *but one* among a number of contending views, each equally plausible. And yet, it was curious that Justice Scalia did not meet that argument head on with the most direct and important refutation that had to be summoned here. His rather oblique approach may have revealed the hesitations of a lawyer and judge who has been diffident, to put it mildly, about the claims of natural law and moral reasoning. He sought then to steer around the main moral argument: The state of Oregon had come to the judgment that the practice of medicine may be extended to encompass assisted suicide, but that move, he said, "does not change the fact that the overwhelming weight of

[51] *Ibid.*, at 785.
[52] *Ibid.*, at 777.

authority (including the 47 States that condemn physician-assisted suicide) confirms that [it has not] yet been so extended. Not even those of our Eighth Amendment cases most generous in discerning an 'evolution' of national standards would have found, on this record, that the concept of 'legitimate medicine' has evolved so far."[53]

Kennedy asserted that the traditional view constituted but one plausible, reasonable view. Scalia simply asserted the opinion of others that the judgment reached in Oregon has not come to be held yet by most other states. That is hardly the answer that the challenge demanded. For example, consider any proposition that has standing as a necessary truth, a truth that cannot be contradicted without falling into contradiction. We can take, as the simplest case, the skeptic who asserts that there is no truth. But that proposition he offers us, not as an opinion, but as an emphatic *truth*. Let's suppose that a judge says, "The claim that there is truth is one reasonable understanding among others." Now would we rebut that claim by taking a survey in the room and reporting that forty-nine out of sixty people think there *is* truth? Or would we seek to show, more aptly, that we are dealing with a necessary truth that cannot be denied without falling into contradiction?

The challenge from Justice Kennedy would have been met more aptly by arguing that this traditional view of the ends of medicine was not simply "one reasonable" view among many, but the only view that reason itself could disclose and justify. But in order to make that argument, Justice Scalia would have had to appeal to an understanding of moral truth that was not finally dependent on a consensus of opinion. Yet any move of that kind, toward objective moral truths, began to touch, of course, on some version of . . . natural law. And Justice Scalia has professed himself to be uneasy about natural law, to put it gently.

But how might the challenge of Justice Kennedy have been met more aptly by an argument cast in terms of natural law? One possibility is that a response could have been made in the version of natural law offered by John Finnis and Robert George.[54] Finnis and George appeal to "basic goods" – those goods

---

[53] *Ibid.*, at 792.

[54] See, most notably, John Finnis, *Natural Law and Natural Rights* (Oxford: Oxford University Press, 1980), e.g., pp. 23–36, 48–49, 59–75, 81–97; *Fundamentals of Ethics* (Washington: Georgetown University Press, 1983); *Moral Absolutes* (Washington: Catholic University of America Press, 1991); Robert George, *Making Men Moral* (Oxford: Oxford University Press, 1995); *In Defense of Natural Law* (Oxford: Oxford University Press, 1999), especially chs. 1, 3–5; and more recently, with Patrick Lee, *Body-Self Dualism in Contemporary Ethics and Politics* (Cambridge: Cambridge University Press, 2008). Cf. reservations about the "new natural law theory," Russell Hittinger,

that are immediately graspable as grounds of action, without any contrived, other interests or concerns to explain them. It would be rather like asking, Why did you fall in love? Why was loving another person worth doing? In the scheme marked off by Finnis and George, the interest in preserving life is one of those basic goods, which require no other reason to explain. And at the same time it is woven in with many other goods. If we need compelling reasons to deprive a person of his liberty, liberty is not even a plausible concern if there is no life, and we should require reasons even more compelling before we deprive people of their lives. People look both ways as they cross a street, absorbing into their acts the premise that their lives are worth preserving. We have campaigns to gather food and contributions for places in Africa beset by famine, and no one needs to explain why it is good to concern ourselves with the preservation of life in distant places, among people we do not know. I used to tell my students of directions that I would give babysitters when they came to sit for the evening with our two young boys. I'd point out that I had a new manuscript on a shelf over my desk. In case of fire, I said, be sure to get that manuscript out of the house. And by the way, make sure you get Peter and Jeremy out as well.

That line was taken as the joke it was because everyone understood that life came first. It was this sense of natural law that we find reflected in the radio shows of my own childhood in the 1940s – for example, in Jack Benny's famous line when he was held up at the point of a gun by a burglar. The burglar said, "Your money or your life." After a long interval of silence, the burglar repeated the question – and elicited Benny's famous reply: "I'm thinking it over!"[55] That joke would not have worked unless a mass audience, on radio, could be counted on as knowing that the interest in life preceded, logically, compellingly, any interest in property.

Scalia might have replied in this vein as well. It is simply unimaginable that we could find an ambulance service, or an emergency medical unit, constituted on the premise that its task was not to heal and to save, and to whisk its patients to places where their lives could be saved. It would be inconceivable to imagine an ambulance service constituted on the premise

---

A Critique of the New Natural Law Theory (Notre Dame, Ind.: Notre Dame University Press, 1987).

But see also some commentaries by David Forte that encompass these varieties in natural law with a wisdom seasoned in law and experience: "The Natural Law Moment" and "Family, Nature and Liberty," in Forte (ed.), *Natural Law and Contemporary Public Policy* (Washington, D.C.: Georgetown University Press, 1998), pp. 3–9, 79–106.

[55] David Forte draws on this well-known bit of comedy as well in "The Natural Law Moment," but with a different twist, worth noting. See Forte, *ibid.*

that, as soon as it gets to the scene, its mission is to dispatch the patient, to speed him to a comfortable death, to relieve him and his relatives of further suffering and debilitating delays.

We know that we have people seriously persuaded by the claims of the Hemlock Society that there is something like a "right," a genuine "right to die." It is entirely imaginable that a young woman, affected by this persuasion, may find herself to be a babysitter in circumstances rather like those I have described. Let us suppose that she has the prospect of getting the children out of a burning house or leaving them there to perish. If the sitter were really convinced that death is a good, a good that stands on the same plane as life, then she would have a moment of perplexity: Why, after all, should she not choose, for the children in her care, what she regards as a genuine "good" – namely, the good of death? But of course no court, and no public, would acquiesce in such a claim. And when they refuse to credit that curious argument, they would back into the recognition that the choice of death simply cannot stand on the same plane as the choice of life, *as though death were in fact a rival good to life*. There is only one choice reasonable for a babysitter to make, as there is only one choice that functional people would regard as reasonable in the circumstances. And yet that point seemed strangely inaccessible to the judges in the majority in *Gonzales v. Oregon*. In the haze they were pleased to cast about them, they seemed to make of themselves, as Henry James would say, the victims of perplexities from which a single spark of direct perception might have spared them.

But at the same time, Justice Scalia came to the edge of a remarkable threshold for someone who has expressed over the years a certain diffidence or deep skepticism over natural law. Three times in the course of his opinion Scalia remarked that the position taken by Attorney General Ashcroft, the position affirming the traditional moral understanding of the ends of medicine, was "*the most natural interpretation*" of the regulation and the statute.[56] But what could it mean to say that the preference for the traditional moral understanding was "the most natural interpretation" for the regulation and the statute governing controlled substances? The phrase could not refer simply to the most natural *reflexes* of people – for example, that people favor their own, and protect their own children. Most do, but regrettably, some will kill their children. As Scalia knew, the Attorney General's predecessor in the Clinton administration, Janet Reno, had taken quite the opposite view – that nothing in the statute barred the state of Oregon from installing a policy in

---

[56] *Gonzales v. Oregon, supra*, note 47, at 779, 782, 784. The emphases here, in the italics, were supplied by Scalia himself.

which doctors could indeed become accomplices in procuring death for their patients. When Scalia said then that Ashcroft's interpretation was "the most natural" interpretation, I surmise that he must have meant *the most reasonable*, the decision most in accord with the canons of reason. They are also the standards of common sense, the standards we use every day in distinguishing between the things that are reasonable or unreasonable, defensible or indefensible.

When we have put these things in place, I think we would have sketched an understanding of the grounds of moral judgment that are rooted in the nature of "a rational creature as such," as Kant put it. Kant is not associated with natural law, at least as natural law was identified with the general tendencies that were thought to be characteristic of human beings, or necessary for the "flourishing" of human beings. Indeed, Kant went out of his way to stress that the ground of obligation "must be sought, not in the nature of man nor in the circumstances of the world in which he is placed, but solely *a priori* in the concepts of pure reason."[57] But at the same time, the principles of pure reason are accessible only to a certain kind of creature – by which some of us would understand a creature of a certain "nature." From that idea of a creature of reason, in the domain of freedom, facing the task of practical judgment, Kant could draw out the principles of right and wrong that could have the standing of real principles: They would not be true only most of the time, or true under certain contingencies; they could be true of necessity, true then under all conditions, true categorically. As Kant observed, "[N]othing but the idea of the law in itself . . . can constitute that preeminent good which we call moral," and that idea of law is "present only in a rational being."[58] Once again, only a being with reason can conceive, in the first place, the notion of a "good" or a principle of justice that may override his own self-interest. And when we connect these points, we may understand the fuller force of what Kant meant when he wrote that "since moral laws have to hold for every rational being as such, we ought . . . to derive our principles from the general concept of a rational being as such. . . .[59]

There is a danger of being ensnared by the tyranny of labels and missing the substance of the teaching. Kant is not linked to the teachers of natural law, but in the substance of the matter he found the ground of moral judgment in the same nature that provided the ground for Aristotle. The enduring, irresistible fact of the matter, taught at the beginning by Aristotle, was that

[57] Kant, *supra*, note 42, p. 57; p. 389 of the RPA ed.
[58] *Ibid.*, p. 69; p. 401 of the RPA ed.
[59] *Ibid.*, p. 79; p. 412 of the RPA ed.

law itself sprung from the nature of a certain kind of creature. If we are dealing with a world of framing reasons and propositions, and respecting the force of principles or propositions beyond our own appetites and wills, we are speaking of creatures with the capacity for reason. It has taken generations of lawyers to make obscure and to forget the most obvious things around us – or within us. But perhaps those primary things are so easily overlooked precisely because they are so evidently with us.

It frequently happens that some of our friends who are most skeptical of natural law discover that they have been practicing it handsomely for many years without quite realizing it – much like that character in Molière who discovers that he has been speaking prose all his life. It is rather like the man who asks, "Can I order coffee without using syntax?" He may not realize that of course he is using syntax and speaking prose without quite recognizing the conceptual world he inhabits, or the understandings that are woven into his own nature. It is no wonder, then, that we find some of our best natural lawyers among the distinguished jurists who have been the most skeptical of natural law. They may go on to discover, as a late colleague once said, that we have principles we have not even used yet. But for many of us, the task of bringing out those principles and explaining them has become, happily, steady work.

In that work we may find our model again in Plato's *Meno*: Socrates feeds the right questions to a slave boy, and – wonder of wonders – the boy is soon working out, step by step, the principles of geometry. As the understanding ran, those principles were already within his comprehension; they merely had to be unlocked. In this charming scheme, knowledge was a matter of remembering. It was a matter of unlocking what is always within us, always there to be discovered anew. And the sense of the matter, experienced by our students today as ever, is that when they discover those things they know, about the grounds of their moral judgment, what is buoying in the experience is the recognition that they have known them all along.

Three

Lochner *and the Cast of Our Law*

I suppose I might have been asked to offer some reflections on the jurisprudence of Darth Vader, or to consider whether I might revisit the subject of dueling and say a few redeeming words for that institution, now faded. Or that is how the assignment might have appeared to many people when my friend, Robert George, asked me to speak in a series of lectures, at Princeton, on "landmark cases" in the law and revisit the legendary case of *Lochner v. New York* (1905). Yet that was an inspiriting offer, and too delicious to forgo. For *Lochner* must surely stand as one of the most reviled – and persistently misunderstood – cases in our constitutional law. And so I remarked to the audience assembled in Princeton that, in a series of lectures quite distinguished, I had received, without any particular merit, an assignment even more distinguished: I had been entrusted with the task of explaining the only case in the series that has been converted into a verb. No one has ever threatened "to Marbury" or "to Dred Scott it," but as Robert Bork has observed, "to Lochnerize" has become a term of derision in those rare circles of people with an interest in constitutional law. Of course, Judge Bork ought to know, because his name too has been converted into a verb, and he has done Lochner one better: His name has become a *transitive* verb: "to bork" a candidate to the Supreme Court is to conduct an orchestrated campaign against confirmation. But in Bork's estimate, the opinion in the *Lochner* case, written by Rufus Peckham, "lives in the law as a symbol, indeed the quintessence, of

An earlier version of this chapter was offered as a lecture at Princeton, on February 4, 1997, as part of a series celebrating the 250th anniversary of the university. It was later published in a volume, edited by Robert P. George, gathering the lectures that were offered in this series at Princeton: *Great Cases in Constitutional Law* (Princeton: Princeton University Press, 2000), ch. 5.

judicial usurpation of power. . . . To this day [says Bork], when a judge simply makes up the Constitution, he is said 'to Lochnerize,' usually by someone who does not like the result."[1]

For the historians, *Lochner* stands for the laissez-faire Court of the late nineteenth century, spilling over into the twentieth. It was, supposedly, a conservative Court, which brought to the cases a deep suspicion of legislators and their motives when they flexed their powers and sought to be overly inventive in regulating business. Even John Noonan, one of the most search-ing and authoritative scholars of the law, recently characterized *Lochner* in a summary fashion as "holding that a state could not constitutionally reg-ulate the hours of work of employees of business."[2] Judge Noonan folded these comments into an argument sweeping toward another purpose, and without his usual modulation. As I'll try to explain in a moment there are ample grounds for doubting all of the ingredients in these familiar caricatures, including the conservatism typically imputed to that Court.

But for Robert Bork, *Lochner* stands also for the evils of "substantive due process": It marks an activist judiciary that was not content to test any law by its formal properties, but was altogether too willing to test, and challenge, the substance of the law itself. Justice Mathews had declared in the old *Yick Wo* case that the judges could not be confined to look merely at the forms, and blind themselves to the substance of what was done.[3] And those who are not trained as lawyers would think there is an elementary sense of justice here: The judges could not be confined to the task of gauging whether a law has been passed in a formally correct way, or whether there have been ample procedures for defendants. The Founders recognized that there could in fact be unjust laws, legal enactments that lacked the substance of justice. And if they understood that, under a constitutional government, the judges would have some leeway to test legislation against the principles of the Constitution, it is quite arguable that there must be implicit, in that vocation, the possibil-ity of judging the rightness, the arbitrariness, or the justification of what is enacted into law. In the annals of our law there is probably no more com-pelling statement on this head than the one offered by Daniel Webster when he was arguing before the Supreme Court in the famous Dartmouth College case. Webster's sense of the matter brought out the principled implications

---

[1] Robert Bork, *The Tempting of America* (New York: Free Press, 1990), p. 44.

[2] John T. Noonan, Jr., *Narrowing the Nation's Power* (Berkeley: University of California Press, 2002), p. 13.

[3] As Mathews wrote, in a moving passage, "the law itself [might] be fair on its face," and yet "it [was] applied and administered by public authority with an evil eye and an unequal hand." *Yick Wo v. Hopkins* 118 U.S. 356, at 373–74 (1886).

contained in that seemingly formal test of "process": it mattered considerably that a regulation or executive order did not spring from the arbitrary discretion of an administrator; that it found its ground of authority in a statute, enacted into law by a legislature, a body that could reconcile the interests at work in the community. But at the same time, as Webster recognized, it made no sense to speak of courts and judges if the judges were confined merely to the question of whether any statute was passed in a formally correct manner. Webster set forth the matter in this way:

> By the law of the land is most clearly intended the general law; a law, which hears before it condemns; which proceeds upon inquiry, and renders judgment only after trial. The meaning is, that every citizen shall hold his life, liberty, property, and immunities, under the protection of the general rules which govern society. Everything which may pass under the form of an enactment, is not, therefore, to be considered the law of the land. If this were so, acts of attainder, bills of pains and penalties, acts of confiscation, acts reversing judgments, and acts directly transferring one man's estate to another, legislative judgments, decrees, and forfeitures, in all possible forms, would be the law of the land. Such a strange construction would render constitutional provisions of the highest importance completely inoperative and void. It would tend directly to establish the union of all powers in the legislature. There would be no general permanent law for courts to administer, or for men to live under. The administration of justice would be an empty form, an idle ceremony.[4]

But with his own, considerable experience as a lawyer, a professor, and a judge, Robert Bork had come to doubt that there could be any reasoned or dispassionate judgment about the arbitrariness, or the justification, of what a legislature would enact. If we go back for a moment to that line I cited earlier, Bork referred to judges who were willing to strike down legislation – or in effect "make up" the Constitution – because they did not "like" the result. Whether it was intentional or merely reflexive, Bork was backing into the language of positivism – the language that reduced reasoned judgments to "emotivism," to matters essentially of "likes" and "dislikes." Judges like Stephen Field or George Sutherland managed to marshal precise reasons, in a compelling way, but at the end of the day, it would all reduce to the translation provided by the positivists. It would mean simply that Field or Sutherland didn't "like" what the legislature had done. To speak of the things that were right or wrong, justified or unjustified, was really to speak of the things that we

---

[4] *Dartmouth College v. Woodward*, 17 U.S. (4 Wheat.) 518 (1819), at 581–82.

simply liked or disliked, or in Humean terms, the things that gave us pleasure or displeasure.

In the case of Robert Bork, I suspect that this language of positivism lingered, even after the assumptions that attended that language had disappeared from his own, richer understanding of the judges and the law. But Bork's characterization offered a fair reflection of Justice Hugo Black, Franklin Roosevelt's first appointment to the Supreme Court, and the most emphatic, the most unreconstructed, opponent of "substantive due" process. He was also, therefore, the most implacable opponent of natural law. On that point, there was no mistake, for Black or for Bork: Behind substantive due process, there had to be some notion of natural law or natural right – some claim to have access to an objective truth, perhaps a truth grounded in nature, or a truth grounded in the laws of reason. But whatever the source from which it sprang, it would be a truth that did not depend on the votes of a majority in a legislature. For after all, if all truth was conventional, then the only measure of truth was to be found in the votes of majorities. And in that case, the function of a judge could only be as Holmes described it: to assure that the herd gets its way – that the majority be allowed to prevail in some decorous way, with the trappings of legality. In one notable case in the 1920s, Justice Holmes dissented and urged his colleagues to hold back their hand, rather than interfere with the authority of a legislature to make laws regulating the economy. As Holmes put it, with his characteristic sharpness, "the legislature may forbid or restrict any business when it has a sufficient force of public opinion behind it."[5] That was, of course, positivism with a vengeance; and it was the voice that rejected, without a tremor of qualification, the jurisprudence of "substantive due process."

In our own day, Bork and William Rehnquist have come closer than any other judges in sharing Hugo Black's perspective, which is why it may be aptly said that Rehnquist and Bork might have been the last judges of the New Deal. Bork, we will remember, got himself into some unexpected trouble because of the criticism he directed at *Griswold v. Connecticut*, with its new doctrines of "privacy." That was of course the case on contraception in 1965, and it would be the prelude, most notably, to *Roe v. Wade* in 1973. It could be said that with *Griswold*, in 1965, and *Roe v. Wade*, liberal jurisprudence moved into a new register. For some people in the law schools, jurisprudence truly begins with *Griswold*: Everything before Griswold is taken to be a reflection of another historic epoch, whose teachings, whose doctrines, bear no validity in this new epoch of our own day. Just a few years ago, in fact, the remark was

---

[5] *Tyson & Brothers v. Banton*, 273 U.S. 418, 445–46 (1927).

reported to me from a young professor of law that *Griswold* and *Roe* are the new touchstones in our jurisprudence: that any theory, any doctrine, of the law that yielded the "wrong" result in *Griswold* or *Roe* would be marked instantly as suspect or invalid. Robert Bork failed of confirmation precisely because he was regarded as a fifth vote to overrule *Roe v. Wade.* It could hardly be an overstatement then to say that *Griswold* and *Roe* mark the center, the core, of liberal jurisprudence in our own time. Yet, it should also be clear that there is the sharpest, most dramatic contrast between modern liberal jurisprudence and the liberal jurisprudence of the New Deal, the jurisprudence that defined itself most crisply in opposition to substantive due process – and *Lochner v. New York.*

And of course the clearest marker here is Justice Black: He was a vigorous dissenter in the *Griswold* case. He was the most emphatic opponent of this jurisprudence of privacy for the reasons that ran back to his own reigning doctrine. Black would explain that doctrine in the most compressed form by quoting Holmes: "a state legislature can do whatever it sees fit to do unless it is restrained by some express prohibition of the Constitution of the United Stats or of the State."[6] For Black, there could not have been the slightest question that a legislature could act to protect unborn children, just as it could act to protect endangered animals, which were not even human. Black certainly understood that the legal protections for the child in the womb had been anchored in the common law, long before this country had even brought forth the Constitution.[7] For Black, it would have been quite clear that there was nothing in the Constitution that prevented a legislature from protecting unborn children, a commitment that had been part of the law in America even before the advent of the Constitution. When Black gave an account of his jurisprudence, he defined himself most sharply by the cases he was rejecting, and first on the list, at all times, was *Lochner v. New York.*

It becomes clear, beyond caviling, that nothing in the liberal jurisprudence of the New Deal could have brought forth, or sustained, the jurisprudence

---

[6] Holmes in *ibid.*, at 445–46; cited by Black in *Ferguson v. Skrupa*, 372 U.S. 726, at 729 (1963).

[7] James Wilson recorded that older understanding in the compelling way in his Lectures on Jurisprudence in the 1790s:

> In the contemplation of law, [wrote Wilson] life begins when the infant is first able to stir in the womb. By the law, life is protected not only from immediate destruction, but from every degree of actual violence, and, in some cases, from every degree of danger.

See James Wilson, "Of the Natural Rights of Individuals," in *The Works of James Wilson* (Cambridge: Harvard University Press, 1967; originally published in 1804), Vol. 2, pp. 585–610, at 597.

of *Griswold* and *Roe v. Wade*. In fact, the irony is that it was quite the opposite: The jurisprudence of *Roe v. Wade* depended on the jurisprudence of those so-called reactionary judges – McReynolds, Sutherland, Butler, Van Devanter – the judges who had resisted Roosevelt and the New Deal in the 1930s. The clues should have been impossible to miss: The proponents of a "right to an abortion" found the ground of that right in a "right of privacy," which was established, in their construal, over four or five cases, and the two leading cases in the series were *Meyer v. Nebraska* (1923)[8] and *Pierce v. Society of Sisters* (1925).[9] Both decisions were written by that cantankerous, anti-Semitic Justice McReynolds.

But this is not to say, of course, that McReynolds and Sutherland were bound to approve of "the right to an abortion." Nor does it suggest that an understanding of "natural rights" would entail, or even support, the right to abortion, or any of the other claims spun out of *Griswold v. Connecticut*. It is simply that the argument for abortion requires an appeal to what may be called at least the "logic of natural rights": It requires an appeal to an understanding of rights that does not depend on the positive law made by majorities voting in legislatures or even the positive law of the Constitution.

But when we speak of the logic of natural rights, or the willingness to go beyond matters of procedure and test the substance of what legislatures enact into law, we are backing once again into the logic of "substantive due process." That is exactly what Justice Black had marshaled all his energies to oppose, and whenever he offered an inventory of the villainies he was resisting, in substantive due process, the case that headed the list was *Lochner v. New York*.

The last time he ran through the litany of cases for his audience, and denounced *Lochner v. New York*, was when his jurisprudence seemed to be at its height. It was 1963; he had just been celebrated the previous year for his twenty-fifth anniversary on the Court; a liberal Democrat was in the White House, and Black could now speak for a unanimous Court in *Ferguson v. Skrupa*.[10] In that case, the state of Kansas had passed a law to restrict those people who made their livings as "debt adjusters," in helping other people to collect and arrange their debts. For some reason, which would probably raise our suspicions, the legislature had come to the judgment that only those possessed of law degrees could engage in this occupation without imperiling the public safety. In the old Court, at the end of the nineteenth century, or the

---

[8] 262 U.S. 390.
[9] 268 U.S. 510.
[10] 372 U.S. 726.

Court in our own day, the judges would have looked at this legislation quite severely. But for Justice Black, the signs of arbitrariness were not to enter into the notice of the judges. No more were we in that dark time, as he said, when judges would presume to challenge the decisions made by representatives of the people. There would be no more inclination, as he said, to strike down acts of legislation because judges "thought them unreasonable, that is, unwise or incompatible with some particular economic or social philosophy."[11]

This was the high tide of Justice Black's jurisprudence, in 1963, only two years before *Griswold* would turn jurisprudence on a different axis, and Black would be left in disbelief. But he had with him, in 1962, a young acolyte in the newly appointed Justice Byron White. Years later, in 1977, White would invoke the memory of Hugo Black for the sake of showing just how much the world had turned between 1963 and 1977. The case was called *Moore v. East Cleveland*,[12] and I offer it here for the sake of highlighting, as White sought to highlight, the dramatic change in structure that had now been absorbed – and settled. The case was hardly momentous, but that made it all the more remarkable that the Court was willing to take in, so readily, a case of this kind. In the suburb of East Cleveland there was an ordinance that sought to confine households to families. Or it sought to avoid the complications brought by gatherings, perhaps even make-shift communes, with a cluster of unrelated people inhabiting the same house. But as the law was applied in this case, it threatened to punish a grandmother who had, within her household, two of her grandchildren, who were cousins but not siblings. (One grandson had come to live with her after his mother had died.) This gathering did not describe then a "family" as it was defined under the local ordinance. The Court had no trouble in judging the ordinance to be invalid. The statute imposed an arbitrary restriction on the freedom of this family to engage in some of the elementary decencies that one might expect of families in caring for their own. Still, Chief Justice Burger thought that there had been no need for the Court to take the case: There had been no appeal to local authorities under the local procedures for appeal, and Burger registered his doubts that any sensible officials at the local level would really have insisted on applying this law, with its full stringency, to a case of this kind. But as to the substance of the judgment – or the fitness of this case to be reviewed by the federal courts – there was not a tremor of doubt.

The deeper doubt was registered by Justice White, who recorded his dissent mainly out of an interest in raising again the flag of the New Deal and of

---

[11] *Ibid.*, at 729.
[12] 431 U.S. 494.

Justice Black. He reminded his colleagues that Justice Black would have been astonished, if not rendered apoplectic, by a decision of this kind. White did not seem to doubt that the local ordinance reached too far, with a hand too heavy, and that it might even have been irrational. But as he recalled to his colleagues, Justice Black had "never embraced the idea that the Due Process Clause empowered the courts to strike down merely unreasonable or arbitrary legislation."[13] So long as an ordinance abridged nothing that was mentioned explicitly in the Constitution, Black would have been willing to sustain it. Apparently, White was willing to flag this case, and this moment, for the sake of conveying the lesson here more sharply: And the lesson was that we had now entered, quite emphatically, perhaps irreversibly, a different phase of our jurisprudence, with a radically different governing doctrine. Between 1963 and 1977, the jurisprudence of the New Deal had clearly been displaced and discredited. Along the way was *Roe v. Wade,* and of course, White, with a lingering attachment to Justice Black, had been one of the two dissenters in *Roe v. Wade.* But if Justice Black had been repudiated, along with the jurisprudence of the New Deal, it should be clear that what was being repudiated now was the rejection of substantive due process. To put it another way, in repudiating Justice Black, the Court in effect had to be installing a new respect for all of those cases that Black himself had repudiated. He had repudiated, most pointedly, *Meyer v. Nebraska* and *Pierce v. Society of Sisters,* on the authority of the family, but again, at the head of the list, as the leading case in this inventory of the objectionable, was *Lochner v. New York.*

I have approached my problem, so far, through this indirect path, for the sake of highlighting dimensions of the case, certain points of significance, that are persistently blocked from sight. Without touching as yet on anything in the substance of *Lochner v. New York,* we may nevertheless reveal a deeper truth about *Lochner* that runs quite beyond the distractions cast up by the case, as we react to the facts that composed it. It is quite possible that, in weighing the claims of the parties, we may be inclined to reach, for reasons notably less than fundamental, a judgment rather different from the one struck off by the Court in 1905. But our judgment there may not dislodge the deeper premises, or principles, on which that judgment was founded. And that point is brought home to us by this preliminary glimpse of *Lochner* threading through the memories and jurisprudence of a later day. Let us suppose for a moment that Justice Black and Judge Bork had it right: that *Lochner* stood for the tradition set against the jurisprudence of the New Deal. If that jurisprudence of the

---

[13] *Ibid.,* at 542.

New Deal has been displaced, decisively, by the liberal jurisprudence of our own day, the jurisprudence of *Griswold* and of *Roe v. Wade*, then there is a deeper truth that does not easily speak its name: that we live today, firmly, within the cast of *Lochner*. That case is ridiculed, derided, by the Right as well as the Left, and yet the structure of jurisprudence marked by that case is the structure that our judges, Left and Right, choose again, choose anew, whenever they are faced with the need to choose. *Lochner v. New York is* our law; it marks the jurisprudence of our own day, even for people who profess to disagree with its result, and who may even fancy that they are rejecting it at its root.

The case arose from Utica, New York, in 1899. It involved a law of New York State that mandated a limit of ten hours in the working day, or rather, ten hours on the average day, in a working week that had to be limited to 60 hours. There was a section of the law that applied these provisions distinctly to bakeries. But one question was whether it applied to bakers as a *labor law*, a law designed to protect vulnerable or ignorant workmen against the dominant power of employers. Or was it to be regarded rather as a species of regulations on health, designed to protect the safety or health of the bakers? As it turned out, that distinction would make a difference, and it might have been telling, in this respect, that the broader statute, containing this section on bakeries, was a major piece of legislation, passed in 1897, and styled "The Labor Law." Joseph Lochner was the owner of a bakery, and he was charged, in a criminal proceeding, for a misdemeanor in violating one section of the "The Labor Law," which read in this way:

> No employee shall be required or permitted to work in a biscuit, bread or cake bakery or confectionery establishment more than sixty hours in any one week or more than ten hours in any one day, unless for the purpose of making a shorter work day on the last day of the week; nor more hours in any one week than will make an average of ten hours per day for the number of days during such week in which such employee shall work.

Lochner was arrested on December 21, 1899, on the complaint of one of his employees, and here is where the record falls into a maddening sketchiness, which is not relieved at any stage. The complaint was not apparently brought by any worker claiming that Lochner had coerced him, against his will, to work longer hours. The action was brought, rather, by a worker who complained that Lochner had permitted another employee to work additional hours, beyond the limit mandated in the law. For some of us looking on, it would make a notable difference as to whether the notion of "permitted" here was a fiction, or whether Lochner really was making a different arrangement with a worker who was genuinely willing to work additional hours for additional, or overtime, pay. But these kinds of details are not contained in the record of any court that heard this case, at any level. What we can say, from the briefs and records, was that Lochner was convicted, that he faced a fine of twenty dollars or twenty days in jail. He paid the fine – and then proceeded to violate the law in the same way, by permitting another worker to work past the mandated hours. He was convicted again, fined this time $50. But now, with his resistance setting in, he launched the series of appeals that would carry him all the way to the Supreme Court. Along the way, he would move through two levels of appellate courts in New York, with the law sustained in each case, but in each case with divided courts.[14]

Of Lochner himself we know little. A search in the newspapers of Utica turned up his obituary in 1939, and brought forth these details: He was an immigrant from Bavaria, born in 1862. He had come to Utica at the age of twenty, where he had worked for eight years as a baker before he eventually established what was called, in the newspapers, a "bakeshop" of his own. This did not exactly sound like a large, corporate bakery, and it was managed by a man who had himself sprung from the class of bakers. We would also suspect that he was still clocking many hours working by the ovens himself, though we still do not know anything about the tenor of his relations with his employees. Again, it made a notable difference as to whether this was a case of protecting workers against a coercive employer, or whether the case involved an interference with a worker who might in fact have wished to work additional hours for added pay. Justice Rufus Peckham was credited by his colleagues at the bar as the most careful, fastidious student of the record, and Peckham seemed to think it was a case of the latter: that the controversy here involved a third party who objected to the fact that another worker had been *permitted* to work overtime.

That understanding of the case became an important lever used by Peckham in his opinion, and yet that is precisely the construction that the unions, or the supporters of the bill, *insisted* upon as they framed this case for a trial. Lochner himself had argued that he was being charged here with two crimes rather than one: He was being charged with the offense of *compelling* his workers, and on the other hand, of merely *permitting* his workers to work.

[14] See *People v. Lochner*, 73 App. Div. [New York] 120 (1902), *People v. Lochner*, 177 N.Y. 145 (1904). In this recounting of the facts, I have found a more detailed account in the briefs for the plaintiff (Lochner), submitted by Frank Harvey Field, in Philip B. Kurland and Gerhard Casper, eds., *Landmark Briefs and Arguments of the Supreme Court* (Arlington, Va.: University Publications of America, 1975), Vol. 14, pp. 654–699, at 654–56.

He argued that they were two quite different things, that he could not be charged at the same time with coercing and permitting. In fact, his argument was that the latter – permitting a worker to work – could not tenably be a crime. And to the extent that the law actually covered the act of "permitting," he contended that the law reached too far. It forbade even willing workers to work additional hours when it served their interests. In this argument, Justice O'Brien, in dissent in the Supreme Court of New York, thought Lochner made a compelling point.[15]

But for the supporters of the law this was not such a bizarre construction. If the law mandates a policy, there is a serious question of whether the law may be subverted through a series of private contracts. We have, right now, laws that forbid discriminations on the basis of race and religion in hiring. A major donor to a university may offer a private bequest and append, as a condition, that no blacks or Jews be hired. But the law could be rendered a nullity if it could be subverted in that way through private contracts, with a university accepting a bequest on the condition that no blacks or Jews be hired. The supporters of the law in New York knew what they were doing then when they insisted on testing the law with its fuller reach. Whatever the circumstances in the case, they wished to present to the courts the law in its completeness, which covered the possibility of *permitting*, and not merely coercing workers, to work additional hours. Justice Peckham could not be faulted then for construing the case as the plaintiffs would have had him construe it.

But that brings us back to Rufus Peckham, and perhaps the key was there: Looking back on what has been written about this case over the years, it struck me that the characterization of the case was often tied in with the characterization of Rufus Peckham. And the supreme caricaturist here, with no peer, was of course, Justice Holmes. As a college student, I recall being dazzled, as most youngsters would be, by the flourish of Holmes's prose, by his feistiness and crisp putdowns. He was a master of aphorism, and he coined the aphorism that would always dog Peckham's opinion in *Lochner*. No line is quoted more often in commentaries on this case than Holmes's quip that "the Fourteenth Amendment did not enact Mr. Herbert Spencer's Social Statics."[16] The further, telling comparison, is that this line is usually quoted

---

[15] Under this construal, as O'Brien said, the law "makes it a crime for the master to permit his servant to do what the servant has a perfect right to do.... [T]he master must see to it, at the peril of committing a crime, that his servants are driven out of the building the moment the clock registers the requisite ten hours." See *People v. Lochner*, 177 N.Y. 145, at 176–78 (1904).

[16] *Lochner v. New York*, 198 U.S. 45, at 75 (1905).

without quoting anything from Peckham's opinion, or setting this aphorism against the body of Peckham's argument. On reading the case a bit later, in graduate school, I found myself embarrassed to have admired Holmes's terse aphorism, for that is all he had offered. But an aphorism does not supply an argument, or show, in measured terms, where a careful argument is deficient. Holmes had not met Peckham's argument; he had merely caricatured the argument, just as he had caricatured Peckham himself in a letter, in a line that became instantly one of my favorites. Offering his recollections of his colleagues, he thought back to Peckham and remarked, "I used to say of him that his major premise was God damn it."[17] The silent implication was that, for Peckham, this premise had proved remarkably serviceable; that it explained, as we say in the social sciences, a "large portion of the variance." It reflected the deep suspicion, cultivated by men steeped in the ways of the world, that behind the enactment of laws were "rent seekers": people trying to use the levers of the law for the sake of imposing their own interests, at the cost of their competitors or the general public. And indeed it may be sobering to consider the portion of cases that could be settled on the strength of this melancholy premise. Still, the caricatures of Peckham may explain then the understanding that became woven about the case, even if the portrait did not exactly fit the person or the arguments.

As to the person, there is a touch of a mystery. Peckham came from an established, connected family in upstate New York. He was sprung from the same, old-line, conservative Democratic families that encompassed the Roosevelts in Dutchess County. Peckham's father had been on the Supreme Court of the state, and Peckham would succeed him there as he had succeeded him in his law firm. But he also had an older brother, Wheeler Hazard Peckham, and he too had cut a noticeable figure in the law. Both brothers had rather independent streaks, and both had been involved in reform politics in New York. But the elder brother had taken an active role in prosecuting the Tweed Ring in New York City. One odd offshoot of that experience came in 1894, when Grover Cleveland nominated Wheeler Peckham to the Supreme Court. And yet, as a result of his abrasions in the politics of New York, he did not

---

[17] The line was confirmed by Charles W. McCurdy in his entry on Rufus Peckham in the *Encyclopedia of the American Constitution*, ed. Levy, Karst, and Mahoney (New York: Macmillan, 1986), p. 1371. I'd like to thank Professor John Robinson of the law school at Notre Dame, who supplied this reference, and confirmed what seemed apparent to me: that this line, which I had remembered from thirty-six years earlier, was not something that a twenty-year-old was likely to have struck off on his own. Still, the reference merely confirms the line without, however, furnishing the source – and the fuller quotation. The mystery remains in the mists of the legend.

have the support of the two Democratic senators of his own state. In a strange turn then, Wheeler Peckham was denied confirmation in the Senate. To make matters even stranger, President Cleveland, the next year, put up the younger brother for another vacancy. As far as anyone could see, their politics were the same, but the personal chemistry was quite different. The two senators from New York were consulted, and Rufus was confirmed. In the Library of Congress, there are papers of the Peckham family, running back to 1837, and labeled as the papers of Rufus Peckham. But in this compilation almost every letter and bill refers to Wheeler. There is virtually nothing of Rufus except copies of some modest memorials rendered at his funeral in Albany in 1909. There was a certain sadness to this life: Peckham and his wife had two sons, and in one of those cruel turns of life, both children died before the parents. I do not know whether Peckham decided to guard his private life in the style of Henry James, but he left us, as I say, with one of the most elusive and mysterious records: a collection of Rufus Peckham Papers almost entirely purged of any papers of a personal nature, and barren of any illumination of their subject.

There may be, in that story, an indirect reflection on the jurisprudence that he would represent; but that jurisprudence would be quite at odds with the caricature offered by Holmes. If I can return for a moment to the characterization left by Holmes, the sense here was that the jurisprudence emanated from the principles of Herbert Spencer, that it represented a pure form of laissez-faire; that Peckham was a cranky, conservative judge, dubious about social experiments, or socialist schemes. In this portrait, in other words, Peckham began with a deep skepticism, with the presumption that schemes regulating business, or abridging the rights of property, were schemes that began in error. They were hatched by well-meaning people who would nevertheless manage to do a considerable public harm. And in this construal, the real vice, for Peckham, was the breach with laissez-faire. The offense was the interference with the rights of property and the regulation of business. But the shorthand expression that covered all of these sins was the abridgement of the "right to contract." That is the ground on which Peckham and the Court would strike down this law of New York State: that it interfered, unseasonably, with the freedom of workers to make contracts with their employers, or their freedom to find the terms of employment that were suitable to their own interests, even if they did not accord precisely with the formulas of the legislation. And of course, in the traditional liberal critique, the "right to contract" covered the freedom of vulnerable workers to make contracts with employers, who presumably had the upper hand. As it was often and mockingly put, the "liberty of contract" meant the liberty of workers to contract to work for more than sixty hours a week at less than a minimum wage. But judges a bit more seasoned in the world understood that there were times when employers, especially in smaller businesses, held little more bargaining power than their workers, for some of them were on the edge of losing their businesses and falling again into the ranks of the employed.[18]

Yet, that was hardly the least of the fictions that seemed to be absorbed as part of the critique of the so-called laissez-faire judges, and this is where John Noonan strayed, I think, from his usual, savvy judgments, when he sought to characterize this case.[19] If we looked back at those judges at the end of the nineteenth century and the beginning of the twentieth – the so-called laissez-faire judges that Peckham and the *Lochner* case are taken to represent – we would find that, in every item in this list, the liberal critique did not get it right. In fact, we would find that the liberal critique was wrong at the center, wrong at the core; and once we are alerted to why it was wrong at the core, we may suddenly become alert to a whole structure in Peckham's opinion in *Lochner* that has gone remarkably unnoticed.

I may sound here like G. K. Chesterton, and in that case I should produce a subtitle like, "Seven or Eight Damnable Lies about the Laissez-Faire Judges." And principal among the truths to be told is that these were not really laissez-faire judges, at least as our own age understands the term. Indeed, they could not be, given the premises that underlay their jurisprudence. After all, they were not yet positivists or "legal realists"; they continued to think that there was a moral ground that underlay the law, and that there had to be a moral ground, especially, for rights, including the rights of property. But then it only stood to reason that the judges who understood a moral ground for the rights of property were quite alert then to the moral limits on those rights of property. No one was a fiercer defender of property rights in that Court of the late nineteenth century than the redoubtable Stephen J. Field, and no one was clearer about the maxim that marked the limit to those rights of property: *sic utere tuo ut alienum non laedas* [use your own for the sake of causing no injury to others]. Under this doctrine, Field and his colleagues were willing to uphold virtually any legislation that bore even a plausible connection to

---

[18] One recalls here George Sutherland's observation in *Adkins v. Children's Hospital*:

> The law is not confined to the great and powerful employers but embraces those whose bargaining power may be as weak as that of the employee. It takes no account of periods of stress and business depression, of crippling losses, which may leave the employer himself without adequate means of livelihood.

See 261 U.S. 525, at 556 (1923).

[19] See *supra*, note 2.

the health, welfare, or safety of the local population. The hidden truth about the judges of "substantive due process" is that they used that weapon very rarely, that their operating inclination was to presume in favor of the validity of laws, and defer to legislators elected by the people. And so Field could suffer not the slightest strain in upholding laws, say, that ordered the closing of businesses on Sunday, and he could be quite clear, as he put it, that these "[l]aws setting aside Sunday as a day of rest are upheld, not from any right of the government to legislate for the promotion of religious observances, but from its right to protect all persons from the physical and moral debasement which comes from uninterrupted labor."[20]

Regulations of business, then, raised no moral strains for the judges. But the jurists also had the wit to recognize those gradations by which a law advertised as a regulation of business turned itself into something else. The judges were not vindicating rights of property in any trifling or narrow sense when they sought to protect the rights of aliens and Chinese, in San Francisco, to practice an ordinary calling in operating laundries. And the judges managed to notice the same vice at work in 1915, when the state of Arizona required that any establishment employing five or more workers had to reserve 80 percent of the jobs for native-born citizens of the United States. The measure was advertised, of course, as regulation of business in favor of

---

[20] *Soon Hing v. Crowley*, 113 U.S. 703, at 710. That sentiment was expressed in one of the cases, emanating from San Francisco, dealing with the regulation of laundries, and that series of cases provides as clear, and dramatic, a statement of my point here as any cluster of cases. The judges were willing to sustain every measure in this series that bore a plausible connection to the public safety – e.g., the concern with "continuous fires," burning all night in order to keep the hot washes going. But the judges were quite acute in noticing when the regulations would cross a line into procedures that were simply aribitrary, and finally driven by an animus toward the Chinese. In that notable case of *Yick Wo v. Hopkins*, the law contained tiers of distinctions: Laundries housed in buildings made of brick and stone would be allowed to operate without restrictions. Laundries contained in wooden buildings would be subject to a different regimen. The owners would have to apply for a license to the Board of Supervisors, who could grant or withhold licenses, based on their judgment of the applicant. But there was apparently no need for the supervisors to justify their decisions, or give reasons that could be examined in a court. The procedures bore all the earmarks of arbitrariness, and the results confirmed the suspicions: The only attribute that connected Yick Wo and the two hundred other applicants rejected by the Board was that they were Chinese. Of the eighty applicants approved by the Board, none was Chinese. The laws might have been fair in their construction, but as Justice Matthews wrote, the laws were administered with "a mind so unequal and oppressive as to amount to a practical denial by the State of the equal protection of the laws." See *Yick Wo v. Hopkins, supra* note 3, at 373–74. For a fuller discussion of these cases involving the Chinese in San Francisco – and a more accurate account of those so-called laissez-faire judges – see my book *The Return of George Sutherland* (Princeton: Princeton University Press, 1994), pp. 60–71.

a social policy – a determination to impose, as they say, "community values" against the prospect of an unregulated capitalism. But this kind of measure should not have been seen as a regulation of business any more than the Nazi legislation in the 1930s that sought to drive Jews from the professions and even from ordinary occupations. The laws in Arizona were an expression, rather, of nativism, and in some cases, of racism. The case was called *Truax v. Raich*,[21] and what the Court saw in this case from Arizona was Mike Raich, an immigrant from Austria, prevented from working at an ordinary job in a restaurant. The Court would vindicate the rights of Mike Raich in this case, but this item in the record of the Court would be charged to the record of the conservative Court in its willingness to fend off the regulation of business. I would suggest that it is not merely an incidental connection, in this respect, that the same labor laws at issue in the *Lochner* case also contained a component that required positions in public employment to be reserved to American citizens. In the same issue of the *New York Times*, reporting on the decision in the *Lochner* case, there was an account of a report submitted by the State Commissioner of Labor, noting with concern that over 60 percent of the employees in New York City were aliens. That situation violated the labor laws of the state. The concern of the unions was deepened when the Corporation Counsel in the city had concluded that the law was a nullity, at least in regard to Italian immigrants – not on constitutional grounds, but because the law might have violated a treaty with the Italian government.[22]

This kind of legislation ran well beyond the breadth of tolerance that the judges were willing to accord to legislation that bore even a plausible connection to the public health and safety. It would have been then a caricature at war with understanding to characterize the reactions of the courts here as a reflex simply to guard businesses against regulation. But at the same time, the judges saw nothing denigrating in the notion that they were defending in these cases rights of property, for those rights were indeed natural rights, or human rights: The right to make a living at an ordinary calling, to enter a legitimate occupation, without arbitrary restrictions, was a right that ran as deep as the right to speak or publish. For ordinary men and women, who were not writers or intellectuals, it might be the right that bore on their lives with a more evident, palpable effect. In his dissenting opinion in the famous *Slaughter-Houses Cases*, Justice Field cited in this vein a decree issued by Louis XVI in France, and written by the estimable Finance Minister, Turgot. In that decree, the king would dismantle the system of monopolies granted by the

---

[21] 239 U.S. 33 (1915).
[22] See the *New York Times*, April 18, 1905, p. 6.

state. He would have the state recede from the exercise of such powers out of a respect for the natural rights of his subjects in the control of their own labor. The explanation in the edict took this form:

> [S]ome persons asserted that the right to work was a royal privilege which the king might sell, and that his subjects were bound to purchase from him. We hasten to correct this error and to repel the conclusion. God in giving to man wants and desires rendering labor necessary for their satisfaction, conferred the right to labor upon all men, and this property is the first, most sacred, and imprescriptible of all.... [Therefore, he regarded it] as the first duty of his justice, and the worthiest act of benevolence, to free his subjects from any restrictions upon this inalienable right of humanity.[23]

To recognize, in this way, the "natural right" of the worker to his own labor was to recognize that his labor did not belong, in the first instance, to the state – or to his employer. It meant, as the first Justice Harlan once explained, that every person had a natural right "to sell his labor upon such terms as he deems proper," and a right "to quit the service of the employer for whatever reason."[24] He could be committed only on the basis of a contract, entered into freely. Which is to say, his labor could be committed, his body comanded, only with his *consent*. For the judges who came out of the antislavery movement, the notion of liberty of contract was another way of recognizing that a man had a primary claim to the ownership of his own labor, as he had a natural claim to the ownership of himself. For these judges, the notion of "liberty of contract" was freighted with the same moral significance that attached to the notion of government by the consent of the governed.

It is curious, in this respect, that when the Thirteenth Amendment was revived in the late 1960s, it was associated with the notion of "contract": As the argument ran, the refusal of private schools, or private companies, to accept black people as clients or customers marked a refusal to enter into contracts with blacks. Therefore that turning away marked a refusal to treat black people with the dignity that attaches to a moral agent, a person competent to enter into contracts, a person who deserves to have his consent sought before he is committed.[25] It is curious, as I say, that the "liberty of contract," in the hands of judges in the 1960s and 1970s is regarded as the mark of a heightened, liberal sensibility; and yet the same concept, understood by judges like Sutherland, Harlan, and Peckham in precisely the same terms, was taken as the mark of reactionaries. The matter might have

---

[23] Quoted by Field in *The Slaughter-House Cases*, 83 U.S. (16 Wallace), at 110–11n.
[24] *Adair v. United States*, 208 U.S. 161, at 174.
[25] See *Runyon v. McCrary*, 427 U.S. 160 (1976).

been crystallized in this way: A right to contract could be claimed only by a "moral agent," as James Madison put it, a being who could deliberate about the grounds for offering, or withdrawing, his consent. But by the same token, a moral agent had access to the understanding of right and wrong; and therefore he would also understand the ends he had no right to pursue, even through the device of a contract. With that understanding, the judges were explicit in pointing out the places in which a person's liberty of contract was very much open to the restraints of the law.

And so Justice Sutherland could say, unequivocally, that "[t]here is, of course, no such thing as absolute freedom of contract. It is subject to a great variety of restraints. . . . The liberty of the individual to do as he pleases, even in innocent matters, is not absolute. It must frequently yield to the common good."[26] And in *Lochner*, Peckham would take the matter to its moral root: He would defend the liberty of contract, but he would note at the same time that "[t]he State . . . has the power to prevent the individual from making certain kinds of contracts . . . [e.g.,] a contract to let one's property for immoral purposes, or to do any other unlawful act."[27] In the jural world of Rufus Peckham and his colleagues, the judges could never be called on to enforce a contract for prostitution, or the "contract" to carry out a murder.

But once those moral premises were in place, it was quite as clear that the law would be justified in restraining, at many points, the freedom of people to inflict harms through their uses of property. And the law would be amply warranted even in restraining a person from injuring himself through his own freedom to contract.[28] Peckham would be charged with a certain flippancy

---

[26] *Adkins v. Children's Hospital, supra,* note 18, at 561.

[27] *Lochner, supra,* note 16, at 53.

[28] And this is what makes all the more bizarre, and quite unaccountable, the characterization of *Lochner* offered by three good friends of mine, ordinarily the most careful and precise of jurists. In their otherwise powerful dissenting opinion in *Planned Parenthood v. Casey* (1992), Chief Justice Rehnquist, joined by Justices Scalia and Thomas, remarked that "the Lochner Court did not base its rule upon the policy judgment that an unregulated market was fundamental to a stable economy; it simply believed, erroneously, that 'liberty' under the Due Process Clause protected the 'right to make a contract.'" The three jurists took *Lochner* to mean an affirmation of "laissez-faire economics." But as I have shown, nothing in the notion of laissez-faire economics as it was understood by the conservative judges meant that commercial or economic relations were beyond the reach of the law when they involved wrongs and injuries that the law could rightly address. Curiously, the three justices took *Lochner* to be challenged by any kind of legislation regulating the economy, including laws mandating minimum wages. They went on then to observe that "these statutes were indeed enacted because of a belief on the part of their sponsors that 'freedom of contract' did not protect the welfare of workers, demonstrating that that belief manifested itself more than a generation before the Great Depression." See 505 U.S. 833, 961. But once again, neither Peckham nor Stephen Field, nor any of the conservative judges, understood "freedom of contract" to mean

in his willingness, in the *Lochner* case, to strike down the policies of a state; and yet, if we look closely at the structure of his argument, we would notice that Peckham was careful to establish the framework by setting in place first the legitimate grounds on which the law may restrict or constrain the liberty of contract. In laying the groundwork in this way, he *assigned the burden of proof to any judge* who would overturn the policies of the legislature. It cannot be strictly right, then, to summarize the holding in *Lochner* by saying that "a state could not constitutionally regulate the hours of work of employees of business."[29] Peckham and his colleagues had already upheld restraints on hours and conditions of work, and they had been utterly clear about the moral grounds of those judgments, sustaining regulations. It is worth recalling, then, even in a sketchy summary, the regulations that this supposed model of laissez-faire judge was willing to uphold as legitimate:

- The limiting of working hours, in underground mines, to eight hours per day ("except in cases of emergency, where life or property is in imminent danger")
- The limiting of hours of work in smelting plants, where a prolonged exposure could pose risks to the health of workers [*Holden v. Hardy* (1898)[30]]
- The requirement, by a state, that the owners of mines redeem coal for cash when workers are paid in kind [*Knoxville Iron v. Harbison* (1901)[31]]
- The provision of vaccinations in a compulsory way, as part of a policy directed to "the public health and the public safety" [*Jacobson v. Massachusetts* (1905)[32]]
- The requirement that barbershops and other establishments be closed on Sundays, even though a policy of that kind, too, would limit the hours that people were free to work [*Petit v. Minnesota* (1900)[33]]

Peckham found in most of these policies an earnest interest in protecting workers from fraud and hazards, and promoting public health. The question

that people may never do immoral or wrongful things through contracts, and that certain contracts could not indeed be regulated or even forbidden by the law. And on the other side of the matter, nothing said by the jurists could possibly establish the notion that the Constitution ignores, as a virtual irrelevance, the premise of a free person, extending or withdrawing his consent to the terms on which he is governed, or the terms on which he commits himself in contracts. If the judges needed any direct jural confirmation of that point, they need only have drawn attention to the recent cases that have vindicated again for black people the standing of blacks as parties competent to enter contracts. See *Runyon v. McCrary, supra*, note 25, at 170–71.

[29] See Noonan, *supra*, note 2, p. 2.
[30] 169 U.S. 366.
[31] 183 U.S. 13.
[32] 197 U.S. 11.
[33] 177 U.S. 164, and see the citations in *Lochner, supra*, note 16, at 54–56.

then was whether this law in New York was aimed plausibly at the public health. As I have suggested, Peckham approached this question with a discipline imparted to him from the traditions of the Court. And with that approach, he was prepared to credit any tenable connection to the public health, along with an apt sympathy for the people who were the objects of protection. But that discipline also brought an aversion to subterfuge, along with a willingness to test, with a critical eye, the restrictions that were imposed upon personal freedom. That sense of freedom, in the understanding of Peckham, was never niggling or narrow, and it was never confined to matters of property. In *Allgeyer v. Louisiana*, in 1897, Peckham articulated one of the most expansive understandings of the range of personal freedom protected under the Fourteenth Amendment:

> The liberty mentioned in that amendment means not only the right of the citizen to be free from the mere physical restraint of his person, as by incarceration, but the term is deemed to embrace *the right of the citizen to be free in the enjoyment of all his faculties*; to be free to use them in all lawful ways; to pursue any livelihood or avocation, and for that purpose to enter into all contracts which may be proper, necessary and essential.[34]

H. L. Mencken once remarked on that curious illusion spun by Justice Holmes, which induced the liberals to believe so readily that he was one of them. "The Liberals," he wrote, "who long for tickling with a great and tragic longing, were occasionally lifted to the heights of ecstasy by the learned judge's operations, and in fact soared so high that they were out of earshot of next day's thwack of the club."[35] And what the illusion camouflaged, in this instance, was that Peckham was far more of a libertarian, or a votary of "rights," than Holmes would ever be. I recall that when I read this case again in graduate school, I wondered how I could have been so dazzled by Holmes that I had missed the real dissent in the case, written by Justice Harlan, and joined by two other colleagues. Holmes had been aphoristic, but Harlan had taken the trouble to lay out an argument, to cite the precedents, to frame the problem far more carefully. But then I must record my deeper surprise and embarrassment, when I returned to this case a while back, and I discovered that there was nothing in the main body of Harlan's argument that Peckham had not already encompassed – and arranged much more tellingly – in his opinion for the majority. When it came to setting in place the moral and

---

[34] 165 U.S. 578, at 589 (1897); italics added.
[35] H. L. Mencken, "Mr. Justice Holmes," in *The Vintage Mencken* (New York: Vintage Books, 1955), pp. 189–97, at 195.

constitutional justification for regulating commerce or placing restrictions on contracts, Peckham had done it all, but even more sharply.

The principal difference between Peckham's opinion and Harlan's was that Harlan had cited reports, or studies, on the hazards that might be facing bakers. He had cited, for example, a study by a Professor Hirt titled "The Diseases of Workers," in which it had been remarked that "the labor of the bakers is among the hardest and most laborious imaginable." Why? Because that labor required a "great deal of physical exertion" in an "overheated workshop," and with the need, often, to perform the work at night, "thus depriving [the worker] of an opportunity to enjoy the necessary rest and sleep, a fact which is highly injurious to his health."[36] Harlan seemed to think it appropriate also to dip into the history of maladies for bakers, suggesting that bakers were somehow more susceptible to the diseases that swept the community (perhaps because they might have been responsible in the past for spreading those diseases!). In any event, he recalled that, in 1720, when the plague ravaged the city of Marseilles, "every baker in the city succumbed to the epidemic."[37]

But to rework an old phrase, what was novel in Harlan's opinion was no longer true, and in fact, it was not even new. It was outdated. There had been much revision of late in the treatises on occupations, and there had been some notable changes in the operations of bakeries since the plague had visited Marseilles. The kneading of dough was done mainly by machinery, especially in an establishment like the National Biscuit Company on 10th Avenue, which covered two city blocks in New York. When the kneading was done by machinery, there was much less flour dust in the air, and the medical authorities were rather divided on the question of whether this state of affairs was hazardous. One treatise, in the 1890s, in England, published the mortality figures in different occupations, and listing them in descending order, in the ranking of hazards, bakers held no prominent place on the list. They were down in the middle of the rankings, well below the dangers faced by coal miners and brewers, laborers on docks, and even servants in inns. There was, of course, a serious concern of health that bore on the sanitary conditions within the bakery, as it affected not only bakers, but the public that consumed the products of the bakeries. Peckham never questioned the aptness of these laws, and indeed Lochner himself, and his lawyers, never contested them. In fact, they conceded them readily, for they thought they formed a dramatic contrast with the rules that were being brought forth

[36] *Lochner, supra*, note 16, at 70.
[37] *Ibid.*, at 71.

now under the guise of the police power. And so, *the lawyers for Lochner* pointed out the provisions that had been put in place, quite rightly, to specify the dimensions of the rooms, the air space and ventilation, the exclusion of domestic animals, the separation of the workplace from sleeping quarters and privies.[38] As Peckham noted, the legislature had already done, in this respect, "all that it could properly do":

> These several sections [of the law] provide for the inspection of the premises where the bakery is carried on, with regard to furnishing proper wash-rooms and water-closets, apart from the bakeroom, also with regard to providing proper drainage, plumbing and painting; the sections, in addition, provide for the height of the ceiling, the cementing or tiling of floors, where necessary in the opinion of the factory inspector, and for other things of that nature.[39]

But once these provisions were in place, the plaintiff and the judges were warranted then in putting the question, in a demanding way, as to why the law should assume that it would be injurious, under any conditions, for a baker to work more than ten hours in any day. As Peckham pointed out, the law was written in such a way that it precluded even the employee who might be willing to work additional hours for especially generous overtime pay.[40] Those suspicions could be aptly raised here, and they were given a deeper resonance by the terms of the statute that finally embarrassed the claims of this legislation as a health measure: According to an official report from the Factory Inspector's Bureau in New York, there were 3,828 bakeries inspected in the state in 1897. Of that number, more than half employed only two, one, or no journeymen bakers.[41] That is, half of the establishments were so small that the owners themselves, or their own families, did the baking. And by the terms of the laws, the owners and their families were not covered by these regulations, since they were classified as employers, rather than employees. But as the lawyers for Lochner aptly argued, if this was a health measure, which was to be imposed even on the worker who wished to work overtime, why

---

[38] See the briefs for the plaintiff (Lochner), *supra*, note 14, at 672.

[39] *Lochner*, at 61–62. In an edition of *The Lancet* in 1895, two English sanitary experts laid out the model regulations in detail:

> [The underground rooms should be] at least eight feet high and a minimum of 500 cubic feet of air space for each workman, and a special allowance for each gas jet. Walls must be kept smooth and dry. Window space must equal one-eighth of the floor and ventilation, light, drainage and lavatory accommodations must be such as to satisfy advanced modern requirements, floors should have nine-inch concrete and drains should be a foot deep lain in concrete.

Briefs, supra, note 14, at 710.

[40] *Lochner, supra*, note 16, at 52.

[41] *Briefs, supra*, note 14, at 668.

was it not applied to the owners and their families? If it were really hazardous for people to work more than ten hours a day, why was there no concern to protect these small businessmen and their families? But then, too, why only the bakers who plied their trade in bakeries? There were people who did precisely the same work, baking in hotels, restaurants, clubs, boardinghouses, and even in private households.[42] Yet, the law did nothing to protect these people, who had to be, as we say, "similarly situated."

One colleague of mine, steeped in the common law, offers as a possible response to these criticisms a perspective drawn from the "natural law": The legislators might have been counting, in part, on the most natural attachments in assuming that people would have a natural inclination to protect their children or other relatives. There would be far less need then for the law to intrude into these small businesses scaled to the size of a family. And yet we know that the same legislators passed and sustained other laws, which ordered the intervention of the law to protect children at the hands of parents who were strikingly inattentive to the health and well-being of their children, or whose reflexes in regard to their own offspring ventured into the murderous. Clearly, the law was not founded in all of its sections on the premise that parents could be counted on, as though driven by a law of nature, to protect their own children. And so, if the law sought to raise to a high level a concern for the safety of people working in bakeries, it hardly made sense to assume that this concern for the health of the workers dissolved if those workers happened to be children working in small establishments for their own parents.

It would appear then that the concern of the law was not so much with the people who worked for long hours near ovens, but with the people who were more likely to be employees and members of the bakers' union. The first call for this restriction of hours had emanated from a meeting of bakers in 1887. It may be a telling sign of the guiding spirit of this legislation that it seemed to have its principal effect in reducing the number of small bakeries, which were of course marked by their want of need for union labor or their inability to afford it. As Bernard Siegan noted, the law seemed to advance the concentration of the baking business, by enlarging the portion of sales taken by the larger, more corporate factories like the National Biscuit Company.[43]

---

[42] *Ibid.*, at 661–62.

[43] See Siegan, *Economic Liberties and the Constitution* (Chicago: University of Chicago Press, 1980), pp. 116–19. Siegan reports that, in 1899, only 2 percent of the baking establishments were owned by corporations, and in 1919 the comparable figure was 7 percent. But in this period, the corporate bakeries enlarged their share of production from 28.7 to 51.8 percent. In the bakeries owned by corporations, the average number

Whatever we may think of the motives that lay behind this legislation, it would have to be conceded, I think, that the judges had ample grounds for considering the argument on the basis of health to be immanently implausible. Indeed, a case might have been made on the issue of health, but evidently the legislators themselves were not honoring that case or taking it seriously. Of course, the judges might have relaxed the stringency of their inquiry, or decided to be affably credulous. But the problem, as Peckham explained, was that the Court could not back itself into a rule of this kind: that it would lapse into a state of benign credulity if a legislature merely invoked the magic words and avowed that any measure was passed out of a concern for "the morals, the health or safety of the people." If the Court were prepared to sustain any piece of legislation so long as those phrases were uttered as invocations, then as Peckham aptly observed, "the Fourteenth Amendment would have no efficacy and the legislatures of the State would have unbounded power."[44] Or to put it another way, a review by the courts would become a ceremony purged of its substance, and what would be lost here is the very notion of a government restrained by a constitution.

Still, Peckham had not exhausted the possibilities for salvaging this legislation. Even if the rationale on the grounds of health was not compelling, the legislation could be regarded as a species of labor law, designed to protect workers who were vulnerable to the power of the employers. But the most telling markers were again absent: The workers here were not composed mainly of children or aliens, of people who were rendered vulnerable by their immaturity or ignorance or want of legal standing as citizens. It has been common, of course, to presume that workers as a class were simply vulnerable to the overwhelming power of people called employers. But judges who bore some experience in the world knew how problematic those suppositions could be. Half of the employers and their families were barely distinguishable from their employees, and many of them were working at such low overheads, with such low margins, that they possessed very little leverage in regard to their workers. There were also periods of tight labor markets, in which workers

of employees was around forty-four, as opposed to a workforce of fewer than three people in the businesses run by their owners. As Siegan estimates, the larger, corporate bakeries found it much easier to absorb the cost of the regulations that were imposed under the labor laws. They might have calculated then that the laws would have the benign effect of squeezing out many of the small, marginal bakeries, operating with very low overhead. As Siegan observes, "The reaction to *Lochner* might have been far less harsh had the critics recognized that the law probably would have reduced considerably the wages of many low-paid workers, and caused others to lose their jobs." *Ibid.*, at p. 118.

[44] *Lochner, supra,* note 16, at 56.

could be choosy, or they could at least have a certain choice in avoiding situations they regarded as far less congenial. The differentials in compensation already indicated that it was necessary to pay people more to enter certain hazardous occupations than to work, say, in libraries or in publishing houses. Under those conditions, judges who were quite sympathetic to the purposes of the law might well wonder whether the law, in this case, was far too sweeping and categorical: Whether it was injurious, or rather profitable, for a worker to work overtime in a bakery would depend on the age, the health, and the situation of the worker. No one could estimate these things more precisely than the workers themselves. What I am suggesting then is that even judges who were concerned about protecting workers could see something quite presumptuous – and quite harmful to the interests of workmen – in legislation that swept in such an undiscriminating way and imposed the same restrictions even in circumstances that admitted a host of exceptions.

Against this prospect, Peckham was disposed to assume that bakers bore as much natural wit as anyone else. His own inclination was to presume that ordinary men and women had the competence to know their own interests and make their own judgments about the terms of employment that met their needs and merited their consent. With the presumption set in that direction, the judge could nevertheless be open to reasons that might weigh compellingly on the other side. He would be willing to search then for the reasons that led him to reach a different conclusion about bakers. But what was at stake here, in the understanding of Peckham and his colleagues, ran well beyond the situation of bakers. If the law could move – shall we say? – less than rigorously in this case, it would be hard to distinguish bakers from many other classes of employees, who could find themselves falling under the same set of restrictions. If the law was applied then with the full reach of the rationale, the reach of the law could end up astonishing even people with the most benign view of regulation. "No trade," said Peckham, "no occupation, no mode of earning one's living, could escape this all-pervading power":

> In our large cities [he continued] there are many buildings into which the sun penetrates for but a short time in each day, and these buildings are occupied by people carrying on the business of bankers, brokers, lawyers, real estate, and many other kinds of business, aided by many clerks, messengers, and other employes. . . . It might be said that it is unhealthy to work more than [a certain number] of hours in an apartment lighted by artificial light during the working hours of the day; that the occupation of the bank clerk, the lawyer's clerk, the real estate clerk, or the broker's clerk in such offices is therefore unhealthy. . . .

> ... Not only the hours of employes, but the hours of employers, could be regulated, and doctors, lawyers, scientists, all professional men, as well as athletes and artisans, could be forbidden to fatigue their brains and bodies by prolonged hours of exercise.[45]

I know more than a few young people who have been put off from the profession of law by the prospect of working sixteen hour days, and eighty- to ninety-hour weeks. We also know of many young people in the academy, working for their tenure, preparing for classes and working on manuscripts, who cannot practicably put a ten-hour limit on their working days. It is not merely that the law does not seek to rescue these young people from these regimens. But rather, we can hardly imagine a law that would try to regulate these matters with a formula that applied equally, uniformly, across the professions – to the young associate in a law firm, fresh from law school; to the graduate student, without his doctorate, teaching his first courses in the nineteenth-century novel; or to the newly minted Ph.D. in molecular biology, launched now in his laboratory. Whether a young scholar needs to work to 2:00 AM may have something to do with his own powers of concentration, or with the presence or absence of writing blocks. A law that sought to confine his limit to ten hours may not impart the spark of insight or deliver him from his writing block. In the meantime, his willingness to put in the longer hours may conduce more readily to his well-being. I know, of course, that we are inclined to make a distinction between the work chosen by academics, because they happen to love it, and the work we may be inclined to regard as rather more prosaic, such as the work done in bakeries. But judges like Peckham seemed to recognize that even people in prosaic callings may find it quite as useful to have the freedom that we are quicker to attribute to the professional classes.

In contrast, there is something to ponder in the report, offered by Bernard Siegan, that there were, in New York City, in the late 1970s, about eight thousand Chinese workers in garment factories, working far longer than the hours stipulated in the law, and at less than the minimum wage. Their situation was known to the authorities and the unions. And yet there was a willingness mainly to look the other way, mainly because these people and their families needed the jobs and the income.[46]

We may recall those early, sociological studies on the injuries suffered by bakers – the kinds of studies earnestly reported by Justice Harlan. But then we might be taken over quickly by the recognition that we could well

---

[45] *Ibid.*, at 59–60.
[46] See Siegan, *supra*, note 43, at pp. 119–20.

hear claims of even more exacting precision in our own day about carpal tunnel syndrome, or the strain on eyes suffered by people compelled to put in long hours staring at computer screens and hammering away at keyboards. Whether those injuries are any more or less serious than the injuries facing bakers, I could not say. My own inclination would be to say, with Peckham, that individuals will be the best judges of the things that cause them strain. I would join Peckham, then, in leaving them the widest freedom for making their own adjustments. But having said that, or having marked my own dubiety, I would not claim that the issue is unarguable: Perhaps the hazards in baking are rather more severe than it seems to me after a detached view of the record. Or perhaps the people working in these establishments were more vulnerable, or far more in need of the sheltering of the law, than it appeared to Peckham and his colleagues at the time. I would preserve the possibility that, in these estimates, Peckham and his colleagues might have reckoned wrongly, or that they might have tipped their judgment, quite as plausibly, to the other side. But my point here is that even if we quarrel with their judgment in *Lochner*, or balance the equities here in a different way, it would not be because we would be acting on moral premises notably at odds with those of the judges. Nor would it be because we brought to the project a wider sympathy for working people than Peckham and his colleagues managed to encompass.

In fact, one of the ironies here is that, if we sought to mount a criticism of Peckham and *Lochner*, it could only be by establishing, as the ground of judgment, the ground that Peckham himself had been so fastidious in setting into place. The situation recalls that fetching passage that Rousseau struck off in the course of his defense of his First Discourse, and offered in response to some criticisms that were composed by the King of Poland. Rousseau remarked that one of the most illustrious popes had once maintained that it was quite an honest and plausible thing to assert the word of God even against the rules of grammar. And yet, he said, the people carried away in the torrents of this argument were constrained to conform themselves to the usage they had condemned.[47] That is to say, their critique would still be carried through with the use of grammar. And so, it was in a manner, as he said, very knowing that most of them declaimed against the progress of science.[48] The irony here is that, if we sought today to quarrel with Peckham, it could only be on

[47] "[I]ls furent contraints de se conformer eux-mêmes a l'usage qu'ils condamnaient."
[48] "[C]e fut d'une maniere tres savante que la plupart d'entre eux declamarent contre le progress des sciences." Rousseau, *Discourse Sur Les Sciences et Les Arts* (Paris: Garnier-Flammarion, 1971), p. 87.

the basis of the jural groundwork that Peckham had written so precisely to sustain. It could certainly not be on the grounds of the positivism that led Holmes and Hugo Black to reject the jurisprudence of *Lochner*. For almost no one, today – not even the jural conservatives – is willing to suspend judgment so uncritically and honor virtually anything that a legislature has "posited" as law through the vote of a majority. And after all, if we credit that litmus put forth earlier as the mark of modern liberal jurisprudence, the critique offered by Holmes and Black was based on a jurisprudence that surely would have yielded the "wrong" result in *Roe v. Wade*. If Holmes and Black had been willing to sustain even arbitrary judgments made by legislatures, they would have found no ground for challenging the judgment of a legislature that there were, in human wombs, nothing other than human beings. And those unborn humans could then be protected by the law, as they had been protected in the common law, long before the beginning of America. The devotees of modern liberal jurisprudence may not find *Lochner* congenial, but it is not clear that they can assemble any *moral* or jural argument against it.

As for Rufus Peckham, I wish I could say that my research had turned up something in his private papers that might dislodge or confirm the characterization that Holmes had offered of him. But even if it were true that his major premise was "God damn it," we can piece together enough from his writings to say that, as a reigning aphorism, it still marked an outlook that made him notably different from people in our own day who have taken as their own reigning aphorism, "God is dead." Rufus Peckham may not have been a clubby fellow, but we can say of him at least this: That he had the most firmly grounded sense that even working people, in the most ordinary and prosaic occupations, merited a presumption of their competence to govern their own lives; that they would not find in our patronizing tenderness the main security for their well-being; and they surely would not find there the source of their rights.[49]

But past the caricature of Rufus Peckham, we seem to be left with a series of misreadings that have worked themselves now into a story line that has

---

[49] Since the time when this lecture was delivered and published, other and younger scholars have revisited the *Lochner* case and the jurisprudence of that "Lochner Era," and given me some new allies in seeing *Lochner* in another, better light and defending anew the jurisprudence of that Court. See, notably, David N. Mayer, "The Myth of 'Laissez-Faire Constitutionalism': Liberty of Contract during the Lochner Era," 36 *Hastings Constitutional Law Quarterly* 217 (2009); Gary D. Rowe, "Lochner Revisionism Revised," 24 *Law and Social Inquiry* 221 (1999); and David Bernstein, *Only One Place of Redress* (Durham and London: Duke University Press, 2001).

proven remarkably durable. There is the catty portrait of Peckham, which might be quite uncharitable in the reading of his character. That portrait would be wildly wrong when set against a close reading of the law he had crafted with arguments precisely tailored. At the same time, a careful reading of the opinion in *Lochner* would yield an understanding quite deeply at odds with the caricature of the case that has been preserved even by scholars writing histories and composing tracts for the law reviews. The deep irony, of course, is that we find people, amply tutored, disdaining a case and, with it, a body of law whose very premises and principles they have come to absorb as their own. And so judges and lawyers may deride *Lochner* without altering the cast that *Lochner* has helped to define for them. Within that cast they continue to function without strain, and continue to dispense their judgments.

Still, I would suggest that there is something strikingly different in a state of affairs in which the judges were led to see the case wrongly, and in that way, tutored the next two or three generations to see a whole series of cases wrongly in the same way, through the same mistaken lens. In that manner, the judges, as teachers, manage to do some serious misteaching. For the doctrines they fashioned would now have become levers in the hands of other judges. The further result is that the judges, armed wrongly, have done serious injuries to persons and to the fabric of the law. Such, I think, has been the wreckage produced by the notion of "prior restraint" as it was taught to us in the 1930s, in the famous case of *Near v. Minnesota*. A phrase was turned into a concept, and then into a doctrine of the law. When that phrase, treated now as a doctrine, was brought to bear on a case as momentous as that of the Pentagon Papers, it would do substantial damage to the national security and endanger the lives of real people. When the Court sought to correct itself a few years later in the case of young Frank Snepp, the judges discreetly altered their judgment without summoning the candor, or honesty, to acknowledge their mistake. The result was to treat shabbily one earnest young man who did not deserve such a rough justice. But that too is a puzzle that deserves some sorting of the strands. I would draw in the reader then to follow me in unfolding, over the next chapters, the story that runs from Near to the Pentagon Papers to the saga of Frank Snepp.

Four

The Strange Case of Prior Restraint:
The Pentagon Papers

The scene: Washington, D.C., in the mid-1980s, a meeting of a panel of the National Endowment for the Humanities. Four professors were sitting with members of the professional staff, reviewing proposals for grants. One proposal, bristling with promise, or at least with pretension, offered a plan for a documentary series on television, dealing with the issue of "prior restraints." Within the space of two broadcasts, the program would move from the landmark case of *Near v. Minnesota* in 1931, to the famous case of the Pentagon Papers in 1971. Each story would have, for the screen, rather colorful characters, with sides dark enough to cast deep shadows and textures. With *Near v. Minnesota*, there was the story of the *Saturday Press*, something down dirtier and lower than what we could call the scandal sheets in our own day, "journals" (if one could call them that) like the *National Enquirer*, sold in supermarkets. Like the sensational tabloids of our own day, the *Saturday Press* trafficked in scandals. But unlike the tabloids sold today in supermarkets, the newspaper in Minneapolis had blackmail as a much more deliberate part of its rationale, or its plan of business. Without taking sides too quickly, we may say that the owners of this newspaper were counting on more than advertising and sales to make their money in publishing. Not to put too fine a point on it, they were counting on their prospective victims to find it to their advantage, on balance, to pay off the editors to forestall the articles in the first place, rather than pay for litigation in suing for libel. The "story," planned for the newspaper, came along then with blackmail, with threats of retaliations, and the actual exchange of gunfire. If this was journalism, it was more in the style of the frontier, with characters like Mose Barnett, Howard Guilford, and Jay Near.

The adventures of the *Saturday Press* were sufficiently disturbing of the public peace that the authorities in Minnesota were finally moved to invoke the laws on criminal libel for the sake of putting this journal under restraint. The use of the laws of libel against the press was, of course, contested as an issue of the First Amendment, and when the case made its way to the Supreme Court, there were, once again, colorful characters in robes. Most notably, for the people planning the documentary for the Endowment, there was the elegant Chief Justice, Charles Evans Hughes, with his striking beard and moustaches. But then the scene would shift, the viewer would leap ahead forty years, to the case of the Pentagon Papers. And there the story could boast the characters who would be stamped vividly for villainy during the days of Watergate. There would be the dour Attorney General John Mitchell, but most of all there would be the dark presence of Richard Nixon.

It was, altogether, quite a colorful canvas for television. There were vivid figures clashing and bringing forth, as part of this morality play, some ringing lessons about censorship of the press and the sacred principle of rejecting all "prior restraints" on publication. It was all so colorful, and quite a confirming package. And it was so staggeringly superficial. As the panel of scholars clustered around the table, one professor remarked with a slight glow of approval that this project had just about everything, all the bells and whistles, the arguments and the characters. But then second thoughts set in with a note of sobriety, and the proposal was put to the side, never to be revived again, at least during the tenure of this panel. In retrospect, I think the melting of the certitude began with the voicing of this simple point: Yes, this project had everything, from the moustaches of Charles Evans Hughes to the agitation over the war in Vietnam – it had everything *except* Mr. Justice Butler's *dissenting* opinion in *Near v. Minnesota*, the opinion pointing out that the Court had radically misconceived the case. As Butler explained, in telling detail, the case before the Court did not really present an instance of "prior restraint" or "previous restraint" on publication, as that notion had come to be known in the law of England and America. In this judgment, Mr. Justice Butler had the support of three other colleagues, including the estimable George Sutherland, who was no trifling scholar of the law. If Butler and his colleagues were right, the Court was not seeing, plainly and accurately, the nature of the case at hand. Many textures, many details quite important to the law, were being screened out. But beyond that, the Court was articulating what would be seen as a new principle. As that principle was carried over into the future, to a train of other cases then, a mistake made by the Court would be amplified into grave mistakes spread to other parts of the law, as the precedent was confirmed and deepened.

I happen to think that Butler and his colleagues got it right that day, in their dissenting opinion. And when the same mistake of the Court was grandly replayed in the Pentagon Papers case, forty years later, the mistakes would come at a heavy price, perhaps even in the actual loss of lives. Yet, apart from the loss of lives, there were the deeper stories of many more lives endangered as a result of the precedent that a hurried Court, rushed to judgment, was willing to put in place in 1971. Faced with a crisis, the Court sought familiar ground and waved again the clichés thought to be settled in the law, clichés about prior restraints. Nine years later, as I'll try to show, the Court repudiated every strand of reasoning that was critical to its judgment in the Pentagon Papers case. And yet, it must stand as a tribute to the liberal filtering of the law, or to the fable spun out in the law schools, that the decision of the Court in *Snepp v. United States* (1980) has never been seen to overrule either the judgment in the Pentagon Papers case or in *Near v. Minnesota*. But why it has not been seen in that way runs rather beyond any chicanery, or manipulative genius, of the law clerks or the professors in the schools of law. It has more to do, I think, with the power of certain words or concepts to fix our perceptions or constrain our imagination. We were presented, in *Near v. Minnesota*, with a rambunctious case, containing some novelties in our law, and it simply was not responsive to the complex of questions posed on that occasion to bring that case under the formula of "prior restraints." It can be accounted only as an exercise in artificial reason to suppose that this formula could offer any sensible help in settling the issues in this case, or supply any guidance for other courts in the future. But the formula, nevertheless, took hold. And so, when professors of law confront cases with injunctions, seeking to restrain publication, the notion of "prior restraint" clicks in, and it seems to block off our vision. It molds our perception of the cases – of the things we see or fail to see – and it alters our view of the legal landscape.

If I might extend this prelude just a bit further, I would recall briefly how the issue played out, in key moments, in the Pentagon Papers case, when the judges were being pressed to render justice in a hurry, and they were acutely aware of the injuries they could do with a decision in either direction. In my own case, it is hard to forget how the news broke upon us, for it came with a jolt on a peaceful Sunday in the beginning of June (the 13th). In an academic town, we had just had the commencement at Amherst, followed by alumni arriving a week later for the time of reunions. The campus was vibrant again with people and celebrations, but on Sunday morning the last stragglers leave, an emphatic calm sets in once again, people settle in with the weekend edition of the *New York Times* – and then the news broke. A minor bomb seemed to be dropped in our laps, for the *Times* had decided to deliver to us this Sunday a story that its reporters and editors had been planning for several weeks and months. With that story, a minor crisis would be triggered. Justices of the Supreme Court, heading out of town with the end of their term, would be summoned back to Washington hurriedly to deal with appeals. Federal court judges, in Washington and New York, would be pressed by the government, by the Nixon administration, to issue injunctions for the sake of halting, at least for a while, any further installments of what was being published now as a series and becoming known as "The Pentagon Papers."

The Papers emerged from a study that had been ordered up by Robert McNamara before he was displaced from his position as Secretary of Defense in the Kennedy-Johnson administrations. In later years McNamara would admit serious doubts about the prospects for prosecuting and winning the war under the schemes produced by his brand of "whiz kids" in charge of managing the military establishment. Curiously, from this pattern of failure and frustration McNamara did not seem to draw many doubts about the wisdom of the strategy. The sense of failure seemed to move him, rather, to flip over into moral doubts about the very justification for the war itself. In this respect, McNamara seemed to absorb the perspectives that inflamed the critics of the war who staged protests against him on the campuses. But even apart from his clumsy efforts to rehabilitate himself in the eyes of the Left, McNamara revealed inadvertently in his memoir something far more telling: As Gilbert and Sullivan might have said, McNamara was teeming with a lot of news about the defects, military and moral, of our allies in South Vietnam. Of the moral defects of the regime we were resisting, the murderous regime ruled from Hanoi, he had not a whisper of criticism.[1] The comparison was unmistakable: McNamara was evidently content to keep hazarding the sons of other people in a war he found no prospect of winning, and for which he bore no moral conviction. For he professed no ground of moral justification for resisting the extension of that regime in North Vietnam. As time wore on, that want of conviction would turn into a surety growing ever firmer about the wrongness of the war. It was a McNamara in the winds of this kind of moral confusion, or moral turning, who ordered up the study of the war within the Pentagon. In any event, a project originating in confusion would then be amplified in its bewilderment by the presence, in the staff, of Dr. Daniel Ellsberg.

Of Ellsberg, with his oscillations and instabilities, we would learn more later. But in the first moments, when we encountered the Pentagon Papers, the striking items that riveted our attention concerned people like John

---

[1] See Robert S. McNamara, *In Retrospect: The Tragedy and Lessons of Vietnam* (New York Times Books, 1995), p. 186.

McNaughton, who had been an Assistant Secretary of Defense. In one memorandum, contained in the Papers, an analyst noted that the President was
moving closer and closer to war, and yet certain "tactical considerations"
were holding him back. Foremost among those "tactical" concerns was that
"the President was in the midst of an election campaign in which he was
presenting himself as the candidate of reason and restraint as opposed to the
quixotic Barry Goldwater."[2] But there were other reasons, too, for holding
back: The government in South Vietnam was still shaky, and there was the
need to prepare a ground in public support before any decisive move into war.
In a memorandum in September 1964, McNaughton described the situation
in this way:

> Special considerations during the next two months. The relevant audiences
> of U.S. actions are the Communists (who must feel strong pressures), the
> South Vietnamese (whose morale must be buoyed), our allies (who must
> trust us as "underwriters"), and the U.S. public (which must support our
> risk-taking with U.S. lives and prestige). During the next two months,
> because of the lack of "rebuttal time" before election to justify particu-
> lar actions which may be distorted to the U.S. public, we must act with
> special care – signaling to the D.R.V. [the so-called Democratic Republic of
> North Vietnam] that initiatives are being taken, to the G.V.N. [Government
> of South Vietnam] that we are behaving energetically despite the restraints
> of our political seasons, and to the U.S. public that we are behaving with
> good purpose and restraint.[3]

"Restraints of our political seasons"? What could those have been other
than the need not to make it known to the public, during the election, that
the administration was gearing up for a widening of the war in Southeast
Asia? That revelation would have dissolved the caricature of Goldwater, as
the bellicose candidate, threatening war, in comparison with the President
who was seeking to avoid a deeper involvement in Vietnam. But then what
could it have meant to convey to the public "that we are behaving with good
purpose and restraint"? If the American government was not plunging into
war, why would there have been any need for dramatic public gestures to
make the point about the restraint shown by the government? The gestures
seemed necessary only if there was a need to preserve the facade of restraint
during "our political seasons." The impression, clearly left in the memo, was

[2] Quoted in Neil Sheehan, Hedrick Smith, E.W. Kenworthy, and Fox Butterfield, *The
Pentagon Papers: The Secret History of the Vietnam War* (New York: Bantam Books,
July 1971), p. 310.
[3] Quoted in *ibid.*, p. 311.

that the administration meant to escalate the war in Vietnam, for the sake of bringing things to a head, after Johnson had come safely through the election. In fact, according to the Papers, the detailed planning for the campaign of bombing began "in earnest" on November 3, 1964, the day that Lyndon Johnson (LBJ) was winning with a landslide.[4]

McNaughton's "office paper" could have been taken to confirm the most lurid accounts of the Johnson administration – and American politics – that would be sounded later by the more unhinged critics: that in manner most cynical, the American political elite had meant to bring America into a war for the sake of resisting socialism and nationalism abroad. In this project, political democracy had been exposed again as a deep fraud, for the people at the ballot box were easily open to manipulation by those men who truly determined when wars were heated up or turned off.

Of course, this display of memos should have been taken with a certain discount. After all, people serving in the middle echelons of an administration are often swollen with their own importance. They have the conceit of acting as though their words and gestures mattered. For them, memoranda may take the place of action in the lives of other people, and they may write those memoranda as though they truly spoke the will of their administration. But the fact that Mr. McNaughton wrote that memorandum cannot be taken on its face to mean that he was accurately reflecting the intentions, or the settled judgments, of Lyndon Johnson, or that Johnson had even been aware of his memorandum. The late John Roche put in a stint for a while as an assistant to LBJ, and Roche would later claim – after a conversation with his former chief – that LBJ had not seen that memorandum, or memoranda remotely like it, until he had heard about the account in the *New York Times.* On the other hand, some recent archival findings suggest that McNaughton, a man of credentials, highly placed, did in fact speak the minds of the people who were directing the administration in this period.[5]

But whether he was aware of them or not, whether the account in the papers was accurate or not, became now Johnson's burden to explain. For there could have been little doubt that if these papers constituted an embarrassment, or a scandal, they were charges on the reputation of Lyndon Johnson and his party. Yet, that sense of the matter was quickly displaced, as the Nixon administration sought to block the publication of the Pentagon Papers. The

---

[4] *Ibid.*, pp. 309–10.
[5] See H. R. McMaster, *Dereliction of Duty: Lyndon Johnson, Robert McNamara, the Joint Chiefs of Staff, and the Lies that Led to Vietnam* (New York: HarperCollins, 1997), pp. 150–51.

war was Johnson's, but Nixon had inherited it. His chances of bringing it to a decent conclusion now would have to be affected by anything that would throw a moral cloud around the conduct of that war. Mr. Nixon then put himself, in effect, in place of Johnson, in the sense that he became willing now to accept Johnson's liabilities as his own. And whether or not the embarrassment would center on Johnson, the publication of these papers had to be seen as an undermining of the Executive authority. Nine years later, when the tensions of the moment had long vanished, the Court was finally able to speak the sober truth that had been expressed at the time only by Mr. Justice Harlan: The very fact that the Executive had to go to court to restrain the publication of these papers, the fact that the Executive had to persuade another branch, the judicial department, to restrain publication – all of this meant, quite plainly, that the American Executive was not in control of its own papers. Not in control, that is, of papers of a confidential kind, bearing on diplomatic and military operations. The late Claire Sterling would discover, in her interviews with people in the intelligence services in Europe, that this unambiguous fact was taken, by observers abroad, as decisive. The French made the decision that there could be no sharing with the Americans of the most sensitive intelligence, bearing on the lives of their agents, because the American Executive clearly did not possess an exclusive control over its own, most sensitive papers.[6]

Whatever the origin of the problem with the Pentagon Papers, their publication clearly impinged now on the interests of Richard Nixon. Apparently, Nixon read the situation initially as an embarrassment for the Johnson administration and the Democrats, in laying out the record of their path to war. His inclination then was not to leap into the fray, but to hold back with some detachment. From the account offered by Robert Haldeman, Nixon's former chief of staff, it was Henry Kissinger who began to react heatedly, and to lay out for Nixon, in terms vivid and pointed, his stake in this misadventure produced by the Democrats and the *Times.* According to Haldeman, Kissinger argued that Nixon's holding back suggested that he did not quite grasp "how dangerous the release of the Pentagon Papers was." Kissinger went on (in Haldman's transcription):

[T]he fact that some idiot can publish all of the diplomatic secrets of this country on his own is damaging to your image, as far as the Soviet are concerned, and it could destroy our ability to conduct foreign policy. If

---

[6] See Claire Sterling, *Time of the Assassins* (New York: Holt, Rinehart and Winston, 1985), p. 196.

other powers feel that we cannot control internal leaks, they will never agree to secret negotiations.[7]

What Kissinger had keenly in mind at this time were the negotiations that he was conducting in trying to make the breakthrough with China. But those negotiations were bound up in turn with the attempts to deal with North Vietnam, steer into the agreements over Strategic Arms Limitation with the Soviet Union, and handle the delicate dance over Berlin.[8] When asked about the matter years later, Kissinger would remark that Nixon finally made his decision to enter the case for the sake of vindicating the "classification system." That is, Nixon had not acted, in this construal, out of a sense of any political blame drawn to himself. In this account, taken seriously by Henry Kissinger, Nixon had acted out of a concern to vindicate the regime of "classification" – the system of holding confidential papers, and ensuring that the Executive did indeed have control of its own papers.[9] But the two accounts had blended into the same thing. As Madison had famously pointed out in the *Federalist Papers*, the institutions of the government would work well when "the interest of the man" could be "connected with the constitutional rights of the place." And in that way, "the private interests of every individual may be a sentinel over the public rights."[10] The Pentagon Papers endangered Nixon's interests, but only as Nixon felt a responsibility to preserve, in turn, the powers and strength of the Executive.

It was too early to tell just how damaging those papers were. But that was all the more reason the national interest would be served by seeking a halt in the process until people in the Executive had the chance to review and consider just what material was being disclosed by the *New York Times* and the *Washington Post*. Still, the initial reports, on the surface, could hardly have been assuring. One student quite close to me was David Eisenhower, even though we were, at the time, in opposing political parties. He was the grandson of Dwight Eisenhower and now the son-in-law of President Nixon, and he told me of the curious report heard at the White House – that the Pentagon Papers had been delivered to three places: the *New York Times*, the *Washington Post* – and the Russian embassy. Whatever that mixture meant, it

---

[7] H. R. Haldeman and Joseph DiMona, *The Ends of Power* (New York: New York Times Book Company, 1978), p. 110.

[8] See, in this respect, Kissinger's memoir, *White House Years* (New York: Little, Brown, 1979), pp. 729–30.

[9] Henry Kissinger, in conversation with the writer, in New York City, May 30, 2000, and again, July 25, 2003.

[10] *Federalist Papers* No. 51 (New York: Random House, n.d.), p. 337.

had all of the earmarks of hostility to the government, and it was understood to mark a willingness to traffic with the enemies of the country.

And so the administration went to court. The first article, in the *Times*, had appeared on Sunday, June 13. Another would appear on Monday, June 14, and on the next day, when yet another appeared, the administration moved into court. Three articles had appeared, and the administration claimed that some of the material had been drawn from documents classified as "Top Secret – Sensitive" and just plain "Top Secret"; that the possession of these papers by the *Times* was unlawful; and that the publication of further articles in this vein would "prejudice the defense interests of the United States and result in irreparable injury to the United States."[11] The government sought a temporary restraining order, blocking the *Times* from publishing any other pieces in this series until the legal process could be completed. Beyond that, the government sought to examine the documents in possession of the *Times*, and asked that they be turned over for review. The *Times* refused, and Judge Gurfein, in the federal district court in New York, granted the temporary restraining order. The government would assert an interest in "discovery," to determine the contents of the papers. But the *Times* would insist in opposition that the government should carry the burden of justification in showing why such access would be needed. Judge Gurfein invited the government to make its most plausible case, but in the absence of the papers, the lawyers for the government found themselves engaged in some stylish mumbling. A general sense of unease, or the awareness of a deep want of impropriety on the part of the *Times* and Ellsberg, did not apparently convey, to Judge Gurfein, a precise case. Nor was Gurfein inclined to help the lawyers emerge from their hazy impressions by letting them see precisely the papers that were at issue. He filed an opinion then on June 19, denying the government's plea for a restraining injunction.

In the meantime, a funny thing happened while the *Times* was under a temporary restraining order. As if responding to a choreographer, the *Washington Post* began to publish articles drawn from the same series, picking up, as it were, where the *Times* left off, before it had been so rudely interrupted by the government and a temporary restraining order. And if that were not enough, other newspapers, like the *New York Post*, began to report on the "story" that was emerging around the Pentagon Papers themselves, including of course one or two choice excerpts from the Papers. The government was

---

[11] Quoted in Alexander Bickel's brief for the *New York Times*, pp. 4–5 (June 24, 1971), reprinted in Philip B. Kurland and Gerhard Casper, eds., *Landmark Briefs and Arguments of the Supreme Court of the United States* (Arlington, Va.: University Publications of America, 1975), Vol. 71, pp. 3–21.

being faced then with a series of leaks, abetted by a free press, and the rather forbidding prospect of trying to plug up all of the spigots. In an earlier day, with other conventions, the Executive might have taken decisive action on its own to close down the publications. But in the conventions settled in our law by the 1970s it appeared that the only thing that could put a sharp, decisive end to the publications was a signal and dramatic judgment, rendered by a court, stamping the *Times* and the *Post* as wrongdoers.

The argument would be heard in later years that the action was unprecedented. There was indeed a serious danger that the national security was being compromised. Still, there was no recollection of any previous case in which an administration had sought to enjoin a newspaper from publishing. But even at the time, the U.S. Attorney in New York, Whitney North Seymour, offered a response that should have registered with the thoughtful. Seymour noted that, in previous cases, the action had been completed with the publication of an article, and it could not have been in the interest of the government to launch a suit that would only draw more attention to the publication. Under the press of time, Seymour did not elaborate on his argument, and it is regrettable, because he could have told the story, always worth telling, of the *Chicago Tribune* and the Battle of Midway during the Second World War. The *Tribune* had published a couple of pieces struck off by the redoubtable Stanley Johnston, newly returned from the Battle of the Coral Sea. Johnston had actually become a hero of sorts, in participating in the rescue of sailors in that battle. When he arrived back in San Diego, he began to assemble his accounts. But then the news began filtering in from another action in the Pacific. By the time Johnston reached Chicago, and drew upon his own, special knowledge, he was able to put together an account of one of the turning points in the war, the Battle of Midway. The Japanese losses were decisive – five carriers destroyed or damaged, by the early accounts, along with serious losses in battleships and cruisers. But when Johnston wove the story together with his own, direct knowledge, he produced a story that was not only precise in its accuracy, but altogether too precise: His account contained the names of the Japanese ships, and it reflected a strikingly accurate awareness of the disposition of the Japanese Navy. This kind of knowledge had been available only because American intelligence had broken the Japanese code. That itself, however, was a piece of intelligence that should not have been revealed to the Japanese. Its disclosure could remove the advantage it offered, and in removing it, imperil the lives and interests that could be guarded through the possession of that vital intelligence.

According to Admiral Ernest King, President Roosevelt's first impulse, when he heard the report, was to send the marines to occupy the Tribune Tower. As FDR calmed down and worked his way to moderation, he pondered a prosecution for treason, directed at his enduring adversary, Colonel Robert McCormick, the publisher of the *Tribune*.[12] But the problem posed then to the government stood as a lesson in prudence for men of affairs who would bear the responsibilities of office: One could hope that the clues, dropped in the course of a dispatch, in one story, might have been overlooked. If they were, there was no real harm done. And if they were not, there was no point in staging a highly visible prosecution of the *Tribune*, which could only have had the effect of a conveying, loudly, to the Japanese, the news they had otherwise missed. In the case, however, of the Pentagon Papers, the papers were being published as a series, with installments coming out every day, scheduled to run for about a week. The concern was that there could be, lurking in those papers, clues that could be revealing to people with tutored eyes, in the KGB or in the intelligence service of North Vietnam. They could be names of places – towns, restaurants, offices, and even the places where troops were being deployed – names that could be known only to people who were engaged in the operations. The mere mention of the names could offer a telling clue to their source. What the administration sought, at the least, was the chance to review those papers before they were published, to see if clues of that kind could be detected by people in the government who were in a position to know.

One of the striking qualities of this case, of course, was that this authority of the government would be treated as problematic. It would be framed as a live issue or question that had to be presented *to a court* in order to receive in turn an authoritative answer. That brute fact, in the very staging of the case, would later be recognized for the grave defect it was. Nine years later, in the *Snepp* case, the Supreme Court would virtually concede the error of sustaining that action in the courts with the Pentagon Papers. But when the matter reached the High Court at the time, it was only Mr. Justice Harlan who recognized this distinct strand of importance in the case: As Harlan observed, with a worldly archness, it did not seem to occur to some of the judges in the lower courts that they were dealing, not with functionaries or bureaucrats, but with a coordinate branch of the government. Indeed, as Harlan pointed out, they were dealing with a constitutional officer bearing a dignity not a shade lower than the dignity that reposed in federal judges.[13] That constitutional officer – the President of the United States – bore an

---

[12] The story is recounted in interesting detail in Richard Norton Smith's biography, *The Colonel: The Life and Legend of Robert R. McCormick* (Boston: Houghton Mifflin, 1997), pp. 429–37, especially 430, 433.

[13] See *New York Times v. United States*, 403 U.S. 713, at 758, and *passim*.

obligation to preserve the Constitution, no less than the obligation borne by the judges. And though it may seem indecorous to point it out, the President also had, annexed to his authority, a virtual apparatus of people seasoned in intelligence, whose capacity to read and decode those papers promised to exceed, by a substantial margin, the competence even of those bright young clerks who made up the chambers of the judges.

In an earlier day, that combination of legal standing and superior competence was likely to have made a more pronounced impression on the minds of judges and their clerks. That was an understanding long settled, and it might have worked in this case to have cautioned the judges. Or, it might have prevented the matter from being posed in the first place as a problem submitted to the Solomonic wisdom of judges. There is a lesson to be gleaned in considering, as a sobering thought-experiment, the way in which the case might have been treated under the Lincoln administration. If this case had arisen under Lincoln, there would have been little likelihood that the government would have seen a need even to trouble the courts. No doubt there would have been a move into the courts, but it would not have been initiated by the government. From what we know of the Lincoln administration, in a time of crisis, I rather imagine that there would have been the equivalent of yellow tape wrapped around the buildings, or the offices, that constituted the *New York Times* and the *Washington Post*. Mr. Arthur Hays Sulzberger, the owner of the *Times*, and Mrs. Katharine Graham, the owner of the *Washington Post*, might have been taken into protective custody, along with a sufficient sample of the editors and reporters who had worked on the Pentagon Papers, for those aides might have continued the work of putting out those papers had the government not intervened in a timely way. The *Times* or *Post* would have been closed down temporarily, with its management under custody, until the government could resolve itself on the issues posing a deadly concern for American soldiers and agents abroad. From their cells, Sulzberger, Graham, and their editors, might have been in touch with their lawyers. The lawyers surely would have come into court, seeking a writ of habeas corpus and the release of their clients. And as the Lincoln administration dealt with such orders from courts during the time of its own crisis, it was likely to inform the agents delivering those orders that it was not in the posture of receiving them. The agents might have been advised then to return to the courts, whence they had been dispatched, with the suggestion that the judges stick to their own knitting. The permanent administration of the country – the one branch of the government that is never out of session and never out of town – would deal with this matter. And the courts, no doubt, would be informed if anything touching the business of courts should arise. In due course, the papers would be examined, and the owners and editors of the papers would be released. They would be returned, that is, to civilian life, made all the more secure for them by their own government, bearing its responsibilities for preserving a framework of lawfulness.[14]

Now if that seems a bit jolting as a prospect, it is worth pondering the question of why it should not have been far more jolting to have settled in with this state of affairs: that powerful corporations may decide on their own to flaunt the laws of the United States on a matter of national security, and reckon themselves just how much it may be worth it to them to endanger American servicemen abroad. According to the Declaration of Independence the existence of the government is justified in the first place by the mission of protecting the lives and liberties of the people. The government bears a direct responsibility to those people, and a direct responsibility to protect ordinary people from unjustified assaults on their lives. A private corporation, even a public-spirited corporation, has no such rationale and no such direct responsibility. If the papers contained nothing damaging, or if the damaging portions were excised, the owners and editors could be returned happily to their offices, without disturbing their lives with a prosecution. But if the papers already published violated the laws on classified materials and compromised the safety of American forces, then these worthy men and women of the press might be charged with violations of the Espionage Act. That may seem, on its face, an astounding sanction, and yet it marked precisely the course that Justice White would later suggest as the most apt response for the government.[15]

But in these pusillanimous times, or in the legal climate that had been shaped for years by *Near v. Minnesota*, it seemed virtually inconceivable that any administration would conceive the problem in this way. And so, it was the government, not the *New York Times* or the *Washington Post*, that went to court. When the problem was framed in that way, the outcome was tilted to

---

[14] This bit of imagining, this license of supposing, may find a confirmation in its main lines in Lincoln's famous Letter to Erastus Corning and the Democrats in Albany [June 12, 1863] in *The Collected Works of Abraham Lincoln*, ed. Roy P. Basler (Brunswick, N.J.: Rutgers University Press, 1953), Vol. 6, pp. 260–69, and in particular the passage dealing with Andrew Jackson during the Battle of New Orleans (p. 268). Still, there was the sense that Lincoln held out Jackson's conduct as an example just a bit too far. Lincoln, with a firmer sense of the moral restraint of the law, would very likely have shown a more demanding level of self-restraint.

[15] Gabriel Schoenfeld has recently shown just how hard it would be to use the Espionage Act even in cases of this kind, where newspeople act with a heedless disregard of the public safety, but with no intention of engaging in actual espionage. See Schoenfeld, "Has the *New York Times* Violated the Espionage Act?" *Commentary* (March 2006).

the side of the newspapers. Judge Gurfein in New York seemed a fair-minded man, and he was willing to put the question earnestly to the government: Could the government point to anything in these papers that could pose a danger to American forces, or to the national security of the country? The government, under the circumstances, had to reply in the most general terms, for there had been no comprehensive review yet of just what the *Times* had selected from the forty-seven volumes of the Pentagon Papers. Still, Judge Gurfein thought he had given the government the chance to offer one or two telling examples, and he probably responded in the style of a streetwise New Yorker when he concluded that there was not much there. The judge held sessions *in camera*, and in that setting the representatives from the Departments of State and Defense and the Joint Chiefs of Staff were invited to register their concerns and point to precise dangers. Apparently, the pointing was not precise enough, for they "did not convince this Court that the publication of these historical documents would seriously breach the national security." And more than that, the judge noted that there would have to be a plausible case of an "irreparable injury" before the equity powers of the government could be engaged and a court could issue a restraining injunction.[16]

Of course, the commonsense question was, Why would such a burden of argument have to be borne by the public interest, or the interest in avoiding harm to American soldiers and agents? Judge Gurfein had cast the problem in the way he had only because the problem had been framed as a case for a court, under the "equity" powers and the requirements that attend the plea for an injunction. This was not at all the way in which the case would have appeared if the Executive, in the style of Lincoln, had simply taken command of the situation himself, seized hold of the papers, and perhaps closed the offending journals. For then the *newspapers* would have been saddled with the burden of seeking a remedy in the courts. The assignment of the burdens of justification was entirely an artifact of the framing of the problem as a case in equity for the courts. And beyond that matter of assigning the burdens of arguments, the deeper problem was that the decision was now so conspicuously – and so decisively – in the hands of judges. Judge Gurfein might have been the most worldly of men, but why should the judgment have turned on *his* reading, or his second-guessing, of the judgments made by people in the departments of State or Defense, or the CIA? He bore no particular expertise in extracting the meaning in these papers. Justice Harlan would later complain, quite aptly, that the judges coming down against the government in these cases did not

[16] *United States v. New York Times*, 328 F. Supp 324, at 330 (1971).

give the Executive "even the deference owing to an administrative agency, much less that owing to a co-equal branch of the Government operating within the field of its constitutional prerogative."[17] In that vein, the problem was only deepened by the recognition that the judges, at all levels, in the district or appellate courts, had never seen any of the documents themselves. This is a matter that would eventually bear with a resounding significance – a significance still not appreciated – when the case would come before the Supreme Court. What propelled the case forward was the sense that there was something portentous in putting newspapers under a prior restraint on publication. Still, Judge Gurfein sensed that he might not have a wisdom coextensive with the problem. He was willing then to continue the injunction, bearing on the *Times*, until the government could go to the Court of Appeals and gain a fuller review.

In the meantime, Judge Gerhard Gesell in the district court in Washington reached substantially the same conclusion as Judge Gurfein, in dealing with the move to restrain the *Washington Post*. But Judge Gesell refused to pre-serve the stay while the case was appealed to a higher court. Gesell remarked that the government had offered "no precise information" to show just where the security of the United States, or American forces, might be imperiled by the publication of the papers. His assumption, again, was that the burden of proof was on the side of the government and the claims of national security (known, in other settings, as "the public interest"). But so tilted were the burdens of proof, in Gesell's understanding, that he ventured the judgment that the government could not plausibly prevail in the case, quite apart from any evidence it could bring forth. In his later study of this litigation, David Rudinstine evidently came to the problem with a distinct leaning toward the freedom of publication; but Rudinstine candidly regarded Gesell's judgment as rather over the top. As Rudinstine wrote, "Judges are always making judg-ments on a less-than-perfect empirical basis, and they routinely make them by assessing factors or variables that are not quantifiable or comparable."[18] But even under the holding of *Near v. Minnesota*, the Supreme Court allowed that some restraints in advance of publication might indeed be justified, especially in time of war. Of course, Rudinstine's criticism still worked in the cast of assuming that this was a matter properly before the court; that the separation of powers raised no serious question about transferring, to the hands of judges, the power to override the President in the management of

---

[17] *New York Times v. United States, supra*, note 13, at 758.
[18] David Rudenstine, *The Day the Presses Stopped: A History of the Pentagon Papers Case* (Berkeley: University of California Press, 1996), p. 189.

diplomacy and the military. And in that same vein, he was willing to glide serenely with the assumption that the judges were competent to the ends of reading, and judging, the papers put before them. In any event, a panel of three judges in the Court of Appeals was content to work for a moment within that same cast – and bounce the case right back to Judge Gesell: The evidence did indeed matter, and two of the three judges thought that Judge Gesell should go on at least to do the work of a judge in weighing the evidence and permitting the government to make its case.

When the parties appeared again in the courtroom of Judge Gesell, the most forceful testimony on the side of the government was offered by Lieutenant General Marvin Zais, who was, at the time, the director of the Operations Directorate of the Joint Chiefs of Staff. Whether Zais was finally warranted or not in his reading of the evidence, there could be no gainsaying that the points he put before the court were as precise in their focus – and as precisely tied to the text – as anything Gesell could have demanded. Zais marked off several documents that exposed, as he said, "two major military operational plans which had been used in 1964 and in 1965" for deploying troops in Southeast Asia. The plans had been measured against the prospect of dealing with a Chinese intervention. But they retained their relevance for the Chinese and others, even now, while the war was still on. As a second point, Zais thought that the publication of these papers could seriously undermine the project of "Vietnamization" in shifting more of the effort in the war to the South Vietnamese and other countries. The revelation of military plans in the public prints could indeed induce a certain skittishness in the governments of Japan, Thailand, and the Philippines, as they were pondering in different ways their contributions to this project. The United States was using airbases in Thailand for American B-52s, planes that were necessary to the "cover" or protection of American troops in Vietnam. But the government of Thailand was not exactly exuberant in advertising, to its potential enemies in the region, its support for the American forces.

The case for the government was rounded out by William Macomber, designated by Robert Mardian in the Department of Justice, to testify in the hearings in New York and Washington. Mardian was, at the time, the Assistant Attorney General heading the Internal Security Division at the Department of Justice. He would become a key figure in the administration, firmly pushing the action in the courts. Macomber sought to bring home to the court that there was no trifling concern in sustaining the promises of the government to protect the confidentiality of its dealings with regimes abroad. He then listed twelve distinct, diplomatic missions, marked off with their code names, all involving other countries, all sheltered from publicity, and running between

May 1964 and February 1968. All of these projects, he averred, were directed to the end of reducing or ending the fighting in Vietnam, gaining the release of American prisoners, or "getting food and medicine and other relief packages to our prisoners of war."[19] In his own estimate, these kinds of initiatives required the cover of confidentiality. To remove, from the Executive, the capacity any longer to protect these operations was to court a "mortal danger" to the "diplomatic process itself." With words of this kind, the witnesses for the government were still floating in a certain haze of abstraction, even as they tried to convey to the judge that this concern for the "diplomatic process" expressed an interest measured in lives and the spilling of blood.[20]

Instructed anew, instructed in some instances for the first time, Judge Gesell managed to surprise no one by serving up essentially the same judgment he had rendered in the first hearing. But his tenacity must be marked, for he held to his position even while he conceded the most critical claim made by the government. Gesell conceded that the publication of the papers could indeed "interfere" with diplomatic negotiations, and with maneuvers growing out of the war. But the interference, he thought, did not spring from anything that emerged clearly from the papers themselves. The live danger arose, rather, from the display, quite evident to all, "that this Government is unable to prevent publication of actual Government communications."[21] One would think that, to grasp that elementary point was to grasp the point that settled the case – and delivered the matter from the hands of judges. For it was a matter that reflected the brute state of affairs in a world of different states, where the problem of foreign policy would always remain, and remain more acute in a world that would ever contain the wicked as well as the saintly. But in a remarkable turn, Gesell was adamantly unwilling to make any concession to those brute facts. For the rights of the press could be subordinated then to an interest in protecting governments abroad from "embarrassing disclosures." Apparently, for Gesell, the aversion to "prior restraints" did in fact ascend to the level of a principle, which could brook exceptions only in the most compelling cases.

And yet, in the sweep of his conviction, he glided past evidence that should have given him pause. Gesell remarked in his opinion that the record brought no reason to think that the papers implicated "contemporary" movements of troops, or that their publication would compromise ongoing projects in "intelligence." But as David Rudinstine noted, General Zais had offered

[19] Quoted in *ibid.*, p. 200.
[20] See *ibid.*, pp. 197–201.
[21] Quoted in *ibid.*, 213.

precise testimony to the contrary on both of these points. Whether Zais was right or wrong, his testimony went unchallenged by the lawyers for the *Post*, and Gesell himself offered no offsetting reasons to rebut those claims. Once again, it deserves to be noted, the authority to decide was confidently exercised by a judge, even in the absence of any claim to offer a reasoned ground for the judgment.

When the case made its way again to the court of appeals, it would encounter a different panel of judges, and the jurists in this second phase proved quite as skittish as Gesell in accepting a restraint on publication in advance. Even the dissenting judges rather suspected that most of the material contained in the Pentagon Papers would pose no serious danger to the national security. But Judges MacKinnon and Wilkey were not prepared to sign on to such a blanket license to publish. Judge Wilkey, for one, thought he found, in the documents, material that, "if published, could clearly result in great harm to the nation":

> When I say "harm," [he continued] I mean the death of soldiers, the destruction of alliances, the greatly increased difficulty of negotiating with our enemies, the inability of our diplomats to negotiate as honest brokers between would-be belligerents.[22]

These reservations, offered in prudence, would be confirmed by the Court nine years later in the *Snepp* case. But right now, they were not enough to break the momentum toward a decision against the government, and in favor of publication. Still, there was a slight difference in the holdings of the two federal courts. In New York, Judge Gurfein's order kept the *Times* under a stay, to prevent publication. In Washington, the *Post* had been delivered from any such encumbrances. This divergence created an awkward legal situation for the two newspapers, and so there would be a need to resolve the conflict. The matter would have to be brought to the Supreme Court, and there was a sense of urgency on either side that the issue be settled at once. The *Times* would not have sprung the publication had the editors not thought that they were launching a major scoop. The government feared that it would be damaging to see this series of articles unfolded in the papers, and so it could not stand back with indifference as the papers dribbled out, day by day.

But there was also a conflict of interest among the allies in publishing, which revealed a separate lesson of its own. While the *Times* was being restrained by Judge Gurfein's order, the *Washington Post* was presumably free to continue

---

[22] *United States v. The Washington Post*, 446 F.2d 1327, at 1330.

publishing the installments of the Pentagon Papers. During the oral argument later before the Supreme Court, the question was posed to Professor Alexander Bickel, arguing on behalf of the *Times*: What if the government had won on appeal in Washington, or the injunction was upheld now by the Supreme Court, and another newspaper picked up the baton and continued with the publishing of the Pentagon Papers? In fact, Judge Wilkey had noted, in the Court of Appeals in Washington, that while the *Times* and *Post* were being restrained, an installment from the papers had appeared in the *Los Angeles Times*. Other installments had already appeared in eight papers in the Knight chain, including the *Philadelphia Inquirer*, the *Detroit Free Press*, and the *Miami Herald*.[23] Still more installments could make it into print, while the government went around the landscape trying to secure injunctions. Faced with this question, Professor Bickel intimated that the *Times* would seek to protect its copyright:[24] That is to say, this august corporation would be audacious enough to *seek an injunction*; it would seek to prevent other journals from publishing, without authorization, these articles in the possession of the *Times*.

The *Times*, in other words, would have sought to do precisely what it denied the right of the government to do. It would have sought the same remedy sought by the government, even when this move would have meant installing a "prior restraint" on publication. Whether the injunction restraining the press is issued in the name of a district attorney or on behalf of a private litigant, the coercive power of the law would be invoked nevertheless to restrain a private newspaper from publishing. Justice White would later make an effort to justify the distinction: White would suggest that it was far more legitimate for a private corporation to protect its interest in copyright, even with a prior restraint, than for the government to seek a prior restraint, with interests that might not be as concrete. That was, as I say, an effort, but it would seem a rather lame one. The two sets of interests were not exactly on the same plane. The interests of the government may seem less concrete but they might plausibly be interests of national security, involving the protection of real lives. If the government could examine the papers, it might also provide a more informed conjecture about the identity of the agents whose lives could be imperiled by the disclosure of the papers. And as an "interest," that must be about as "concrete" as they come. But without venturing into those speculations, the contrast, or the distinction, was remarkable: The interests of a private corporation were presumptively legitimate, even when it came to ordering up prior restraints, while the interests of the national

---

[23] *Ibid.*, at 1332.
[24] See *supra*, note 13, at 749, note 1.

government, encompassing the safety of the nation and its military forces, were presumptively illegitimate. A person more innocent of the law might have been forgiven for wondering just why the lives of American soldiers or citizens did not claim the same weight and seriousness in our law as the property of a corporation in its copyright.

But this was hardly the only time, in the rocky story of this case, that a moral obtuseness became manifest on the part of the newspapers and their lawyers. And by that I mean an unfeigned inability to see, with detachment, their own claims, or to notice that the principles they were advancing so earnestly were engaged even more powerfully on the side of the government. There was probably no better example in that vein than the objections cast up by the *Post* when the government simply sought to examine the papers. The manifest interest of the government was simply to gauge the seriousness of the problem posed by the publication of those papers. The lawyers for the *Post* raised an alarm: Such a disclosure to the government could reveal the identity of the *Post's* sources! But if we were to credit the same lawyers, it was apparently inconceivable to them – or beneath their notice – that the concern of the government was precisely the same: that the publication of the papers would reveal sources or agents for American intelligence within Vietnam, or within other governments. And the dangers, in that case, ran well beyond the loss of a job.

The same obtuseness, whether willful or innocent, showed itself rather sharply on the question of why the case required this rush to judgment. On that point, Chief Justice Burger and Justice Harlan were quite vexed. They seemed to wonder just why the pressing interests of a corporation should force the Supreme Court out of the procedures that were more fitly measured to the dignity of the Court and the importance of its cases. Those were procedures geared to a more sedate reflection, more likely to produce cases adequately prepared and more thoroughly argued. Burger could point out then that the *Times* had held these papers for about four months, as the editors and writers worked over them. The *Times* had been free, that is, to ponder at relative leisure the best way of presenting the papers, and the most strategic time to spring them on the public. But the interests of the *Times* in seeking its advantage here did not encompass a comparable willingness to let the government gauge the interests it had at stake in these papers – or the interest of the country in having the judges deal with this matter in the most careful and judicious way.

Justice Blackmun was still fairly new to the Court, appointed just a year earlier by President Nixon, following upon the appointment of Warren Burger as Chief Justice. Both men were from Minnesota, and they seemed close enough, personally and politically, that they had been dubbed at the time "the Minnesota Twins." This was all before *Roe v. Wade*, and the turn, taken by Blackmun, that would move him ever more firmly to the liberal side and find him celebrated for his "growth." This was all long before Blackmun recast himself, and so his reactions to this case seemed strikingly similar to those of Burger. In the conference held by the justices, as they were discussing the case and taking a vote, Blackmun ventured to say that the action of the *Times*, in publishing the Papers, was "reprehensible." He thought the Papers were likely to contain "dangerous material that will harm the nation," and he went on to say that he had "nothing but contempt for the *Times*."[25] In the opinion he would finally publish, he would be far more modulated, but his arguments would follow along the path marked out by Harlan and Burger.

That sardonic edge to the commentaries of Harlan and Burger reflected the temper of the conservative judges in these cases, but that archness, that slant on the problem, conveyed a sense of the substance of the matter as well: The conservative judges objected to all of the hurry and manipulation, to the manufacture of a "crisis," because they were willing at least to consider that there might be serious national interests endangered in this case; interests that could even justify some restraints on the press. As Justice Harlan observed, even an aversion to prior restraints should not prevent the courts from "maintaining the status quo" long enough to allow the government to examine the papers.[26] Alone among the judges, Harlan had the wit to see that the very need of the government to go into court was itself already a telling, and possibly damaging, sign to governments abroad that the American Executive was not in control of its official papers.

Of course, it seemed indecorous at the time to note the obvious: Just three years into the Nixon administration, it was to be expected that the newly appointed justices, Burger and Blackmun, would be willing at least to credit the Nixon administration with decent motives. With that stance, the conservative judges could express more readily the moral outrage that would spring from a commonsense reading of the case: As the Chief Justice noted, these papers were, after all, "stolen property," and documents held, by law, in a condition of secrecy, barred from public broadcast. In that case, said Burger,

> it is hardly believable that a newspaper long regarded as a great institution in American life would fail to perform some of the most basic and simple

---

[25] Cited in Rudinstine, *supra*, note 18, at 299.
[26] *New York Times v. United States*, *supra*, note 13, at 759.

duties of every citizen with respect to the discovery or possession of stolen property or secret government documents. That duty, I had thought – perhaps naively – was to report forthwith, to responsible public officers. That duty rests on taxi drivers, Justices, and the *New York Times.*[27]

In discussing these cases put before the courts for judgment, I rarely find myself dwelling on the box score, by focusing on the vote rather than the reasons. But here, as Leo Strauss used to say, it may be useful to begin on the surface of things, because the surface may lead us back to the heart of things. We would be pointed, I think, to some critical defects in the reasoning of the judges if we worked our way back from the box score, by mapping out the votes, and noticed what that vote on the Court revealed about *the structure of the argument* in this case. It matters profoundly that three of the Republican judges were in firm dissent in this case. They recognized an abiding concern with "prior restraints," but they were not prepared to rule out a restraint in advance of publication in all cases, especially in cases that involved the endangering of lives. Even in *Near v. Minnesota*, when Chief Justice Hughes had penned his argument against prior restraints, Hughes had marked off a notable exception for times of war: It could be quite reasonable, he thought, to bar newspapers from printing the names of ships, or the schedules for their comings and goings.[28] In the case of the Pentagon Papers, the conservative judges were not prepared yet to say that a restraint of that kind would be justified. But they thought it reasonable at least to restrain the publication long enough to give the government a chance to estimate the imminence of any dangers.

To come down then so decisively against the government required the six remaining votes, and among those six the rationale for the decision would have to be found. And yet, it could not be found. The six remaining judges could not settle on a set of reasons that could command a majority of five votes. And therein lies the deeper story here. It is no accident that two of the justices – Harlan and Blackmun – cited Justice Holmes's famous dictum, "Great cases like hard cases make bad law." Those cases make bad law because they induce divisions or splits, and make it harder for the judges to come to an agreement on the reasons that finally govern their judgment in the case at hand. The result in this particular case was that the Court in fact *created no law*: All it could do was announce a result – that the injunction, sought by the government, would not be granted; that the stays, granted so far, would

---

[27] *Ibid.*, at 751.
[28] See *Near v. Minnesota*, 283 U.S. 697, at 716.

be dissolved. That was all. And that judgment, expressed in one paragraph, was put forth as an opinion per curiam. It was the proclaimed decision of the Court, with no justice speaking for the Court or a majority.

What followed then was something closer to the presentation that took place in the days before John Marshall persuaded his colleagues to produce a unified judgment of the Court: The opinion of each judge was printed separately, seriatim, in order of the seniority of the judge, except of course for the dissenting side, where the Chief Justice would be given precedence. The lead opinion on the side of the majority would come from the most senior member of the Court, Justice Hugo Black, and that lead, followed by Justice Douglas, would instantly reveal the problem afflicting the judges. Black had become famous over the years for his supposedly "absolutist" position on the First Amendment. In this construction, virtually peculiar to Justice Black – and even to him, not all of the time – the First Amendment would brook no restraints on speech or publication, not even the restraints that were contained in the traditional laws of libel. At certain moments, Black's absolutism would suddenly show a remarkable flexibility – as when he upheld restraints on demonstrators outside the home of Mayor Daley in Chicago,[29] or when he thought that the First Amendment offered no protection to armbands worn by students in a public school.[30] Armbands, he could say, represented conduct and not speech, and as for the demonstrators in front of the Mayor's home, Black could still insist that people had an absolute right to engage in political speech – but only in those places where they had a right to be.[31] When it came, say, to pornography and obscenity, Black's colleagues busied themselves in work they professed to regard as uncongenial, in viewing pornographic movies, in order to judge each case on its merits. But Black would have neither the entertainment nor the strain of judgment: He did not think that the government should censor in any degree. And he certainly did not think that the censorship should be transferred from the local authorities to federal judges – or even worse, shifted to the highest court in the land.

For Black, the words "Congress shall make no law" abridging freedom of speech and of the press meant precisely "no law." But with the intervention of the Fourteenth Amendment, Black was wholly convinced that the plain words of the First Amendment now applied, with the same stringency, to the

---

[29] *Gregory v. Chicago*, 394 U.S. 111, 113 (1969).

[30] See Black's dissent in *Tinker v. Des Moines*, 393 U.S. 503, 515–25.

[31] Cf. Black's remark in *Cox v. Louisiana*: "The First and Fourteenth Amendments take away from government, state and federal, all power to restriction freedom of speech, press, and assembly *where people have a right to be for such purposes.*" 379 U.S. 536, at 578 (1965); italics added.

states as well. In his construal, then, governments at all levels in the United States were barred from making laws that abridged the freedom of the press. Quoting James Madison, Black simply insisted that the freedom of the press was "inviolable." In other words, we could put aside entirely the question of restraining publications in advance: For Black, Congress could literally make no law restricting the freedom of the press, even if that law sought to punish people *after the fact* for the injuries they had inflicted through publication. In that case, it was even more unthinkable, for Black, that "the courts should take it upon themselves to 'make' a law abridging freedom of the press in the name of equity"[32] – that is, that the courts would now use their equity powers to fashion, through injunctions, a power to restrain publication, a power that even the Congress could not rightly exercise.

The Solicitor General, Edwin Griswold of Harvard, handled the oral argument for the government, and in an exchange with Justice Black he remarked that the views of the Justice were by now "well known":

> You say that no law means no law, and that should be obvious. I can only say, Mr. Justice, that to me it is equally obvious that "no law" does not mean "no law," and I would seek to persuade the Court that that is true. . . . There are other parts of the Constitution that grant powers and responsibilities to the Executive, and . . . the First Amendment was not intended to make it impossible for the Executive to function or to protect the security of the United States.[33]

Black himself quoted this line for the sake of drawing the contrast ever more sharply between his own, advanced views and the diminished understanding that he persistently encountered among his colleagues and other lawyers. For Black, his absolutism would always be attended by expressions of deep disbelief, bordering on revulsion, that his views, so eminently clear, were not shared by his other colleagues. In the case of the Pentagon Papers, his disappointment with his colleagues was quite severe, and that deploring of his colleagues became a key to the case. For among his colleagues, there was only one who seemed close to his position: Justice Douglas, ever given to sweeping gestures, proclaimed now that the First Amendment "leaves, in my view, no room for governmental restraint on the press."

Douglas was willing, however, to venture further into the recesses of the problem, and in that way separate himself a bit from Black. The remaining colleagues on their side expressed a willingness to punish the publishers *after the fact* if the publication resulted in any demonstrable harms. What they were

---

[32] *New York Times v. United States, supra*, note 13, at 718.
[33] Quoted in *ibid.*, at 717–18.

not willing to do was restrain a newspaper in advance of publication. Justice White, in particular, put a heavy accent on the Espionage Act. In a move rather rare among the judges, White virtually announced his willingness to uphold prosecutions under that Act after the Pentagon Papers were published, and the results could be assessed. But Douglas argued now that the Espionage Act could not be applied rightly to the press. In his reading, the Espionage Act involved the delivery, or communication, to an enemy of vital information with a military significance. He thought it would be a stretch to apply this statute, carried over from World War I, to sustain prosecutions against the press. And yet, Douglas's opinion entailed no conclusion as to what he would do if Congress had amended the Espionage Act to clear up any doubts and apply the law to the press. In that event, the case could have been, for Douglas, quite a different matter. This seasoned judge, who had been willing to hold back his hand when the Executive rounded up the Japanese in California in the aftermath of Pearl Harbor, might well have deferred again to the political branches on matters of national security.[34] But for Justice Black, even a change in the Espionage Act by Congress would not have made the slightest difference.

Again, let me recall the box score as it stood so far: Three judges were willing to sustain the injunction and restrain the publication of the papers, at least for a short while. Of the remaining six, two were willing to regard the First Amendment as containing an absolute, or nearly absolute, bar on any move of that kind to impose a restraint in advance of publication. Black's disappointment with his colleagues offered a clear reflection of the differences: The four judges in the middle, the judges who would be pivotal to the case, were emphatically not willing to join Black in any *categorical* rejection of "prior restraints." They were willing to quash the move for an injunction in this case, but they all admitted the possibility that, under certain circumstances, a

---

[34] In the famous *Korematsu* case, on the sequestering of Japanese-Americans during the Second World War, the decision of the Court, sustaining the removal of the Japanese from their homes in California, elicited three precise and even stirring dissents from Justices Roberts, Murphy, and Jackson. But Justice Douglas joined Justice Black in supporting the Commander-in-Chief who appointed him. Neither of them was as close to FDR as Robert Jackson. Yet it must be said that while Jackson dissented, he wished mainly for the Court to avert its eyes from these decisions taken under the heading of military necessity. That is to say, he would not have had the courts interfere with the removal of the Japanese by the military. He would have sought simply to avoid any arrangement in which the Court would be asked to put an imprimatur of constitutional "rightness" on the decisions taken by the Executive under "military necessity." See *Korematsu v. U.S.*, 323 U.S. 214 (1944), especially 242–48 (Jackson).

restraint in advance of publication could indeed be justified. In the differences among these judges, we find the shades of reason that were finally decisive in the case. The clearest lessons emanated from three of the judges: Brennan, Stewart, and White.

Justice Brennan conceded that, in the case law created by the Court, there was "a single, extremely narrow class of cases in which the First Amendment's ban on prior judicial restraint may be overridden." That class would be defined by Chief Justice Hughes's line in *Near v. Minnesota*: "no one would question but that a government might prevent actual obstruction to its recruiting service or the publication of the sailing dates of transports or the number and location of troops."[35] But that was in fact rather close to the claim made by the government. Brennan remarked, in a curious passage, that "even if the present world situation were assumed to be tantamount to a time of war," the government had not presented or alleged that the publication of these items would have that kind of effect. "Tantamount to a time of war"? Had it somehow escaped Brennan's notice that there was an actual, shooting war going on in Vietnam? It was not a condition *tantamount* to a war, but a *war*, with real shells and bombs, real deaths and casualties. Nothing in Hughes's opinion suggested that it was legitimate to protect American troops only when they were fighting in a *declared* war, as opposed to one of those interventions, numbering nearly two hundred, where American troops had been ordered into action by the Executive. But from a murky discussion, Brennan extracted the most extravagant conclusion: "Thus," he said (while his readers might wonder just what reasons had furnished the grounds for the "thus"),

> only governmental allegation and proof that publication must inevitably, directly, and immediately cause the occurrence of an event kindred to imperiling the safety of a transport already at sea can support even the issuance of an interim restraining order.[36]

The government may protect soldiers and sailors boarding a ship – but only if the ship is "already at sea"? Not while the sailors are boarding the ship, or being scheduled for their boarding and sailing? Beyond that, the evidence linking the disclosure to the bombing must show a connection that is "inevitable . . . direct . . . immediate"? Those are severe tests – but from what do they emanate? None of these things was mentioned in the text of the Constitution, or in the Espionage Act. If they were words pronounced by

---

[35] 283 U.S. 697, at 716 (1931), cited in *New York Times v. United States, supra*, note 13, at 726.
[36] *Ibid.*, at 726–27.

the judges in earlier cases, we might ask, By what authority did the judges pronounce those tests or criteria as though they stemmed from the Constitution itself? Were they logical implications contained in the text? If so, that required some explanation, to see how these implications were derived. Brennan did seem to be propounding his criteria of judgment as though they were necessary implications, embedded in the logic of the First Amendment. And yet, there are ample grounds to contest them all. Publishing the names of transports and their time of departure may be freighted with danger. If there is an explosion on the ship, it may be impossible to chart a clear connection between the planting of the bomb and the disclosure of its location and schedule. But that is precisely why prudent people simply use a broader rule, advising servicemen not to speak of these things, and imploring journalists not to publish them. It is hard, though, to see what moral principle would put the burden of justification on the side of people who would act to protect the lives of American servicemen. Why would the government be obliged to carry such a heavy burden of proof, in showing an *immediate* and *necessary* connection between the publication and the harm before it could act to protect American servicemen and agents?

By any strict measure, nothing in the principles of moral judgment, the provisions of the Constitution, or the character of the First Amendment entails the kind of conclusion that Brennan announced with such unequivocal surety. And yet, this was almost exactly the line taken by Justice Stewart, even though Stewart questioned the propriety of the judges standing in the place of the Executive in this kind of case. More than that, Stewart treated as eminently plausible, or even likely, the dangers that Brennan regarded as mere speculations. Stewart found a persisting reason in the traditional understanding: The Executive was constituted to deal with these problems in the national security in a way that the courts were not. The Executive was deeply enmeshed in the operations that formed the stuff of intelligence and military operations. For that reason, the Executive had access to sources of information that had to be inaccessible to officers outside the Executive. That was not because people under the President were smarter in any way, but because certain things were simply known distinctly to those who were involved in the chain of operations, in the relations of command and control. In this case, it was the tentative judgment of the Executive that the national interest could be injured by the publication of some of these papers, and Stewart was frank to say, "I am convinced that the Executive is correct with respect to some of the documents involved."

Why then was he voting with Black and Douglas, rather than with Burger, Blackmun, and Harlan? He held back, as he put it, because "I cannot say that disclosure of any of [the papers] will surely result in direct, immediate, and irreparable damage to our Nation or its people."[37] That is to say, to Brennan's solecism he was willing to add a howler of his own. He had still not established just what logic of a moral principle saddled the government with the need to carry such a burden of justification. But putting that aside, he had just expended his efforts in pointing out anew why the Executive had a competence in this realm that exceeded the competence of judges. He had also been unaffected by any doubt that the Executive had a preeminent claim, under the Constitution, to deal with cases involving diplomacy and foreign affairs. And yet, he would end by transferring *that power* to himself and his colleagues: "I cannot say" that the disclosure of the paper would result in "direct, immediate, and irreparable damage." He had confessed his want of competence in making a judgment, and yet the matter would turn now on *his* own – and by his own admission – uninformed intuitions. He had conceded that the Executive had the preeminent standing as a constitutional officer in making these kinds of judgments, but did the Executive have that standing only after he had been cleared by the judges to exercise that authority? Or did he have that authority under the Constitution itself, unmediated by any permissions granted by the judges? In any case, as Stewart seemed readily to assume now, the judges would exercise that control over the President even while his staff bore a competence in this field that the judges and their clerks did not.

Compared with Stewart, Justice White offered a truer portrait of a judge strained by the puzzles of rendering justice. During the oral argument, White put the question earnestly to Professor Alexander Bickel, arguing for the *New York Times*:

> THE COURT: [L]et me give you a hypothetical case. Let us assume that when the members of the Court go back and open up this sealed record, we find something there that absolutely convinces us that its disclosure would result in the sentencing to death of 100 young men whose only offense had been that they were 19 years old, and had low draft numbers. What should we do?

White's question evidently took hold of Bickel, for he revealed, in his response, that he grasped the moral core of the question, even as he sought to dodge its import and preserve his argument for the *Times*:

> MR. BICKEL: Mr. Justice, I wish there were a statute that covered it.
> THE COURT: Well there isn't, we agree – or you submit – so I'm asking in this case, what should we do?
> . . . .

---

[37] *Ibid.*, at 730.

> MR. BICKEL: ... [I]t's a case in which the chain of causation between the act
> of publication and the feared event – the death of these 100 young men – is
> obvious, direct, immediate –
> THE COURT: That's what I'm assuming in my hypothetical.
> MR. BICKEL: I would only say, as to that, that it is a case in which, in the absence
> of the statute, I suppose most of us would say –
> THE COURT: You would say the Constitution requires that it be published, and
> that these men die? Is that it?[38]

The moral core of the argument was that innocent lives could be at stake –
lives that were put in danger precisely by the acts of the government. And
when weighed in the scales of judgment, would that interest not be grave
enough to justify that same government in restraining publication? In contrast, there was nothing *intrinsically* right or wrong about the restraint on
publication. The rightness or wrongness of that restraint would always have
to depend on whether it might be justified under the circumstances. White
was raising the most plausible question, then, of why in fact the government
that put its servicemen in danger would not be justified in protecting them.
In the presence of doubt, there would seem to be a prima facie case for
presuming in favor of protecting the men until the dangers had diminished.
We cannot suppose, of course, that White was willing to offer a license to
any government to put soldiers in harm's way and then use that action as a
predicate for silencing the press. The problem had to assume persons acting
with reason and restraint. But when the question was posed with a certain
moral rigor, or a measure of common sense, it required the most strained
efforts at constitutional theory in order to explain why it was more important
to keep the *Times* unconstrained than to protect Americans in the service.
Bickel implicitly recognized the force of that argument, and pleaded his case
mainly at the margins. When White asked if the Constitution required the
Court to leave the men unprotected, to let them die, Bickel responded:

> MR. BICKEL: No, I'm afraid I'd have – I'm afraid my inclinations of humanity
> overcome the somewhat more abstract devotion to the First Amendment, in a
> case of that sort. I would wish that Congress took a look to the seldom-used,
> and not-in-very-good-shape Espionage Acts and clean them up some, so that
> we could have statutes that are clearly applicable within the vagueness rules
> and whatnot, so that we don't have to rely on Presidential powers....

This accomplished man seemed not to have grasped the depth of what he
was conceding in his remarkably imprecise language – that the "inclinations

---

[38] Transcript of the oral argument, in Kurland and Caspar, eds., *supra*, note 11, pp. 239–40.

of humanity" overrode the "somewhat more abstract devotion to the First Amendment." The First Amendment appeared more "abstract" here because it contained no substantive principle that could bar, categorically, all restraints on speech and publication, as members of the Founding generation amply understood.[39] What Bickel conceded on the face of things was that there could well be, under certain circumstances, a compelling moral case for restricting the press – most notably, for the sake of saving lives. Against that moral core of the problem, all of his concerns about the presence of statutes, or the separation of powers, reduced to a kind of dancing around the moral question. It was stylish dancing, or talk informed by serious questions of constitutional theory, but the exposition, built on that earnest talk, was morally out of scale: That talk, with intimations of depth about the law, could not finally explain why it was justified to put servicemen in danger rather than impose a temporary restraint on the *New York Times*.

When White offered the hypothetical case of saving one hundred men, he called to mind at once Abraham negotiating with God over Sodom and Gomorrah: "Shall not the Judge of all the earth do right?" Would He destroy the righteous with the wicked? "Peradventure there be fifty righteous within the city: will thou also destroy and not spare the place for the fifty righteous that are therein?" God agrees to spare the city if there are as many as fifty righteous men within it. "Peradventure there shall lack five of the fifty righteous: will thou destroy all the city for lack of five?" Abraham continues in this way, in increments of five, driving God down to a test of ten decent or righteous men. When White posed the question of the one hundred men, he seemed to be preparing the ground for pressing Bickel, step by step, in increments of five. One hundred wanting five? Wanting ten? What if there were ninety men endangered? If Bickel could go for one hundred, would he not go for ninety? Or ten wanting one – nine? Without replicating that ancient exchange, Chief Justice Burger seemed to move along a comparable line by shifting slightly the magnitude of the danger:

> THE COURT: Professor Bickel, let me alter the illustration a little bit, the hypothetical. Suppose the information was sufficient that judges could be satisfied that the disclosure of a link – the identity of a person engaged in delicate negotiations having to do with the possible release of prisoners of war – that

---

[39] Hence John Marshall's observation, struck off with no particular sense of the remarkable, that anyone who publishes a libel in this country may be "sue or indicted." See Marshall's speech on the constitutionality of the Alien and Sedition Acts: "Report of the Minority on the Virginia Resolutions" (January 22, 1799), *J. House of Delegates (Va.)* 6:93–95 1798–99, reprinted in Philip B. Kurland and Ralph Lerner, eds., *The Founders' Constitution* (Chicago: University of Chicago Press, 1987), Vol. 5, no. 20.

the disclosure of this, would delay the release of those prisoners for a substantial period of time? Now this I am posing so that it is not "immediate." Is that, or is that not in your view, a matter that should stop the publication, and therefore avoid the delay in the release of the prisoners?

MR. BICKEL: Mr. Chief Justice, on that question . . . I can only say that unless, which I can't imagine can be possible, the link of causation is made "direct and immediate" – even though the event might be somewhat distant – but, unless it can be demonstrated that it is really true, that if you published this that would happen, or there is a "high probability," rather than "as is typical of those events" – there are 17 causes feeding into them, three of those, any one of those other than publications is entirely capable of being the single, effective cause – then the real argument is: "Well, you add publication to that, and it makes it a little more difficult." I think, Mr. Chief Justice, that that is a risk that the First Amendment signifies that this society is willing to take. That is part of the risk of freedom that I would certainly take.[40]

Of course, it stands to reason that, in the matter of gauging the effects of speech, there must be a minimal test of "directness": After all, it could always be argued that the presence of serious criticism, directed at the government, might suggest division and weakness, and embolden our enemies abroad to attack. But speculation of that kind, no matter how plausible, could not be acceptable as a ground for restricting the freedom to debate the policies of the government. Yet, Bickel's test of directness, applied in this setting, was no test at all. It merely offered a formula for fending off any attempt to impose even prudential restraints on publication. The concern for protecting the lives of American servicemen would labor under a burden of justification that would be virtually impossible to meet in most cases. It was curious, then, that White let himself be drawn along the path of that argument and away from his own, much firmer argument in weighing the interests at stake. In the aftermath of the case, there were rumors heard at the CIA that the agency had lost several agents as a result of the publication of the Pentagon Papers; a legend, or estimate, I have not been able to confirm.[41] But it was evident that White

---

[40] *Ibid.*, at p. 240.

[41] One of my favorite students, in the Class of 1970, entered the CIA, and he remarked to me, in a lunch at the agency, early in his training, that the word going about the CIA was that the United States had lost around eleven agents as a result of the Pentagon Papers. Thirty years later, as I went back to my notes, I sought the help of veterans, retired from the CIA. They had heard nothing to confirm that earlier estimate, and they put me in touch with a couple of other people who "should know," along with a newsletter for former members of the foreign and intelligence services. Those inquiries elicited no precise memories to confirm that old rumor. Finally, I was in touch with my former student, in the spring of 2003. He had trained in Arabic, he had gone on to become the CIA section chief in Beirut, in turbulent times, and he was now one of the chief

did not regard the papers, or their publication, as harmless. And that sense of the matter afflicted him as he settled his judgment in the case.

White joined his liberal colleagues in refusing to issue the injunction and restraining the press. But no one, in the majority or the minority, revealed a fuller acceptance of the government's case – or a fuller certitude that harms would indeed be done, that the lives of agents would be endangered by the publication of these papers. White would not say, with Justice Black, that the First Amendment would never permit an injunction against publishing the plans or operations of the government. Nor would he deny what his colleagues treated as implausible on the face of things – "that the revelation of these documents will do substantial damage to public interests." In fact, as he said, "I am confident that the disclosure will have that result."[42] It was, altogether, the most bizarre confession, and it revealed a judgment dramatically at odds with its reasoning: He agreed that publication might be restrained in advance with justification – which is to say, the restraint would be compatible with the First Amendment and the Constitution. The matter would hinge then on whether serious harms were in prospect. He was *virtually certain* that the publication would be productive of those serious harms. And yet he refused to issue the injunction.

What held him back, as he said, was the "concededly extraordinary protection against prior restraint," a protection that emanated from the Court rather than the Constitution. But this reluctance was deepened by an unwillingness to ascribe, either to the Executive or the courts, an inherent power to seek injunctions and restrain the freedom of persons, in the absence of a statute. As White pointed out, there were ample precedents for "prior restraints," established through legislation: Congress had authorized, in effect, a scheme of prior restraints when it authorized the National Labor Relations Board to issue cease-and-desist orders against employers who had threatened or coerced their employees in the exercise of their rights. The Federal Trade Commission was authorized to issue cease-and-desist orders in its own domain, and in

experts of the CIA, dealing with terrorism and negotiations in the Middle East. In an e-mail to me, he confessed that he no longer remembered that older conversation, and he had heard nothing, apparently, to confirm the estimate he had passed on to me years earlier. On the other side, my friend Angelo Codevilla, had spent years as a key staffer on the Senate Committee on Intelligence, and he had cultivated the deepest dubiety about most things served up, with conviction, from the CIA. The report on losing agents might indeed have been correct; but he was inclined himself to regard it as a typical bit of CIA story-telling – the kind of tall tale that heightens the drama, and deepens the legends of the CIA, but a tale, finally, that was empty of substance.

[42] *New York Times v. United States, supra*, note 13, at 731.

the field of copyrights it seemed to be accepted, without strain, that newspapers or printers could be enjoined from publishing when they were arguably violating a copyright.[43]

Even in 1971, then, Justice White had known enough to know that there were many defensible reasons for courts to issue injunctions that restrained publications. Under the conditions of a dramatic crisis, newly contrived, even the most seasoned judges might begin to fear that understandings long settled may suddenly be out the window, or strikingly inapt. Still, White had more than enough examples at hand to make him wise at least to this point: that there was no real principle engaged here on the matter of prior restraints. He knew that there were times when restraint could be imposed in advance with substantial justification, and by his own words, he seemed to recognize, also, that the ingredients that justified a restraint were present in this case. After all, the danger to the lives of American servicemen had to exceed the dangers of violating a copyright. Why would there not be sufficient, residual authority in the Executive or the courts to issue an injunction, then, to avert the injury? When broken down in this way, into its component parts, White's aversion to the use of the injunction became not only baffling but unaccountable.

And yet, if White had an aversion to restraining people in advance, out of a speculation as to what they might do, those hesitations dissolved as soon as the act was performed. In a passage freighted with meaning, White remarked that the

> failure by the Government to justify prior restraints does not measure its constitutional entitlement to a conviction for criminal publication. That the Government mistakenly chose to proceed by injunction does not mean that it could not successfully proceed in another way.[44]

White might have regarded the use of an injunction as portentous, but he was ready to see criminal prosecutions brought against people who were willing to publish recklessly, even when it meant endangering men in the armed forces. Perhaps picking up on the persistent suggestions of Professor Bickel, White thought that the preeminent vehicle for these prosecutions might be found in the Espionage Act. When that Act was drafted in 1917, the Congress had withheld from the President the broad powers to proscribe whole categories of publication that might bear on the national defense. The bill had been drafted rather narrowly, to focus on the disclosure of intelligence, or plans of operation in the military. But even so, White thought

---

[43] See *ibid.*, at 731, n. 1.
[44] *Ibid.*, at 733.

that the Espionage Act could still encompass the kinds of injuries that were potentially at stake in the Pentagon Papers. Publications that reveal the codes or intelligence of the government could run afoul of the Act. In one passage White regarded as relevant, the Act addressed anyone who

> knowingly and willfully communicates, furnishes, transmits, or otherwise makes available to an unauthorized person, or publishes, or uses in any manner prejudicial to the safety or interest of the United States or for the benefit of any foreign government to the detriment of the United States any classified information. . . . [45]

The Act carried penalties of $10,000 and a term of imprisonment up to ten years. That fine, for the *New York Times* and the *Washington Post,* could have been regarded as a mere trifle. But a criminal prosecution brought against the owners and editors of the newspapers would have been no trifling thing. In fact, its portentousness was an apt guide to the deep unlikelihood that this sanction would ever be used. If White had been more sensitive to that practical matter, or that gauge of prudence, he might have recognized just what was morally skewed in the position he was staking out with apparent anguish, as he strained to avoid a "prior restraint." Nine years later, in the *Snepp* case, the recognition would come crashing in on him, and he *silently recanted every argument he would make here.* That is to say, he would join a Court that would explicitly repudiate every argument that seemed decisive to him with the Pentagon Papers. With the advantage of time and detachment, it would become clearer that what he had been offering, in the case of the Pentagon Papers, was no remedy: Putting Katharine Graham or Arthur Hays Sulzberger into jail offered no apt response to the case. It would help to avert no injury to agents or servicemen in the field; and for those who were killed, the jailing of the publishers or editors offered no fit compensation for their loss. Nor would a cash award bear any resemblance to the wounds suffered by the government – and the community – as the courts demonstrated quite dramatically to the world that the American Executive's control over its own intelligence, or its own confidential papers, was quite compromised.

When these kinds of comparisons were made, the use of an injunction should not have appeared as a draconian device, but quite the contrary. It was the most measured and sensitive of tools: The government had no interest in putting the owners and editors of the newspapers in jail. Its dominant interest was in protecting the national interest as that was measured, concretely, in its own operations, directed to legitimate ends, and the safety of

---

[45] *Ibid.*, at 736, n. 6.

American servicemen and citizens. The government merely sought to restrain publication – not block it indefinitely, but halt it long enough to have some consultation and review of the papers, the kind of consultation and restraint that the *Times* and other papers had accepted in the past, without evident strain. In the scale of things, the move for an injunction was among the most moderate and measured things that a government, in these circumstances, might do. That path offered the prospect of safeguarding the interests of the country, while respecting the liberties of the press and the public.

Yet, that was not the way in which the matter was presented to the country at the time, or the way in which it has been presented to this day in academic commentaries and histories. The remarkable thing, in retrospect, was the way in which the judges contorted themselves for the sake of averting an injunction, an arrangement they seemed to regard as nearly shameful. To order restraints on the *New York Times* seemed to be regarded as a step so portentous that it would be understood by the public as a virtual abandonment of the Constitution. Some of these contortions might be attributed, no doubt, to the atmosphere of crisis, and the uncommon pressures placed on the Court to act in haste. But it would mark a distraction on our own part if we labored under the illusion that the mistakes that befell the judges were the result mainly of a political situation that deprived them of the "sedate reflection" that befitted judges. What was revealed, rather, in the fragmentation of opinions, was that the judges fell into confusion, not because of time, but because they were surprisingly at sea when it came to the axioms or the propositional logic that should have anchored their judgments.

For White, the warnings and bells should have sounded when he invested so much of his passion, and his jural skills, in justifying the distinction between imposing a prior restraint and using the criminal law to punish people, after the fact, for the harms they might inflict with publication. *Before the fact*, White would do anything to avoid a prior restraint. But *after* publication, White seemed willing to see prosecutions brought on the very next day. The reigning dictum here was drawn from Blackstone: the liberty of the press "consists in laying no previous restraints upon publications, and not in the freedom from censure for criminal matter when published." In this construal, every free man should be at liberty to lay his sentiments before the public, but as Blackstone remarked, in a phrase that would resound in the law books, "he must take the consequence of his own temerity."[46]

---

[46] See Blackstone's *Commentaries*, Vol. 4, at 151, 152; quoted in *Near v. Minnesota*, 283 U.S. 697, at 713–14.

With that sense of the matter, White seemed ready to sustain a prosecution directed at the *Times* and the *Post* on the day they finished publishing the Pentagon Papers. But how would the problem have been eased in any way as a result of handling the case in that manner? The concern that always attached to restraints in advance of publication is that the authorities might have to act on the strength of speculation or conjecture alone. By holding back and waiting for the publication, the authorities would not interfere with the content of what is published, and they would be in a better position to gauge the effects, or the injuries, that they anticipate. But let us say, for example, that the government feared the effects of publicizing, in advance, the name of a ship scheduled to depart the next day, carrying troops abroad. Let us suppose that the government knows that a newspaper is about to publish the name of the ship. And yet, the government decides instead, in the style of Justice White, to wait for the sailing of the ship and see if anything happens. Let us imagine that, a day or two later, a bomb goes off in that ship at sea. Would the government now be in a position to launch a prosecution against the editors and writers who had identified the ship and its mission? Or would the government not run again into the arguments posed by Justices Brennan and Stewart? The fact that a bomb was planted on the ship would not be enough in itself to establish that the bombing had been "caused" or facilitated by the newspaper in publishing the name of the ship. The court could not merely assume a causal connection. Justices Brennan and Stewart could insist on proving a *direct and immediate* connection between the publication and the harm. But the lines of causation may be quite hard to draw. Bombs, after all, are planted in stealth, and it may be hard to find the witnesses or collect the evidence to show the connection.

The difficulties that emerge here may only suggest why these matters have not been handled through the processes of the criminal law. They have had to be handled, rather, with prudence and measures preventive: All things being equal, it is better not to mention the names and schedules of ships carrying troops; for while the withholding of information may inconvenience the families of the soldiers, that advantage is readily overborne by the concern for their safety. The use of the injunction responds to the same understanding: better to take precautions and restrain the publication, rather than work with criminal prosecutions later, especially when those prosecutions can at best mete out punishment. For anyone anchored in common sense, those prosecutions will never stand out as the remedy of choice because they cannot save the lives of the men who were being imperiled.

Acting *after the fact*, then, with a prosecution, does nothing to render easier, or more tractable, the problem of assembling and assessing the evidence. The assessments would still have to be made here, as they are in other parts of the law, and they would have to be made in this way: The court would have to take testimony of people in a position to know just how bombs could have been assembled and placed, or how the knowledge of the ship and its schedule could have facilitated the plot. In the case of the Pentagon Papers, the court would have required the practiced eye, or the special knowledge, of people who could decode the references in the papers. Why, for example, would the naming of a particular restaurant in Saigon indicate, to those who knew, the persons who had to be the source of the information? This kind of knowledge was indeed rather special and "local." It was likely to be supplied only by people who were familiar with the operations – very likely because they had been engaged in the planning, or because they had been in the chain of command dealing with the operations.

But to say things of that kind is to come back to the elementary point that the judges and their clerks simply could not have had the competence, unaided, to decode and assess these papers. To make that point is to say nothing demeaning about the judges and the courts. It is a matter simply of recognizing the special knowledge that must flow distinctly to people who are intimately involved in the operations and alert to many particular fragments of information that would elude even the most brilliant jurist. Whether the government acts, then, after the fact, or whether it moves to avert an injury in advance, the judgment will have to *pivot on the same knowledge, in the hands of the same men and women in the Executive.* And again, the problem of proving the case or assessing the damage would not necessarily be rendered any clearer, or more manageable, the day *after* than the day *before.* But if that is the case, the argument made by Justice White falls into a moral bewilderment: White apparently harbored no doubts that a serious injury was at stake, an injury or a wrong that would justify the full force of a criminal prosecution. But if there was a wrong there that deserved to be prosecuted and punished; and if it were no easier to prove that wrong the day after than the day before; then why would it not have been warranted to act even earlier, to avert the harm, rather than wait until the harm had become irreparable?

In short, the problem may simply come down to that axiom recognized by Lincoln and the Founders: that there can be no such thing as a "right to do a wrong." If White was clear that the publication of the Pentagon Papers was *punishable,* that was the mark of wrongdoing, as John Stuart Mill explained many years ago.[47] If the publication was "wrong," there could not have been,

---

[47] As Mill observed in his classic book *Utilitarianism,* "[W]e do not call anything wrong unless we mean to imply that a person ought to be punished in some way or other for doing it." See Mill, *Utilitarianism* (Indianapolis: Bobbs-Merrill, 1957 [1861]), p. 61.

strictly speaking, a "right" to have published those papers. In that case, why was it not as morally justified to restrain the publication, and avoid the harm, as to risk the loss of life and the damage to the interests of the country? But to say these things is to back again into the very axioms that mark the equity powers. If it is wrong for Smith to kill Jones, then it would be justified to punish Smith for the murder – and even restrain him from the murder if that becomes possible. If Smith has no right to kill Jones, then he has no "right to be unimpeded" up to the moment he kills Jones. If the law may punish the killing of Jones, the law may also act, where it can, to prevent or restrain Smith from committing that wrong. The axioms I briefly recall here are not in the least novel; and yet they might have spared Justice White the moral strain that he had suffered – a strain that would not dissolve for him until nine years later in the *Snepp* case. He should not have labored for two minutes in the thrall of this particular confusion: that he knew enough already to suggest the plausibility of bringing a criminal prosecution against the owners and editors of the *Times* and the *Post*, but that he had no tenable ground for seeking to restrain these newspapers from continuing along a course leading, he was convinced, to a grave wrong.

But if these points managed to elude the judges, working as they did under pressure, the structure of argument they produced at the end should have set off all of the alarms. The judges might have been far from the Venn diagrams of their school days or their courses in logic, but something in the sensibility of judges should have alerted them to the jerry-built structure that emerged when their separate opinions were strung together. Consider again: Three judges were in dissent, and only one judge (Black) took the position of ruling out, categorically, any "prior restraints" on publication. For the rest of the judges who made up the majority, the judgment had to be *contingent*, not categorical: Prior restraints, they conceded, might indeed be justified under certain circumstances, if the dangers were real enough, and the ends weighty enough to justify the restraints. The wrong of prior restraints could not then be *categorical*; it had to be *contingent* upon circumstances. The decision had to be made by considering, in every case, the details that could make a restraint on publication justified or unjustified. In this instance, it would have been necessary to consider then the Papers themselves: What exactly did they contain? What was in them that could have been of use to the North Vietnamese and their Communist allies? And what was it that, if known, could endanger American agents and servicemen?

If the judgment in the case was, of necessity, a *contingent* matter, a decision could be made only by reading and assessing the Papers themselves on these points. But was that done? A telling sign was contained in Chief Justice

Burger's opinion, though it might have been overlooked as part of the surging wave of his complaints. As he surveyed the case, against the pressure to hurry the Court to judgment, he remarked that "we literally do not know what we are acting on."[48] That might have been seen as hyperbole, but the complaint took on a different complexion when it was added to his observation, earlier in the opinion, that "No District Judge knew all the facts [of the case]. No Court of Appeals judge knew all the facts. No member of this Court knows all the facts."[49] There was an echo here of Judges MacKinnon and Wilkey in the Court of Appeals in the District of Columbia. Judge MacKinnon had noted that the case "comes to us on a blind record in which the actual documents in the possession of the newspaper are not before us." Judge Wilkey noted that the judges had not been furnished with any of the "original documents." He pointed out that "the trial court dealt only in generalities, because that was necessarily the Government's case" – and it was necessarily the government's case because the government did not have a list of the papers that were in the possession of the *Times*. The result was that the government was virtually constrained from making its case.[50] Throughout the proceedings, in the district and appellate courts, most of the judges were willing to conclude that the Papers contained nothing really damaging, *even as the judges never examined the papers themselves*. In each instance, the judges concluded that the government made only a vague case for its position, while they steadily denied the government the chance to review the documents and make the grounds of concern more precise.

It should not have been surprising that, as the matter advanced through appellate courts, the higher courts would be even more distant from the facts of the case. Justice White crystallized the problem: Even as the Court held that the government had not met its burden of justification, the Court did not demand for itself the time that was necessary to take anything more than a cursory look at the papers. That "material," as White said, "remains sealed in court records and it is properly not discussed in today's opinion."[51] By that, White did not apparently mean that the papers were wholly inaccessible to the judges, for White himself and Justice Brennan had dipped into the papers.[52] What he seemed to mean, rather, was that the judges were constrained from a probing inquiry into the papers, and they were restrained, most of all,

---

[48] *New York Times v. U.S.*, supra, note 13, at 751.

[49] *Ibid.*, at 748.

[50] See Judges MacKinnon and Wilkey in *United States v. The Washington Post*, 446 F.2d 1327, at 1329–30.

[51] *New York Times v. U.S.*, supra, note 13, at 732–33.

[52] Brennan's perusal of the papers was reported in Rudinstine, *supra*, note 18, p. 265.

by the prospect of laying out, on the public record, what they might have learned from a reading of the papers. But to recognize, in that way, that this material might well be productive of harms, was *essentially to confirm the case for the government*. That prudent assumption, folded into the case, contained already the understanding that should have been sufficient in itself to resolve the case on the side of the government and restrain publication, even if only temporarily.

Still, I should not be drawn away, by that notable contradiction, to the point of neglecting again the underlying structure of the Court's argument here. Let me restate it: All but one of the judges making up the majority refused to credit the notion that there was a true principle at work that ruled out all prior restraints on publication. The judges did not think that prior restraints were categorically wrong, wrong in all instances, and under all circumstances. They held that the rightness or wrongness of a prior restraint must always be contingent upon the circumstances, and upon the ends that justified a restraint on publication. The judgment could be rendered then only in particular cases, by gauging the publication and the circumstances. In the case of the Pentagon Papers, then, the seriousness of the danger, to persons or to the interests of the country, could be gauged only by a precise examination of the Papers themselves. But this the Court never undertook. As the judges themselves understood the logical requirements of the judgment, they never did the very thing that, by their own account, was necessary to the rendering of the judgment. They held themselves back from examining the materials that were absolutely essential in reaching a judgment, under the circumstances, in the case at hand. And yet, the majority of the judges proceeded nevertheless . . . to pronounce a judgment.

We might aptly ask, Have we missed something? Or had the judges themselves missed something, under the conditions of high politics and crisis? What they missed was the fact that they had conspicuously violated the very terms of argument, the properties of judgment, that they themselves had put in place. With this move, the Court talked itself into a state of incoherence that has few matches, even in the checkered history produced by judges who remain, even with their robes, creatures quite as far from flawless genius as the rest of us. Of course, this species of embarrassment stands out, persistently, in the work of judges, because judges are the only officials whose vocation involves a painstaking explanation, in public, of the reasons that justify their decisions. And in fairness to the judges, it is arguable that the grievous mistake they made in this case was itself molded by their institution. Left to themselves, any of these judges, viewing the record from the outside, might have been quite as dubious about the arguments of the majority as I have been. Something else got in the way, I think, something that cast up distractions or blinders, or prevented the judges from seeing through the problem by seeing the logical structure of the argument they were arranging. And that thing, that source of distraction, is precisely the object of these essays: What distracted the Court, or altered its vision, were the understandings, or formulas, that had been formed over the years around its own precedents. After all, the function of precedents is to form concepts, or propositions that acquire the force of principles. Those concepts shape the understanding, which means then that they alter the angle of vision, or they shape the lens, that the judges bring to the cases that come before them. Justice White twisted himself as he sought to explain why he could not make himself support an injunction in this case, even while his sense of the world, and his moral intuitions, told him that a restraint on publication would have been quite warranted. Indeed, his own sense was that the absence of that restraint was likely to produce serious harm. What got in the way for him, then? Nothing, apparently, apart from the conviction, long settled among the judges, that there was something deeply portentous, constitutionally noxious, in the notion of a "prior restraint" on publication.

As I will try to show, the Court would later repudiate, in the *Snepp* case, every strand of reasoning that had been decisive in the case of the Pentagon Papers. Years earlier, in *Near v. Minnesota*, the Court thought it saw the presence of "prior restraints." That sense of the matter seemed to fix a lens, and that lens would affect the way in which judges and professors would view the cases that came later. It accounted, more than anything else, for the way in which Justice White viewed the problem in the Pentagon Papers. And the same lens would block from sight the turn that the Court, with White, would take in the Snepp case, as they moved away from their holding on the Pentagon Papers.

Justice White's service on the Court extended well past the *Snepp* case, and through this run of cases he might have satisfied himself that the law was finally being settled on terms far more defensible than the terms that had caused him so much moral strain in 1971. White had supported, in the Pentagon Papers, a decision he evidently regarded as morally wrong. He did it because he apparently thought there was a deeper wisdom contained in that precedent of *Near v. Minnesota*, confirmed by a succession of judges over forty years. It was there, in *Near*, that the Court brought to a new level of articulation the concern for prior restraints on the press. The Court had imparted to this concept a new standing, as nothing less than a principle, at the heart of the First Amendment and the Constitution itself.

And yet, it seems to have been forgotten that the decision in *Near* came through a divided Court. It was issued against the background of a forceful dissent by Justice Butler, supported by Justice Sutherland and other colleagues. The core of Butler's argument was that the Court had made a notable mistake: that what the judges were encountering, in *Near*, was not really a previous restraint on publication as that term had been understood in the English law. And indeed it was hard to see how the arrangements would describe any coherent understanding of a "previous restraint." If Butler was right, the Court had grafted onto our law a serious mistake, and as that mistake took the standing of a precedent, it shaped the vision in turn of the judges who would come later. That settled view would then be relayed, and amplified, into the next generation; and when the issue was posed again, forty years later, in a matter of consequence for the national security, judges like Byron White would find themselves caught in the coil of these mistakes. Or to switch the figure, White could not help looking out on the world with the "lens" that had been shaped by *Near v. Minnesota*. He could not help it even though the view through that lens brought him to conclusions that he could not regard as anything but troubling. Just how much that lens, or that jural vision, had been reshaped cannot be grasped unless one returns to *Near v. Minnesota* and looks at that case anew. And by that I mean, not look at the case with the assumptions that the case has managed by now to congeal. I mean rather that we look at the case, if we can, with fresh eyes, as though the statute in Minnesota, and the issue it raised, were coming to us, on their own terms, for the first time.

Five

Near *Revisited*

Every textbook in psychology will have, under "perception" or "cognition," a small picture of what looks like a black-and-white silhouette. The viewer may look at the picture and see an urn, in white, against a background of black. Or that is what the viewer may see until it is pointed out that the shape on the page might also appear to be a woman wearing a large hat. The figure is used to illustrate the tricks of perception, and often, once the viewer finally sees in the shapes the woman with the hat, he or she can no longer see the urn. I would suggest that something like that has been at work over the years with *Near v. Minnesota* (1931) and its lingering effects on our law. Chief Justice Hughes and four of his colleagues looked at the case, involving the trial of libels in a lurid scandal sheet, and the use of an injunction to restrain publication. And what they saw was an instance, or example, of "prior restraint." Justice Butler and three other colleagues looked at the same case and saw nothing that really fitted the model of "previous restraints" on publication. The force of their dissent was that Hughes had seriously misconceived the character of the case before him. In describing the case inaccurately (the argument might continue) Hughes and his colleagues had failed to see the parts of the case that were quite novel, and which gave this case its moral or jural significance. Instead of coming to grips with the real jural questions, they invented a new formula, which quickly became a cliché. But more than that: This new formula would shape the lens through which the Court viewed other cases arising in the future. My contention here is that the Court saw the case wrongly in *Near*, and it committed itself thereafter to seeing other cases wrongly in the same way. But in doing that, in altering its jural vision with a lens that was not apt or accurate, it continued to take a rather strange view of the legal landscape. The lens used by the Court picked out certain features in that landscape as familiar, and when they were noticed, they would produce, from the Court, the same conclusion. But at the same time, that lens seriously screened or truncated the judges' view of the legal landscape. Matters of even deeper significance would simply go unnoticed while the Court had trained itself to see things through the formulas of *Near v. Minnesota.*

With that sense of the problem, let me try to set in place a description of the case, first with some bare facts, but then in the way that the pattern of facts was seen by Chief Justice Hughes. The action in the case was brought against the publishers of a journal called the *Saturday Press* in Minneapolis. It was an action for libel, based on articles printed in nine separate issues of the journal, between September and November 1927. The complaint was that the issues in question had formed a pattern of "malicious, scandalous and defamatory articles," and the remedy sought in this case was to "enjoin" the further publication of material of this kind. The newspaper would not be put out of business. Rather, it would be placed under the enduring supervision of a court, to assure that the paper would not continue to publish the kind of material that was judged, in a trial, to be an injurious use of speech or publication. These features in the action were not exactly spelled out by the Chief Justice, even though they involved items that made a difference to the understanding of the case. And in the same way, Hughes seemed to miss the significance of one item he did mention: that the action was brought by the county attorney. That is, this was not an action for personal damages, brought by one of the parties who claimed to be injured. It was not, in other words, in the style of a civil case for personal injury and personal damages, which has been quite the most familiar style in actions over libel. This was not an action for personal damages, because that was not the remedy measured to the offense that was alleged in this case. This was an action brought, not by a party alleging injury, but by the public prosecutor or the district attorney. In form, then, it would count as a *criminal* libel: It was brought by a *public officer,* in the name of the people of Minnesota. Murders, after all, are prosecuted as public wrongs, not merely as private tort actions, brought by the relatives of the victim, or by those who could afford to launch a private suit. The prosecution for murder implies that, though the crime was quite definite and personal in its target, the public as a whole has an interest to be vindicated, in punishing this kind of wrong as an offense against the public order as well as the private victim. That was the sense that had to attach to this form of the law of libel in Minnesota – a form that has become rather unfamiliar in our own time, owing perhaps for the most part to the decision in *Near v. Minnesota.*

But at the time, there was nothing patently strange about this mode of proceeding over libel, for the Chief Justice in his opinion for the majority professed at least to be aware, and accepting, of the concept. Hughes was emphatically not of the persuasion that would be dramatized years later by Justice Black, who professed to think that the First Amendment precluded any attempt to restrain or punish speech, even when it came to punishing people for libels and the harms that can be wrought through the destruction of reputations. Hughes was quite clear in rejecting that outlook. For Hughes, the freedom of speech and publication could not mean that publishers and writers could be insulated from the consequences they produced, and put beyond the reach of the law. And so, citing Blackstone, Hughes made a point of remarking:

> [I]t is recognized that punishment for the abuse of the liberty accorded to the press is essential to the protection of the public, and that the common-law rules that subject the libeler to responsibility for the public offense, as well as for the private injury, are not abolished by the protection extended in our Constitutions.... The law of criminal libel rests upon that secure foundation.[1]

Hughes accepted, then – or at least he professed to accept – the notion of a criminal libel. But he would proceed in the rest of his opinion to cast serious doubt on whether he truly understood what he seemed to accept here so breezily. Just why a criminal libel was especially apt in this case became clearer as one looked at the list, proffered by the state, of the people who were the alleged targets of the libel. They included Charles G. Davis, Frank W. Brunskill, the *Minneapolis Tribune*, the *Minneapolis Jounal*, Melvin C. Passolt, George E. Leach, the Jewish Race, and the members of the grand jury of Hennepin County impaneled in November 1927. Leach was the mayor of Minneapolis, Davis was a special law enforcement officer employed by what was called a "civic organization," Brunskill was the chief of police, and Floyd Olson was the county attorney, who was at the same time bringing the case as the public prosecutor. Olson would go on to become the governor of the state. But the references to the "Jewish Race" rather pervaded the articles, in substance and tone. ("Practically every vendor of vile hooch, every owner of a moonshine still, every snake-faced gangster and embryonic yegg in the Twin Cities is a JEW.")

To fill in these ingredients from the case would already suggest why the form of a "criminal libel" seemed appropriate at the time. It would also mark

---

[1] 283 U.S. 697, at 715 (1931).

the features of the case that would make the use of the law even more suspect to civil libertarians of our own day. For the prosecutions could be summarized here under the terms "seditious libel" and "group libel." There was not to be found here, for the most part, an attack on private reputations. The attacks were directed rather at institutions, like the *Minneapolis Tribune* and *Journal*; to racial groups; to a group identified by its public function (the jury); and to individuals who became objects of attack because of their performance in *public office*. The civil libertarian would react in the first instance with a certain wariness at charges of libeling people in public office. To threaten the use of the libel laws in cases of that kind might merely put powerful tools in the hands of men in office to silence their critics in the public. The Supreme Court articulated a strong position against "seditious libel," or defaming the government, in 1964, in *New York Times v. Sullivan*.[2] And the late Harry Kalven, Jr., remarked that this was the place at which the First Amendment should begin: Whatever else the First Amendment could mean (as that formula usually goes) it must mean that people in office should not be able to make casual use of the laws of libel for the sake of silencing their citizen-critics.[3] As for the defamation of racial groups, the complaint of Justice Black and other libertarians has been that the charge is too diffuse to be tried: By this argument, a trial for libel takes on a critical discipline when it is connected to allegations of harm and injury against a particular person. When the attack is spread over groups, it becomes that much harder to assess whether anyone in fact has suffered injury as a result of the speech or publication.

But as I have argued at length in another place, the notion of racial defamation draws on a logic that is hard to efface. Whether or not the laws contain statutes on the defamation of racial groups, judges will find themselves backing into the logic of racial defamation as they try to make sense of restraints on "hate speech" and verbal assaults on groups.[4] A cross is burned, say, in a neighborhood where black families live. The gesture of intimidation, the attempt to terrorize, can be understood instantly for what it is, and the act is not softened in any way by the fact that it is not directed against any person in particular. It can be understood as a verbal assault for the same reason that

[2] 376 U.S. 254 (1964).
[3] See Harry Kalven, Jr., "The New York Times Case: A Note on the Central Meaning of the First Amendment," in Philip B. Kurland, ed., *The Supreme Court Review 1964* (Chicago: University of Chicago Press, 1965), pp. 191 ff.
[4] See, on this point, my own book, *The Philosopher in the City* (Princeton: Princeton University Press, 1981), Chs. 2–3, but especially, pp. 74–82, and in another section, pp. 328–31.

letters of extortion and threat have been understood as menacing gestures. These "expressive acts" may be actionable in the law in the same way, even if they do not produce any material injuries, and indeed even if the menacing gestures involve no bodily touching. We are reminded here that an "assault," in the law, does not strictly require the laying on of hands. Assailants may shoot and deliberately miss, or hold an unloaded gun near someone's head and pull the trigger. Whether the action constituted an "assault," a menacing act without justification, is something that people of ordinary wit can judge. And the ingredients of judgment are essentially the same when we move the problem to an assault on racial groups. If we had to explain the wrong of assaulting all members of a racial group, we would draw upon precisely the same ground on which we had explained the wrongness of racial discrimination: In both instances, the wrongdoer would fall back upon a theory of racial "determinism." He would have to assume that race "determined" the moral character of every member of that race, and made it intelligible then to recoil, in general, from members of that ethnic or racial group. It is to assume that on the basis of race alone, it is possible to draw inferences about the goodness or badness of people, and whether their presence should be welcomed or shunned.

As I have written on this matter on other occasions, I have sought to show, along the way, that the case against racial discrimination must be understood as a case grounded in principle, not a case that depends on conjecture about material injuries. A black family may be turned away from a house on the basis of race, and they may find a better house in the same neighborhood at a better price. We have had famous examples approximating that case, and I've already cited the notable case of Cecil Partee, who managed to cut an important figure as a black politician in the legendary Democratic organization of Cook County, Illinois.[5] Partee was barred from attending a public law school in Arkansas because the state made no provision of a law school for blacks. He was given a voucher that could be used for law schools even outside the state, and so Partee was able to choose between the law schools at Northwestern and the University of Chicago. Partee had not suffered a material injury as a result of being barred, on the basis of race, from the law school in Arkansas. But he was nevertheless *wronged*. As I put it earlier, he was treated according to the maxims of an unjust principle.[6]

---

[5] See Chapter 2, supra.

[6] The story of Cecil Partee is told in a book done by Milton Rakove: *We Don't Want Nobody Nobody Sent* (Bloomington: Indiana University Press, 1979), p. 156. For a fuller statement of the argument in principle on racial defamation and racial discrimination – an argument that bears in principle on "racial preferences" as well – see my book, *First Things* (Princeton: Princeton University Press, 1986), pp. 92–99.

My main point here, though, is that the notion of group libel cannot be resisted in principle without removing many features that are utterly necessary to our law: for one thing, that there are standards of judging verbal assaults as real assaults. But then also, that assaults do not require material injuries in order to come within the reach of the law; that there is a distinct wrong in visiting punishments, and directing attacks, upon whole groups of people defined by their race. We may take it as one of the usual ironies popping up often in our own time that the same libertarians who reject "group libel" have only rediscovered the logic of group libel when they have made the case, of late, for laws dealing severely with "hate speech." The labels have shifted, but hate speech evidently involves speech directed at people on the basis of groups defined, say, by race, ethnicity, and sex. During the debates over the Alien and Sedition Acts in the 1790s, John Marshall recognized that what we call "seditious libel" often involves group libel: Seditious libel could involve the creation or churning of tumults in the community, the kinds of tumults and disorders that unsettle established governments.[7] Quite often those assaults take the form of calumnies directed against local minorities. Those minorities may, of course, be "the rich" or "creditors," but most often they are minorities defined by religion or race. The most notorious example, of course, was that of the "blood libels" directed recurrently against the Jews, who were accused of using the blood of Christian children in making unleavened bread. A notable case arose in 1593, in London, with libels directed against foreigners, who were accused of gaining a stranglehold on the local economy. And so there were attacks on the "beastly brutes the Belgians," the "faint-hearted Flemings," the "fraudulent Father Frenchmen," the crafty, calculating Netherlanders, and – no surprise – the Jews. The crime of these foreigners, apparently, was that they achieved their prosperity, not evidently at the expense of the locals, but in a manner that noticeably exceeded that of the natives. It was complained, in one instance, that the foreigners "contented not themselves with manufactures and warehouses, but would keep shops and retail all manner of goods." One libeler set down lines in this vein:

Your Machiavellian merchant spoils the state,
Your usury doth leave us all for dead,
Your artifex & craftsman works our fate,
And like the Jews you eat us up as bread.

---

[7] See Marshall's speech on the constitutionality of the Alien and Sedition Acts: "Report of the Minority on the Virginia Resolutions" (January 22, 1799), *J. House of Delegates (Va.)* 6:93–95 1798–99, reprinted in Philip B. Kurland and Ralph Lerner, eds., *The Founders' Constitution* (Chicago: University of Chicago Press, 1987), Vol. 5, no. 20.

These attacks were taken seriously by the authorities precisely because they were understood as a species of seditious libel. They were attacks on groups identified by their nationality or ethnicity; they were the kinds of attacks that fed animosities and threatened to rend the civic peace. And so the Queen was informed. A commission was appointed; inquests were held; and the most serious punishments would be meted out.[8]

Seditious libel and group libel have often then run together. But even apart from that, it is not so clear that the regime of the First Amendment must remove people in public office from the protections of the laws of libel. In spite of all of the hand-wringing in recent years over "negative advertising," politics will always involve personal attacks, as long as politics deals with matters of moral consequence. When there is something at stake, in matters of justice, politics becomes a proper theater for the expression of outrage, and the leveling of moral condemnations. All of this simply "comes with the territory," as most politicians understand. Still, there is a point at which a campaign of personal attack may be highly destructive of personal reputations, and we should not be astonished that even political men and women will be sensitive to these injuries. The loss of honor may be sufficient in itself as an injury to a man or woman of honor. But even the utilitarians appreciate the damage that can be done then in disrupting families and impairing the capacity of a libeled man to earn his living. And so, not all democracies have been as quick as we have been, in the United States, to rule out the freedom of politicians to make use of the laws of libel. In Britain, it is still considered quite legitimate for politicians to vindicate their personal reputations by suing the libelers.

All of this is worth recalling, in setting in place the framework of judgment in the case, but also because even the majority in *Near v. Minnesota* did not contest these points. Hughes and his colleagues might have had deep reservations about the use of the law in Minnesota, but we ought to be clear that their opposition, at least ostensibly, did not run to the root of the laws of libel. By Hughes's own declaration, the Court fully understood

- that serious harms could be done through speech and publication;
- that the laws may vindicate those harms, in the same way that they may cast protections for individuals and groups against other kinds of harms;
- that the laws on libel may be criminal as well as civil – that is to say, the laws of libel may offer damages for the injuries sustained by discrete persons, or

---

[8] For an account of these troubles, see Charles Nicholl's book on the murder of Christopher Marlowe, *The Reckoning* (New York: Harcourt Brace, 1992), pp. 138–47, especially 139–41.

they may offer punishment for malicious speech directed at groups, even if it is hard to assess damage to particular persons, and even though the law awards no damages, in recompense, to persons.

The objections of the Court had to focus then on the statute in Minnesota, and the situation to which that statute had been addressed. But this is one of those instances in which we would actually understand the statute more readily if we knew something more about the persons and journal in the case. For it was in contemplation of the kinds of editors involved here, and the kind of journal they produced, that the statute was framed. Justice Butler would later remark in dissent that the publications and their history virtually "disclose the need and propriety of the legislation." The offending newspaper in this case was known as the *Saturday Press*; but its character ran back to the buccaneers who had launched its progenitor, the *Twin City Reporter*. Butler drew out the telling points in that history in this summary:

> In 1913 one [Howard] Guilford, originally a defendant in this suit, commenced the publication of a scandal sheet called the *Twin City Reporter*. In 1916 Near joined him in the enterprise, later bought him out, and engaged the services of one [Jack] Bevans. In 1919 Bevans acquired Near's interest, and has since, alone or with others, continued the publication. Defendants admit that they published some reprehensible articles in the *Twin City Reporter*, deny that they personally used it for blackmailing purposes, admit that, by reason of their connection with the paper, their reputation did become tainted, and state that Bevans, while so associated with Near, did use the paper for blackmailing purposes. And Near says it was for that reason he sold his interest to Bevans.
>
> In a number of the editions, defendants charge that, ever since Near sold his interest to Bevans in 1919, the *Twin City Reporter* has been used for blackmail, to dominate public gambling and other criminal activities, and as well to exert a kind of control over public officers and the government of the city.
>
> The articles in question also state that, when defendants announced their intention to publish the *Saturday Press*, they were threatened, and that soon after the first publication Guilford was waylaid and shot down before he could use the firearm which he had at hand for the purpose of defending himself against anticipated assaults. It also appears that Near apprehended violence and was not unprepared to repel it. There is much more of like significance.
>
> The long criminal career of the *Twin City Reporter* – if it is in fact as described by defendants – and the arming and shooting arising out of the publication of the *Saturday Press*, serve to illustrate the kind of conditions in respect of the business of publishing malicious, scandalous, and defamatory

periodicals by which the state Legislature presumably was moved to enact the law in question. It must be deemed appropriate to deal with conditions existing in Minnesota.[9]

In the 1950s, there would be the familiar scandal sheets, printing stories about sexual affairs and escapades that would not be printed in the more respectable newspapers. That difference in character marked the style of the scandal sheets – and their niche in the market. But as the story in Minnesota suggests, that character also marked another dimension of their business: In the 1950s the threat to expose celebrities as homosexuals could be a fatal threat, which ended careers, especially of those stars who were billed by their studios as leading men. When the evidence was clinching or plausible, the businessmen in charge of the studios would move to protect their investment, not by contesting the notoriety in a court, but by paying in effect blackmail to suppress the story. That realistic sense of the other dimensions to the business of publishing cannot be ruled out in the understanding of this case. As to the sensibilities of the editors who ran the *Saturday Press*, and the kind of civic life they were helping to shape in Minneapolis, the clearest evidence could be found in their own publication. I take it as revealing that the Chief Justice never thought it useful or pertinent to cite that material. And so the only gritty account that lingers in the law is the one offered by Justice Butler in his footnotes, as he sought to leave some record of the real words and conduct that marked the *Saturday Press*. Butler drew these samples from articles that appeared in the last edition of the paper, published on November 19, 1927:

> "I am a bosom friend of Mr. Olson," snorted a gentleman of Yiddish blood, "and I want to protest against your article," and blah, blah, blah, ad infinitum, ad nauseam.
> I am not taking orders from men of Barnett faith, at least right now. There have been too many men in this city and especially those in official life, who HAVE been taking orders and suggestions from JEW GANGSTERS, therefore we HAVE Jew Gangsters, practically ruling Minneapolis.
> It was buzzards of the Barnett stripe who shot down my buddy. It was Barnett gunmen who staged the assault on Samuel Shapiro. It is Jew thugs who have "pulled" practically every robbery in this city. It was a member of the Barnett gang who shot down George Rubenstein (Ruby) while he stood in the shelter of Mose Barnett's ham-cavern on Hennepin avenue. It was Mose Barnett himself who shot down Roy Rogers on Hennepin avenue. It was at Mose Barnett's place of "business" that the "13 dollar Jew" found a

[9] *Near v. Minnesota, supra,* note 1, at 731–32.

refuge while the police of New York were combing the country for him. It was a gang of Jew gunmen who boasted that for five hundred dollars they would kill any man in the city. It was Mose Barnett, a Jew, who boasted that he held the chief of police of Minneapolis in his hand – had bought and paid for him.

It is Jewish men and women – pliant tools of the Jew gangster, Mose Barnett, who stand charged with having falsified the election records and returns in the Third ward. And it is Mose Barnett himself, who, indicted for his part in the Shapiro assault, is a fugitive from justice today.

Practically every vendor of vile hooch, every owner of a moonshine still, every snake-faced gangster and embryonic yegg in the Twin Cities is a JEW.

Having these examples before me, I feel that I am justified in my refusal to take orders from a Jew who boasts that he is a "bosom friend" of Mr. Olson.

I find in the mail at least twice per week, letters from gentlemen of Jewish faith who advise me against "launching an attack on the Jewish people." These gentlemen have the cart before the horse. I am launching, nor is Mr. Guilford, no attack [*sic*] against any race, BUT:

When I find men of a certain race banding themselves together for the purpose of preying upon Gentile or Jew; gunmen, KILLERS, roaming our streets shooting down men against whom they have no personal grudge (or happen to have); defying OUR laws; corrupting OUR officials; assaulting business men; beating up unarmed citizens; spreading a reign of terror through every walk of life, then I say to you in all sincerity, that I refuse to back up a single step from that "issue" – if they choose to make it so.

If the people of Jewish faith in Minneapolis wish to avoid criticism of these vermin whom I rightfully call "Jews" they can easily do so BY THEM-SELVES CLEANING HOUSE.

I'm not out to cleanse Israel of the filth that clings to Israel's skirts. I'm out to "hew to the line, let the chips fly where they may."

I simply state a fact when I say that ninety per cent of the crimes committed against society in this city are committed by Jew gangsters.

It was a Jew who employed JEWS to shoot down Mr. Guilford. It was a Jew who employed a Jew to intimidate Mr. Shapiro and a Jew who employed JEWS to assault that gentleman when he refused to yield to their threats. It was a JEW who wheedled or employed Jews to manipulate the election records and returns in the Third ward in flagrant violation of law. It was a Jew who left two hundred dollars with another Jew to pay to our chief of police just before the last municipal election, and:

It is Jew, Jew, as long as one cares to comb over the records.

I am launching no attack against the Jewish people AS A RACE. I am merely calling attention to a FACT. And if the people of that race and faith wish to rid themselvs of the odium and stigma THE RODENTS OF THEIR OWN RACE HAVE BROUGHT UPON THEM, they need only to step to the front and help the decent citizens of Minneapolis rid the city of these criminal Jews.

Either Mr. Guilford or myself stand ready to do battle for a MAN, regardless of his race, color or creed, but neither of us will step one inch out of our chosen path to avoid a fight IF the Jews want to battle.

Both of us have some mighty loyal friends among the Jewish people but not one of them comes whining to ask that we "lay off" criticism of Jewish gangsters and none of them who comes carping to us of their "bosom friendship" for any public official now under our journalistic guns.

GIL'S (Guilford's) CHATTERBOX.

I headed into the city on September 26th, ran across three Jews in a Chevrolet; stopped a lot of lead and won a bed for myself in St. Barnabas Hospital for six weeks. . . .

Whereupon I have withdrawn all allegiance to anything with a hook nose that eats herring. I have adopted the sparrow as my national bird until Davis' law enforcement league or the K. K. K. hammers the eagle's beak out straight. So if I seem to act crazy as I ankle down the street, bear in mind that I am merely saluting MY national emblem.

All of which has nothing to do with the present whereabouts of Big Mose Barnett. Methinks he headed the local delegation to the new Palestine-for-Jews-only. He went ahead of the boys so he could do a little fixing with the Yiddish chief of police and get his twenty-five per cent of the gambling take-off. Boys will be boys and "ganefs" will be ganefs.[10]

The tone of these offerings was rather evident, though one point of curiosity is that they contained ingredients rather rare in group defamation: They disclaimed any intention of suggesting that all Jews were criminals. Still, that mild disclaimer hardly offset the sense of the piece, which was to cast a calumny against Jews as people bearing a culture that nurtured criminality. But of course, that is not all there was to it. As Butler suggested, there was a richer weave, involving the commercial uses of defamation. It was defamation as a business, and that business could be productive of profit even when the journal did not publish. Indeed, it could turn its main profit by offering *not* to publish, and find in that gesture of restraint a sustaining commerce in

---

[10] *Ibid.*, at n. 1.

blackmail. Beyond the assault on particular politicians, or the churning of racial hatred, that weave of defamation and blackmail was probably decisive in bringing forth the prosecution.

Chief Justice Hughes spoke the truth of the matter – without apparently realizing the depth of the truth he spoke – when he noted that "the object of the statute is not punishment, in the ordinary sense, but suppression of the offending newspaper or periodical."[11] Indeed, the editors of the newspapers were not being faced with punishment, in the ordinary sense. But instead of considering just what alternative the statute offered to punishment – and the reasons that lay behind that alternative – Hughes's strange inclination was to see, in the absence of punishment, something even more sinister lurking: namely, suppression and censorship. There was no attempt in the statute to assess damages for the injuries done to particular persons. And yet, Hughes found in that feature the absence of those ingredients that lent precision or discipline to an action for libel. Hughes professed to accept the notion of a criminal libel, dealing with the libel of groups, but when the problem was focused precisely in that way here – rather than dealing with injuries done to particular persons – Hughes seemed to forget the things that made it plausible to have a "criminal" action for libel, dealing with assaults on racial groups. His attention was diverted rather by the fact that the assault issued from a kind of journal or newspaper. His interest shifted then to a concern that newspapers could become hostages to anyone who formed a powerful dislike of a newspaper and was willing to characterize it as a "nuisance." And so, Hughes could put this construction on what was taking place in Minnesota:

> Describing the business of publication as a public nuisance does not obscure the substance of the proceeding which the statute authorizes. It is the continued publication of scandalous and defamatory matter that constitutes the business and the declared nuisance. In the case of public officers, it is the reiteration of charges of official misconduct, and the fact that the newspaper or periodical is principally devoted to that purpose, that exposes it to suppression. In the present instance, the proof was that nine editions of the newspaper or periodical in question were published on successive dates, and that they were chiefly devoted to charges against public officers and in relation to the prevalence and protection of crime. In such a case, these officers are not left to their ordinary remedy in a suit for libel, or the authorities to a prosecution for criminal libel. Under this statute, a publisher of a newspaper or periodical, undertaking to conduct a campaign to expose and to

[11] *Ibid.*, at 711.

censure official derelictions, and devoting his publication principally to that purpose, must face not simply the possibility of a verdict against him in a suit or prosecution for libel, but a determination that his newspaper or periodical is a public nuisance to be abated, and that this abatement and suppression will follow unless he is prepared with legal evidence to prove the truth of the charges and also to satisfy the court that, in addition to being true, the matter was published with good motives and for justifiable ends.[12]

Hughes makes it sound like a rather remarkable and unmanageable burden that someone should be asked to repel charges of libel by arguing (1) the truth of the publication, or (2) that it was published for "good motives and . . . justifiable ends." But those were precisely – and properly – the modes of defense in trials for libel. A charge of libel could be dispelled foremost by showing that the condemnations leveled against a person were not warranted, because they were untrue. Or, in certain cases, some embarrassing things revealed about a person might be true, but the public had no pressing or legitimate business in knowing them. A writer might reveal parts of the personal diary, say, of President Ford, or a photographer for a newspaper might have taken pictures of Jacqueline Kennedy swimming in the nude. The items might have been "true," but the papers would have been put under a burden of showing why they could have been justified in publishing these rather private facts. In the case from Minnesota, the complaint would appear to be that Near and his colleagues were given the chance offered to everyone else in a trial of libel, to rebut the charges against them. What Hughes sailed past then – and quickly overlooked – was the fact that the statute offered the occasion for a trial, with all of the discipline of proof and justification that comes into play with a trial. Justice Butler would later remark in dissent that the plaintiff had offered ample evidence at the trial to support the complaint. Whether or not he was correct in that assessment, the fact of the matter was that there had been a trial, a point one might have had trouble in inferring if one had seen the case only through the account offered by Hughes. And as Butler would point out at length, there was no basis for the suggestion that Near had been barred from offering every defense that was available to a defendant in an action for libel, including the claim of "fair comment on public affairs." That doctrine of "fair comment" offered a certain protection to newspapers in pursuing criticisms, even when it turned out that some of their charges were not strictly true. And even if Near lost on that claim in a court tied in to those local politicians, there was a prospect of taking the case on appeal to courts at another level.

[12] *Ibid.*, at 711–12.

In other words, it was not at all clear that the discipline attaching to trials for libel was missing in this case, or that it was not contained as amply here as in any other case. Yet, the impression arose from Hughes's account that the state had bypassed the usual discipline of a trial for libel by simply putting Near and his magazine under the restraint of an injunction. But Hughes was able to give that kind of account because Near himself had virtually foreclosed the trial. Near had taken the line that the statute itself, as a restraint on publication, violated the First Amendment. Therefore, as he argued, it was wholly unnecessary to move, in the usual modes of rebuttal, in proving the truth of the publication or the justification for publishing. In fact, Near was willing to concede that there was nothing imprecise or overly broad about the injunctions: They were, he owned, as they should be, and (in Hughes's report) "what was done was properly done if the statute is valid."[13] For the sake of shaping his version of the case, Near was willing to concede that he was open to all of the risks of trial and prosecution for libel. He would not claim, in the style of Justice Black later, that it was illegitimate under the First Amendment, to have such things as laws of libel. But he insisted that he could be punished properly only *after the fact*, only after he had published. Presumably, it was only *after the fact* that one could know whether the offenses anticipated were actually committed, and whether the injuries anticipated had actually taken place. The distinction that Near and his lawyers sought to emphasize was picked up and amplified by Hughes, as he invoked the authority of Blackstone in the *Commentaries*:

> The liberty of the press is indeed essential to the nature of a free state; but this consists in laying no previous restraints upon publications, and not in freedom from censure for criminal matter when published. Every freeman has an undoubted right to lay what sentiments he pleases before the public; to forbid this, is to destroy the freedom of the press; but if he publishes what is improper, mischievous or illegal, he must take the consequence of his own temerity. (4 Bl. Com. 151, 152; see Story on the Constitution, 1884, 1889)[14]

With these resounding lines, Hughes could endorse the curious version of the case as framed by Near, and with that kind of construction, he could reduce the case to this description – and this indictment of the authorities in Minnesota:

> If we cut through mere details of procedure, the operation and effect of the statute in substance is that public authorities may bring the owner or publisher of a newspaper or periodical before a judge upon a charge of

---

[13] *Ibid.*, at 708.
[14] Cited in *ibid.*, at 713–14.

conducting a business of publishing scandalous and defamatory matter –
in particular that the matter consists of charges against public officers of
official dereliction – and, unless the owner or publisher is able and disposed
to bring competent evidence to satisfy the judge that the charges are true
and are published with good motives and for justifiable ends, his newspaper
or periodical is suppressed and further publication is made punishable as a
contempt. This is of the essence of censorship.[15]

John Marshall once remarked that anyone who publishes a libel in this
country may be "sued *or* indicted" – that is, he could be subject to a civil suit
for personal damages, or he could be prosecuted for a criminal libel.[16] What
then was the novelty that Hughes found so striking – and so repellent in its
novelty? We might offer a translation of Hughes's argument in this way: A
man accused of publishing a libel is subject to a trial, either for damages or for
criminal libel, but in either event a court has to be satisfied that the writing
would meet the sense of a defamation understood by ordinary people, the
kind of people who fill out a jury. And even after that point is established,
the accused would have the chance to justify his conduct by showing the
truth of the publication or the reasons that made it justified to publish the
material. What then was so striking or unsettling in the case of Near? Did
the case not come well within these formulas and conventions, long known?
The only thing different in the end was that the accused was not (a) saddled
with a knockout award for damages that could bankrupt him or put him
out of business, or (b) put in jail. What is different in the case is that the
newspaper or publication is "suppressed," as Hughes put it. But even there
his language offered no calibrations or qualifications, and he might have
been giving here an account quite misleading: For what was it, exactly, that
was being "suppressed"? Here it apparently suited both Near and the Chief
Justice to preserve a certain haziness about this problem, a haziness that was
not warranted.

The case for Near, and the case made by Hughes, did indeed hinge on the
claim that the publication was being suppressed, or subjected to the kind of

---

[15] *Ibid.*, at 713.

[16] Again, Marshall in his defense of the Alien and Sedition Acts, *supra*, note 7:

> If by freedom of the press is meant a perfect exemption from all punishment for
> whatever may be published, that freedom never has, and most probably never will
> exist. It is known to all, that the person who writes or publishes a libel, may be
> both sued and indicted, and must bear the penalty which the judgment of his country
> inflicts upon him. It is also known to all that the person who shall libel the government
> of the state, is for that offence, punishable in the like manner. Yet this liability to
> punishment for slanderous and malicious publications has never been considered as
> detracting from the liberty of the press.

control known in the past, in English law, as a "previous restraint" on publication. Justice Butler would argue in dissent that neither argument, in fact,
was true. One oddity in the case was that Hughes himself recorded the facts
or arguments that should have told, quite critically, against his own account
of the case here. But apparently he did not grasp himself the significance
of what he was recording. And so, he seemed to neglect the import of the
argument made by the Supreme Court of Minnesota as it denied, point by
point, Near's construal of the case. On the matter of suppression, the High
Court in Minnesota observed that there was no reason "for defendants to
construe the judgment as restraining them from operating a newspaper in
harmony with the public welfare, to which all must yield."[17] That is, the trial
for libel did not result in a judgment at law to close down the newspaper.
There had been no "suppression" in that hard sense. No such penalty had
been part of the law. Nor did the judgment offer the kind of award for damages that would put the newspaper out of business. The inference made by
the Supreme Court of Minnesota was the most reasonable inference: The
newspaper would still be in business, where it could function as a legitimate
newspaper, and it could do that by the simple expedient of refraining from
publishing a series of libels, the kind of writing that the law may rightly punish and forbid. The *Saturday Press* could simply refrain from publishing the
kinds of articles that were judged, in this case, to be defamatory. Libel is an
illegitimate form of publication. A newspaper that publishes libels as a regular
part of its business is an illegitimate enterprise, as would be any enterprise
that incorporates, in its ongoing operations, things that the law forbids. A
school, for example, that incorporates training in pickpocketry or prostitution
would cease to be a legitimate school. It could possibly establish itself again
as a legitimate school by purging, from its offerings, the things that were
unlawful. In these understandings there was nothing novel. And as I will try
to show, neither was there anything really novel in the remedy offered under
the laws of Minnesota. Presumably, the newspaper could have continued as
a legitimate paper by purging itself of the things that were illegitimate, the
things that had been judged as defamatory in a court of law. The ingredient
that seems novel in this case – though not, as it turns out, in others – is that
the newspaper would be subject to the *continuing* supervision of a court.

But might that mean that the newspaper would now be under the arbitrary
judgment of a judge? If the concern is that judgments here will depend
on the vagaries of persons, on the mistakes made by judges and jurors in
judging, ... well yes, but that would be a hazard that attends everything else

[17] Cited in *Near, supra*, note 1, at 706.

in the law. If the question, though, is whether the standards at work in the screening of the paper are arbitrary, that point had already been addressed–and essentially rejected both by Hughes and by Near. Both of them, after all, had conceded that courts have access to standards of judgment that allow both judges and jurors to make tenable, defensible judgments in distinguishing between the publications that are libelous and defamatory, and those that are not. Whether the action for libel is civil or criminal, the plausibility of that action depends on the assumption that those standards of judgment are in place. If there were no such standards, or if the standards were essentially arbitrary, then there could not be, in any intelligible sense, a law of libel. Hughes and Near were both conceding that the standards in judging the presence of libel were indeed there and intelligible. Otherwise, it made no sense at all for them to concede the legitimacy of having laws on libel. But in that case, there is no inscrutable problem before us when the question is posed, Where do the judges draw the standards that would guide them as they maintain a continuing supervision over the newspaper? For the answer would have to be: They would use precisely the same standards they had used in the first place to gauge whether the publications set before them for judgment had indeed been defamatory and actionable. If we concede that judges and juries knew enough, in the first instance, to make those judgments, then we would have to concede that they knew everything they needed to know for that second tier of judgments in the case. They knew enough at least to say: "We will recognize the same thing when we see it again. You are free to publish in that wide range of subjects treated by newspapers, and you are enjoined simply to avoid publishing more of the same material that was judged to be defamatory in the first place."

My contention has been that Hughes had not seen this case rightly, that he seemed to have been thrown off precisely because the action in Minnesota had not involved, as he said, "punishment, in the ordinary sense." Because of that, he seemed to assume that the law in Minnesota was also getting around the vexing matter of offering a trial, with its sober assessment of the evidence. But the angle on the case may be altered critically as soon as one recognizes that there was indeed punishment here, and there had been a trial. In a curious trick-of-the-eye, Hughes seemed to have overlooked the presence of the trial because he had not seen the punishment. He seemed to have the sense that something novel was at work, and in the presence of a novelty he was disposed to suspect the presence of something unwholesome. In fact, there might have been novelty at work, but he strangely managed to miss what was arguably sensible in that novelty. He might have seen more clearly what was before him if he had bothered to reflect again on the purposes of laws on criminal libel or the defamation of groups. For he might have taken more seriously then the purposes of the law in Minnesota and the reasons that it was shaped the way it was. What Hughes had failed to see was that the restraints imposed here by statute were not a "previous restraint" on publication. They were in fact the punishment that was administered *after* a serious trial at law, with all of the ingredients that add discipline and precision to that kind of trial. As Justice Butler pointed out, the injunction was not a restraint imposed in anticipation of a wrong that might be done in the future. It was a form of reproach and punishment for the wrongs that had already been committed; the wrongs constituted by nine articles, making up a pattern. And what that pattern described was an enterprise that lived off and through the generating of scandal and blackmail.

The restraint imposed on the newspaper was thought to be the remedy most aptly applied in treating the harms that the law sought to reach. In the case of the Pentagon Papers, nothing at stake for the government could have been ameliorated by putting the owners of the *New York Times* and the *Washington Post* into jail. In the case in Minnesota, the concerns of the law, or the safety of the community, might conceivably have been advanced by putting the owners of the *Saturday Press* in jail, but the law did not seek a remedy so drastic. Nor did it seek to provide damages to people who suffered losses through defamation. The traditional laws on defamation were available for that concern. But this law in Minnesota had a different concern, expressing itself in a rather different form of remedy. Once again, and oddly enough, Chief Justice Hughes managed to encompass the explanation of that design, without quite grasping it. The explanation came in the form of a passage he cited from the Supreme Court of Minnesota, in sustaining the law in Minnesota:

> It is a matter of common knowledge that prosecutions under the criminal libel statutes do not result in efficient repression or suppression of the evils of scandal. Men who are the victims of such assaults seldom resort to the courts. This is especially true if their sins are exposed and the only question relates to whether it was done with good motive and for justifiable ends. This law is not for the protection of the person attacked nor to punish the wrongdoer. It is for the protection of the public welfare.[18]

The rationale behind the law in Minnesota is still not exactly obvious, but it begins, as the jurists on the High Court began here, with the most

[18] *Ibid.*, at 710.

commonsense understanding of the problems that beset the law of libel: If we are dealing with civil libel and personal actions for damages, there are powerful disincentives for people to take on the burdens of a lawsuit even if they have been severely damaged. For one thing, if there is a concern about broadcasting specious charges, it may hardly make sense to contest those charges visibly and loudly in public. The result may only be to broadcast the defamation even more widely to people who had never heard it in the first place. Beyond that, it may take a special courage and resolve – to say nothing of deep financial resources – in order to bear the expenses and persevere through all of the stages of litigation, exacting more and more of an emotional cost. That is why Ms. Carol Burnett made a notable impression years ago – and a reputation for grittiness – when she stood up against stories printed about her in one of those tabloids sold at supermarkets. It was, of course, one of those papers that takes as its standard fare the retailing of sexual escapades and embarrassments. In that vein, a story was told to me, secondhand, years ago by the late Yosal Rogat. It was a story about a young lawyer, newly graduated from the law school at Harvard and settled as an associate, in his first year, in an established firm in New York. One day, the young man was surprised when he was summoned to the office of one of the most senior partners. And there, sitting in the office, was the then-governor of New York. The governor was evidently quite tense, with an anger barely suppressed. The senior partner handed the young man a column that appeared that day in one of the dailies in New York, and that was apparently the piece that had so vexed the governor. The new associate scanned the piece, and remarked that it was quite wretched. Was it defamatory and potentially actionable? Yes, he thought, quite clearly. Would he advise therefore that the governor sue? No, he said; for if anyone had not read the morning paper, and seen the charges, it would simply abet the same wrong by publicizing the story and spreading the libel then even more widely. The senior partner listened to this advice with a confirming smile, as though he was satisfied at once with the wisdom shown by his young associate. And the young lawyer, taking in the scene, noticing the reaction of the senior partner, suddenly had visions of his own, precocious ascent. His office could be enlarged, he would be moved closer to the center of authority in the firm, his salary notably elevated into another register . . . when the senior partner turned to the governor and said, "Do you see? What did I tell you? Even a kid right out of Harvard will tell you the same thing!"

As the Court in Minnesota said, it was rare that the people smeared in libels had an incentive to vindicate the wrong done to them by taking up the burdens of suing. The statute did not make sense unless we understand that it was designed to deal with a different kind of problem. This statute would not offer damages for the harms suffered by the libels already punished, and it would not seek to put in jail the reporters and editors who had been guilty of the libel. It would deal with the problem in another way, without punishing in the ordinary sense, and without placing on ordinary people the burdens of litigation. Under the statute, the complaint could indeed be brought by a person claiming to be injured; but it could also be brought by a public officer (a district attorney), and it could be brought by any other citizen. These people could not plausibly be invoking the law in order to seek a judgment, and damages, for the wrongs already done to themselves or other known persons. They had to be acting, rather, for the sake of other persons, not yet picked out of the broader public and made into victims. A citizen may be decently concerned for members of the community who may be picked out in that way as targets for a campaign of vilification. I would suggest that the statute finally comes down to this rationale: The aim was not to offer redress for particular persons for the injuries they sustained as a result of libels already published. The aim, rather, was *to protect those members of the public as yet unnamed, but sure to be identified and named in the weeks and months ahead.* For the business in question was a business that lived off and through the destruction of reputations. That was the way the editors and writers made their living. That victims would be named over the course of weeks or months was unshakably predictable, as sure a prediction as could be made in this world. The surety of the expectation lay in the very character and *purpose* of the enterprise. Nor was it open to the authorities simply to brand any publication a public nuisance. The burden still fell to the law to establish that it was dealing with a journal of that character. It would do that in part by collecting evidence or accounts of blackmail, but in critical part, also, by discovering that there was not just one, aberrant slip in a journal characterized by the most consistent rectitude, or the most fastidious care to get things right. The judgment of the law would come into play more firmly when the law could establish, as it did in this case, that the libels were not one-shot affairs, playing on one day and one day only. In this case, the law could cite a pattern, a systematic design of libel, which was marked off unmistakably in a series of nine separate publications, drawn over weeks. And what was described, again, in this pattern, was an enterprise that made libel its business, a source of expected, predictable revenue.

Chief Justice Hughes, then, had misconceived the case. Or, he had not seen what was plainly before him. There was no restraint applied in advance of publication, as though the law anticipated that wrongs would be done, and on the basis of nothing more than speculation, had closed down a paper. What Hughes had failed to see was that *there was no restraint in advance of publication.* The restraint that came into play here was a form of punishment for a whole series of libels *already published.* Again, it appears that he did not see the punishment because the statute did not inflict the familiar punishments of awards for damages or terms in jail – though of course Near could have been sent to jail for failing to submit to the decrees of the court. Hughes had apparently failed to see that the injunctions actually offered a milder form of remedy or punishment, and he missed that point perhaps because he might have forgotten, or failed to grasp, the different purpose and rationale that came along with a "criminal libel." In the most remarkable way, all of that slipped past his vision. And only because it slipped past his sight so fully could he fly to the assumption that the *Saturday Press* was suffering under a "prior restraint" on publication.

That term, "prior restraint," drew its significance because it drew upon the understanding of a "previous restraint" on publication as it became known in English law, and even more famous through the commentaries of Blackstone. But Justice Butler pointed out – in what should have been a decisive and devastating commentary – that nothing in this case even remotely exhibited the features that defined a "previous restraint" as it was known in the English law. Butler drew his account of the "licensing system," or the system of "previous restraints," from Justice Story's account in his *Commentaries.* And since Story's account was quite detached from the controversy in *Near*, it is worth recalling. A close attention to the details would suggest what separates the licensing system, as it was known in England, from the regime of injunctions that was in place in Minnesota. As Justice Story recalled:

> The art of printing soon after its introduction, we are told, was looked upon, as well in England as in other countries, as merely a matter of state, and subject to the coercion of the crown. It was, therefore, regulated in England by the king's proclamations, prohibitions, charters of privilege, and licenses, and finally by the decrees of the Court of Star-Chamber, which limited the number of printers and of presses which each should employ, and prohibited new publications, unless previously approved by proper licensers. On the demolition of this odious jurisdiction, in 1641, the Long Parliament of Charles the First, after their rupture with that prince, assumed the same powers which the Star-Chamber exercised with respect to licensing books; and during the Commonwealth (such is human frailty and the love of power even in republics!) they issued their ordinances for that purpose, founded principally upon a Star-Chamber decree of 1637. After the restoration of Charles the Second, a statute on the same subject was passed, copied, with

some few alterations, from the parliamentary ordinances. The act expired in 1679, and was revived and continued for a few years after the revolution of 1688. Many attempts were made by the government to keep it in force; but it was so strongly resisted by Parliament that it expired in 1694, and has never since been revived.[19]

Under the odious system of "previous restraints," the government was understood to have a monopoly on the claim to legitimate publication – of anything. The standing presumption then was that, in the absence of an explicit permission from the government, there was no rightful freedom to publish. That is already a striking difference from a regime of liberty, in which people had a presumptive claim to their personal freedom in all parts of their lives, and the burden would fall then to the government to justify any restraints through the law. In America, in the absence of a law on any subject, people were presumed free to act – as they were presumed to be free to publish unless they had done something wrong. If they were charged with wrongdoing – as with claims of libel – then charges had to be filed. The matter would have to go to trial, or come before a legal tribunal, before there could be a restraint on publication. If there were a trial, charges would have to be sustained or confirmed by a jury. If there was a judgment from a judge, then that judgment had to be justified, and in most cases it would be subject to appeal and review by a higher court. That is to say, the very notion of an appeal served to test the justification for the judgment below. And once again, the burden of justification would fall to those who would restrain speech or publication or encumber those freedoms with punishments.

All of that stood in the most striking contrast to the system of previous restraints. In that system, the burden was entirely on the people who would exercise a freedom to publish. There could be no publication without submitting the material in advance to a licensor (or censor, in the strictest sense). And there the matter might sit. Dr. Johnson once inveighed against the typical dilatory performance of the licensor in his day, sitting for weeks on an application to produce a play.[20] In the absence of any explicit approval

---

[19] Cited in *ibid.*, at 734. It is instructive also to see the original statute on licensing: An Act for Preventing the Frequent Abuses in Printing Seditious Treasonable and Unlicensed Books and Pamphlets and for Regulating Printing and Printing Presses, 14, Ch. 2, c. 33, 1662. The statute is reprinted in Philip B. Kurland and Ralph Lerner, eds., *The Founders' Constitution, supra,* note 7, Volume 5, Amendment I (Speech and Press), Document 1.

[20] Samuel Johnson, "A Compleat Vindication of the Licensers of the Stage [1739], *Works of Samuel Johnson,* Vol. X ("Political Writings"), pp. 52–73. "Let the press remember when they appear before the licenser, or his deputy, that they stand at the tribunal from which there is no appeal permitted, and where nothing will so well become them as reverence and submission." P. 61.

from the licensor, nothing could be published or produced as a public performance. There was evidently no obligation on the part of the censor to come forth with reasons, or to offer an explicit justification for his decision. A justification, published, merely invites the public, and adversaries, to enter into a critical examination of those reasons. It invites further controversy and litigation. But the object of the licensing system was not to produce litigation and controversy; its purpose was to maintain control. It was an arrangement rather close to what Max Weber called "Kadi-justice": What would issue was only the judgment, and not a set of reasons or justifications.[21] This was not only a form of control; it was a form of diffuse control. If a licensor offered a precise account of why a book failed to elicit the permission to publish, the licensor would be offering, in effect, guidelines. Clever people could then adhere to the letter of those guidelines while finding subtle ways of getting round them. The burden then would fall to the licensor to explain why that clever effort should not be allowed. But under the licensing system, all of those restraints were nicely averted and the burdens reversed. It would fall now to writers, editors, printers, to discern where the boundaries were. If they could not be sure, they were given a powerful incentive then to steer a wider course away from the kind of material that could offend. Hence, the control was, as I say, diffuse, not precise and limited. All of that was a far cry from a regime in which editors and writers enjoyed a presumptive right to publish; where the burdens of restraint fell upon the government; where decisions to restrain would always have to bear the burden of justification; and where the rendering of judgments would merely open the reasoning of the judge to inspection, review – and reversal – by judges standing above them.

These matters are worth drawing out at length, because they may not explain themselves, and so there would be a point in unpacking, as we say, the fuller import of what Justice Butler was seeking to convey when he summed up the differences:

> The Minnesota statute does not operate as a previous restraint on publication within the proper meaning of that phrase. *It does not authorize administrative control in advance* such as was formerly exercised by the licensers and censors, but prescribes a remedy to be enforced by a suit in equity. In this case there was previous publication made in the course of the business of regularly producing malicious, scandalous, and defamatory periodicals. The

---

[21] See *From Max Weber: Essays in Sociology*, trans. and ed. H. H. Gerth and C. Wright Mills (New York: Oxford University Press, 1946), pp. 216, 220–21; and *Max Weber: The Theory of Social and Ecnomic Organization*, ed. Talcott Parsons (Glencoe: Free Press, 1947), pp. 361–62.

business and publications unquestionably constitute an abuse of the right of free press. . . . *The restraint authorized is only in respect of continuing to do what has been duly adjudged to constitute a nuisance. . . . There is nothing in the statute purporting to prohibit publications that have not been adjudged to constitute a nuisance.* It is fanciful to suggest similarity between the granting or enforcement of the decree authorized by this statute to prevent further publication of malicious, scandalous, and defamatory articles and the previous restraint upon the press by licensers as referred to by Blackstone and described in the history of the times to which he alludes.[22]

The very fact that the case came before a series of courts on appeal should have been already a decisive point of evidence that the arrangements in Minnesota could not possibly have satisfied the description of a "previous restraint" on publication. No such reviews, no such examination and judgment on the reasons for the restraint, were ever part of the system of "previous restraints." It is curious that some of these recognitions were actually absorbed by the judges as the Supreme Court careened over the years from case to case. Almost every scheme of control on obscenity, or the licensing of public places, could lead to charges of "prior restraint." For after all, the law would bar people in advance from entertainments thought lewd or at least inappropriate for a public place. In fact, in the world as the judges had known it, at the time of *Near*, nothing seemed as close to the system of "previous restraints" as the system of licensing movies for distribution. The system was not coordinated from a single, national center, but installed in different cities, with boards of censorship or licensing, depending on the ethic that prevailed in the local community. No one could mistake the differences that marked, say, Chicago and St. Louis, as more open towns, in comparison with cities like Boston. And yet almost all large cities had licensing boards of some kind. Even New York City, perhaps the most liberal, big city in America had a licensing board that took its mandate quite seriously. What makes that situation especially interesting in retrospect was that this very system of licensing was contained in the statute before the Court in *Near v. Minnesota*. And as Justice Butler pointed out, the majority made no move to challenge it. The statute read in this way:

Section 1. Any person who, as an individual, or as a member or employee of a firm, or association or organization, or as an officer, director, member or employee of a corporation, shall be engaged in the business of regularly

---

[22] *Near v. Minnesota*, supra, note 1, at 736–37; italics added.

or customarily producing, publishing or circulating, having in possession, selling or giving away.

(a) an obscene, lewd and lascivious newspaper, magazine, or other periodical, or

(b) a malicious, scandalous and defamatory newspaper, magazine or other
periodical,

is guilty of a nuisance, and all persons guilty of such nuisance may be enjoined, as hereinafter provided.[23]

At the end of his dissenting opinion Butler reminded his colleagues that the statute contained both (a) and (b). Of course the case centered on the problem of (b) a newspaper charged with becoming a nuisance because of a pattern of malice, scandal, and defamation. But surely, everything said about the wrongness of "previous restraints" would apply with comparable aptness in (a) as well, with magazines engaged in lewdness and obscenity. And so, as Butler observed:

The opinion seems to concede that under clause (a) of the Minnesota law the business of regularly publishing and circulating an obscene periodical may be enjoined as a nuisance. It is difficult to perceive any distinction, having any relation to constitutionality, between clause (a) and clause (b) under which this action was brought. Both nuisances are offensive to morals, order and good government. As that resulting from lewd publications constitutionally may be enjoined it is hard to understand why the one resulting from a regular business of malicious defamation may not.[24]

In other words, the decision in *Near* should have called into question at once all of those licensing boards in the cities dealing with movies and with entertainments ever bordering on raciness and lewdness. That understanding, made public, would have sounded the alarms – it would have brought home to the public the full, principled implications of what the Court was doing. And in making the holding dramatically manifest, that news, breaking out to the public, might have drawn attention precisely to the things that were most problematic in the judgment of the Court. But of course, it was not exactly in the interests of the press to raise grave doubts in public about a decision that seemed to give newspapers a larger measure of insulation from the regulations of the law.

And yet, as people were quite aware at the time, the problem of obscenity was manifesting itself in the most conspicuous way with the movies. Anything

[23] *Ibid.*, at 701.
[24] *Ibid.*, at 737.

said about previous restraints would have applied with even more force to the regulation of the movies, for nothing came closer to the system of previous restraints than that scheme for licensing and censoring movies. As the years wore on, the Court would be confronted with more cases challenging the regulation of the movies, and little by little the recognition would break in that the cases raised in a plausible form the issue of "prior restraints." But what was even more revealing was that the Court was still reluctant to deny altogether the legitimacy of restraining in advance certain obscene displays. Once again, the judges did not seem to notice that even this lingering form of licensing or censorship did not strictly satisfy the definition of "previous restraint" as that regime had been known in England. That is, even forty and more years of experience did not lead the judges to see what Butler had sought so patiently to lay out for them, in the way of instruction, in *Near*.

Nevertheless, it was an interesting spectacle to behold the judges, over the years, insisting that not every restraint in advance could be regarded as wrong. At one moment, in a case in 1961, the judges backed themselves into an axiom they should have grasped long ago when they rejected, with a certain high-flown disdain, this audacious claim made by one distributor of movies: that the "constitutional protection includes complete and absolute freedom to exhibit, at least once, any and every kind of motion picture . . . even if this film contains the basest type of pornography, or incitement to riot, or forceful overthrow of orderly government."[25] That far the judges would not go. Yet, at the same time, they seemed to miss the point that, in rejecting this argument, they were affirming, by indirection, that it may indeed be legitimate to prevent certain movies or publications from being exhibited even once. They preferred to fasten rather on the problem of censors or licensing authorities keeping films or theatrical productions blocked indefinitely, without the need to give reasons, justify their decisions, or have their judgments tested in a court. And so, in *Freedman v. Maryland* in 1965, Justice Brennan and his colleagues found fault with an arrangement in Maryland in which the owner of a theater had to seek permission to exhibit a film (*Revenge at Daybreak*). In that particular case, the official board came under no "time limit" for rendering a decision, and no obligation to reach that decision. The burden fell to the exhibitor to seek a decision, or carry the expense of an appeal.[26] The Court claimed to find a similar situation, fifteen years later, in a case in Texas involving an owner of a theater showing so-called adult films (*Vance v. Universal Amusement Co.*). The county attorney sought an injunction to

---

[25] See *Times Film Corp. v. City of Chicago*, 365 U.S. 43, at 46, 47 (1961).
[26] See *Freedman v. Maryland*, 381 U.S. 51, at 55 (1965).

abate the theater as a "public nuisance." A federal court of appeals read the statute in Texas to authorize a prior restraint with an indefinite duration.[27] But as Justice White pointed out in dissent, the injunction could not have been enforced without a prosecution for criminal contempt. At a trial of that kind, the state would have borne the burden of proving that the film in question was obscene.[28] In other words, the injunction could be challenged, the challenge would force the issue away from the county attorney or a board of censors, and into the hands of a court, operating under the restraints and discipline of the Constitution. With that kind of a shift, the situation was removed decisively from anything that resembled the old system of licensing or "previous restraints." But if the judges could have been sensitive to that cardinal point, they would have recognized just why the arrangements in *Near v. Minnesota* had not really fit the model of a "prior restraint." They would have grasped, that is, what Justice Butler had been trying to explain to his colleagues almost fifty years earlier as they had become distracted by the puzzles of the *Near* case.[29]

My argument here has been that Chief Justice Hughes fell into a serious mistake, that he misconceived what was before him, and he misread the case precisely because he was unclear, at the root, about the logic that attaches to a criminal libel. He was remarkably uncomprehending, then, of the rather different ends that the statute in Minnesota had sought to achieve. What was different about this law, and made it, at the same time, a policy of *moderation*, seemed to pass him by entirely. If that is a stern judgment on that accomplished jurist, it can be said at least that it was not a judgment rendered only in hindsight. As Justice Butler managed to show, four of Hughes's

---

[27] See *Vance v. Universal Amusement Co.*, 445 U.S. 308, at 309 (1980), per curiam.

[28] *Ibid.*, at 322–23.

[29] Just a few years before the Vance case, the judges faced a case of obscenity unalloyed, undisguised – a production of the rock musical *Hair*, applying for an arena in Chattanooga, Tennessee. In describing the show and its lyrics, Justice White noted that the play involved "not only nudity but repeated 'simulated acts of anal intercourse, frontal intercourse, heterosexual intercourse, homosexual intercourse, and group intercourse.'" See, for example, *Southeastern Promotions, Ltd. v. Conrad*, 420 U.S. 546, at 566 (1975). The project was offered to the directors of the Chattanooga Memorial Auditorium, who did not think that the production was fitting for a public arena, operated by the city. *But nothing in that decision barred the producers from seeking to stage the show at any other auditorium, privately owned.* Still, Justice Blackmun was able to find in this situation the rudiments of censorship and prior restraint. Justice White, in dissent, pointed out that the show quite clearly violated the laws in Chattanooga on obscenity, and that the city would have been well within its powers to ban the show entirely, instead of merely declining to stage it at a public facility.

colleagues were quite alert to the mistake he was making even at the time, and Butler had offered enough, in his dissenting opinion, to lead Hughes to a more accurate reading.

But for the sake of fairness, in turn, to Hughes and Justice Brandeis and the other judges in the majority, it would be useful to turn the case around yet again, and consider how those seasoned lawyers could have missed the points I have set forth here and seen the case in quite a different way. If we stop to turn the lens around again, we might try an account from this angle: Butler, Sutherland, and their colleagues understood the rationale of the law; and because they grasped its logic, they did not see that the faults attributed to the law here were anything more than accidents arising out of this case. Near and his lawyers foreclosed a trial, but *nothing in the statute had foreclosed a trial.* The Supreme Court in Minnesota saw nothing in the statute that entailed, or made necessary, the closing of the newspaper, or a flat prohibition on the freedom of the publishers to publish. In practice, however, a temporary restraining order was put in place by a court, and while the litigation proceeded, that injunction held. By the time that the trial court pronounced the *Saturday Press* to be a "nuisance," the *Press* had been under the restraining order for twenty-six months, or more than two years. If that was not a flat prohibition on publishing, it became hard to distinguish that version from the real thing. Was it a case then of the law describing a certain vision in theory, while the practical working of the law described a radically different state of affairs? And was it so implausible to think that this state of affairs rather confirmed the judgment reached by Hughes: that allies of the political class had used this law as a device for thoroughly silencing their critics?

That perspective has to be taken seriously, for woven into this case were serious allegations of an unsavory alliance between the underworld in Minneapolis and a political establishment that included the mayor and the chief of police. If that part of the case could be disentangled from the tawdry features of retailing scandals and generating blackmail, we might take a different view of the case. But that disentangling might well have been revealed if Near and his lawyers had been willing to mount a defense and argue the justification for their reports as "fair comment" on the conduct of public officials. And yet, for reasons of strategy, they avoided the trial and held back from making those arguments. That judgment proved successful in gaining their ends, though it might have created a lingering haze about the law and the issues at stake in this case. For Butler and his colleagues, the issues had to be disentangled, and if they were not, Butler was not willing to leap to some abstract charge of "suppressing" a newspaper. He was not willing to blind himself to the brute facts that the statute had sought to address – namely, that a publisher could well be running a blackmail operation in the guise of a journal.

So many things depended then on the strategy adopted by Near: that he would reject categorically the law in Minnesota and refuse to use the forum of a trial in order to show that the lurid charges made by the journal were possibly true and justified. That Near's defense took such a categorical view of the matter is something that could be attributed to his peculiar backing in this trial. That backing, from powerful sources outside the state, may also explain why Near was able to keep this litigation going for twenty-six months, rather than settling earlier. If he had settled earlier, he might have managed to show how it was possible to resume publication while adhering to the judgment made against him on criminal libel. Everything then is connected, and the connections lead back to Colonel Robert R. McCormick, the redoubtable publisher of the *Chicago Tribune*.

Near's cause had been taken up first by Roger Baldwin of the American Civil Liberties Union, who committed a critical $150 for Near's legal defense. But Baldwin gave way to an angel, or backer, with far larger means when Colonel McCormick took a serious interest in this case. With that interest came the continuing involvement of McCormick's lawyer, Weymouth Kirkland, one of the founding partners of the firm that would be known later as Kirkland and Ellis. For McCormick, the case offered the chance to produce a ringing, categorical judgment on the freedom of the press; a judgment that clothed his own particular business with a protection, or sanctity, that attached to no other private business. McCormick entered the case, with his substantial resources, in September 1928, when the case was already under way. But what seemed to propel him was his experience in two notable cases in which he himself had been involved. One had been a libel action directed against him by Henry Ford, the industrialist, in 1916. Ford had elicited the contempt and derision of the *Tribune* in the aftermath of President Wilson's deployment of troops on the Mexican border. Wilson had called up national guardsmen, and some of them had been working for Ford in Michigan. Ford, however, refused to make allowances for their national service, and refused to give them back their jobs on their return. For this bit of insensitivity, the *Tribune* branded Ford an "anarchist" and urged him to move his factories into Mexico. Ford sued for libel, and a jury in Michigan gave him a nominal victory: The *Tribune* was found guilty of libel, but Ford was allowed only six cents in costs. For the *Tribune*, however, the legal bills summed up to about a half-million dollars.[30]

---

[30] The story of the litigation is recounted in Fred Friendly, *Minnesota Rag* (New York: Random House, 1981), pp. 70–73.

Both sides claimed exoneration, but Allan Nevins and Frank Hill, in their biography of Ford, remarked that the verdict stung the *Tribune*. The paper had been found guilty of "reckless and spiteful utterance."[31] Yet, striking even closer to home, for McCormick, was the litigation that was launched against the *Tribune* by Mayor "Big Bill" Thompson in Chicago. McCormick and Thompson had been allies at different moments, but it was only to be expected that the ways of a political machine would draw the outrage of the *Tribune*, with its tradition of Protestant rectitude and reform.[32] Both Thompson and McCormick had shared a certain prejudice against England, but Thompson preserved his animosity during the First World War, and the *Tribune* began to roast him for being pro-German. He was also accused of fronting an administration that looted the treasury and brought the city to the edge of bankruptcy. By 1918, the accumulated charges finally brought four libel suits by Thompson, directed at the *Tribune*. Thompson sought personal damages totaling $1,350,000, but in addition he claimed that McCormick's attacks had impaired the credit rating of the city, and for that injury to the city, he sought damages of about $10 million. Once again, the law seemed to be taking seriously the notion of "seditious libel," or defaming the government. McCormick thought that such actions had ended with the trial of John Peter Zenger before the American Revolution, but now he feared that the political class was combining against him. In a town with a vibrant political machine, the judges and the politicians could be linked in a common family, and they could use against him now the weapon of the law.

But to McCormick's astonishment and relief, his reading of the political scene proved wrong. Or he had underestimated the hold that the traditional doctrines of the law – and the traditional tests of the law of libel – were still capable of exerting. For even in a court in Cook County, the mayor did not prevail. Judge Harry Fisher threw out this charge of "seditious libel," and offered a full-bodied defense of the press in a republic.[33]

Still, the experience rather concentrated McCormick's mind. It seemed to make him ever more sensitive to the powerful weapon that could be wielded

---

[31] *Ibid.*, p. 73.

[32] The fascinating, stormy, and litigious relations between McCormick and Thompson were spun out, in loving detail, by the late Frank Waldrop in *McCormick of Chicago* (Englewood Cliffs, N.J.: Prentice Hall, 1966), pp. 70–72, 182–94, 235, 279. And I record the note with a certain keenness of recollection because, as a graduate student at the University of Chicago, I was enlisted from afar by Waldrop in the research on this book.

[33] "[The press] has become the eyes and ears of the world, and to a great extent, its voice. It is the substance which puts humanity in contact with all its parts. . . . It holds up for review the acts of our officials. . . . It is the force which mirrors public sentiment." Cited in Friendly, *supra*, note 30, at 75.

by entrenched local politicians who extended their controls to the courts. When the case arose then in Minnesota, it seemed to awaken again fears long absorbed by McCormick, and his lawyer pointed up to him the interests that the *Tribune* could have at stake in this episode:

> [I]f this decision stands, any newspaper in Minnesota which starts a crusade against gambling, vice or other evils, may be closed down . . . without a trial by jury. . . . If this decision is sustained in the Supreme Court, how easy it would be for a "small" administration, through control of the legislature, to pass a like statute in Illinois or some other state.[34]

Kirkland went on to recall McCormick's apprehension "that a method of curbing the press having been found in one state would be copied in other states whenever the corruption and effrontery of the politicians in power reached a sufficient debasement."[35] When the issue was conceived in that way, the sense of satisfaction felt after the case seemed to swell, in the same measure. In a rare move, McCormick would later write to Chief Justice Hughes, to convey his gratitude for what was done:

> I think your decision in the Gag Law case will forever remain one of the buttresses of free government. Heaven knows we err constantly and there are those among us who are not guiltless of deliberate misbehavior.
>   I will welcome well studied measures to protect citizens from the views of arbitrary newspaper men but the method proposed in Minnesota would have destroyed the only check we have upon corrupt government.[36]

And yet, when we make allowance for the hyperbole, and McCormick's proper satisfaction, it may nevertheless be quite striking that other major newspapers at the time did not see the outcome in the same way. They did not apparently think that something critical to their own freedom had been preserved. Nor did they think that an insubstantial interest of the public was cast aside when the law in Minnesota was struck down, and its purposes swept away. When the litigation was under way, the *Christian Science Monitor* remarked that any menace to the freedom of the press here "comes from the unscrupulous within the ranks of the profession"; and if responsible journalism was to preserve its character, it had to "repudiate activities of the sensation-seeking newspaper."[37] In Minnesota, at any rate, the newspapers were not responding with glee, as though *their* interests had been safeguarded

---

[34] Cited in *ibid.*, p. 78.
[35] *Ibid.*
[36] Cited in *ibid.*, p. 161.
[37] Cited in *ibid.*, p. 89.

by this victory for another newspaper. The *Minneapolis Tribune* anticipated that the decision would be celebrated by other newspapers in the country, but it did not join the celebration. An editorial remarked that the celebration would be muted in Minneapolis because the state was so "fertile in the production of blackmailing and scandal sheets. The suppression law put an end to them, but no doubt they will be back with us, now that the law has been declared unconstitutional." The next day, the paper ran another editorial, urging the bar to find some other means "whereby these scandal and blackmailing sheets may be put out of existence."[38]

In recalling these commentaries on the case, I have been able to draw on the late Fred Friendly, in his book in 1981, aptly called *Minnesota Rag.* In that book, Friendly virtually incorporated every cliché about this case that it has been my purpose here to overcome. The "Four Horsemen" of the Supreme Court, who were in dissent here – Sutherland, McReynolds, Van Devanter, and Butler – he tarnished with the familiar brushes of caricature. Their opinions in dealing with cases of economic regulation he reduced to a set of familiar slogans.[39] And in a manner that reflected the journalism of his day Friendly saw, and celebrated, the connection between *Near v. Minnesota* and the Pentagon Papers case. To his credit, he cited commentaries and facts that could call his own analysis into question. But as with Chief Justice Hughes, he managed to miss the significance of the evidence that was, as it were, under his nose. The evidence comes back into sight if one asks that most obvious of questions, What was the result? What happened to Near after he had won the case? Friendly's own account offers as telling a commentary as one could devise, while at the same time being curiously oblivious to what the commentary reveals.

In October 1932, the *Saturday Press* was back on the streets, with a resounding caption: "The Paper That Refused to Stay Gagged." Near was back in business, back in charge. But as Friendly concedes, "The character of the paper hadn't changed much, and neither had its editor":

> He was still broke, was still spreading scandal and was even more bitter. He had managed to eke out an existence in the intervening years by being a "poison pen for hire," resurrecting his career as a propagandist and ghost

---

[38] *Ibid.*, pp. 158–59.
[39] Here I have that firm prejudice of one who has written on these cases, and so I would merely invite the reader to test the point by comparing the account of the Adkins case offered in *ibid.*, pp. 144–45, with the account offered in Arkes, *The Return of George Sutherland* (Princeton: Princeton University Press, 1994), pp. 20–22, 71–80.

writer, this time for Ray P. Chase, a notorious, vicious anti-Semite and unsuccessful gubernatorial candidate on the Minnesota Republican ticket. Near's self-styled mission, devised by the candidate's brother, Roe, was to run a smear campaign depicting Governor Floyd Olson as the willing tool of "Jew pigs," "thugs," and "Communists." His correspondence and writings for Chase reveal Near to be an unprincipled bigot, with no aim other than to get rid of Olson and "godless communism." . . . Finally, after saving a little money, Near began to publish again.[40]

But Near was at the edge of his resources, and so he felt compelled to take back his old partner, Howard Guilford. With Guilford, however, came the same-old same-old: the same flamboyant charges, skirting the edges of obscenity – or barreling past them – and the same spurring on of violence. Near had never been burdened with a sensibility overly refined, but even for him, this further round of mayhem proved altogether too much. At the end of August he wrote to Ray Chase:

> I severed my connection with the *Saturday Press* yesterday morning. For weeks, Guilford has growled and snarled about my writing these . . . articles and in the current issue, he insisted that scandal so vile it stunk should fill the paper. I made him take my name off the masthead and quit, cold. If I can't make a living without turning what little ability I have or may have to no better purpose than smearing sex filth I'll quit and dive off a bridge.[41]

Guilford tried running the paper on his own, but within a year he was out, and Near was back. Guilford struck off in 1934, then, to run for mayor, and he promised a stream of commentaries on the radio in which he would "tell the whole story of Governor Floyd Olson's connection with the Twin Cities underworld." But the commentaries never ran, for in a replay of his earlier escapades, he was waylaid and shot by gunmen. This time the shot, near at hand from a shotgun, proved fatal. There were no witnesses, no indictments. Near, as ever, put his own construction on the story, with the same blending of the obvious and the fanciful: "Howard was undoubtedly killed by hired assassins, and I think the killers were hired by communists."

For people whose vision was not shaped by clichés, the experience might merely have confirmed what had been so enduringly seamy and vicious in the paper run by Near and Guilford. Even for other people in the business, it was no particular strain to imagine a world of journalism without the *Saturday Press*. That Fred Friendly, and other commentators, would identify the

---

[40] Friendly, *supra*, note 30, pp. 163–64.
[41] Quoted in *ibid.*, pp. 164–65.

preservation of the *Saturday Press* with the interests of all other newspapers, and with the very standing of a "free press" marks, in itself, a serious moral confusion. For it suggests an unwillingness to take seriously the moral distinction between freedom and its abuse, as though there were no rightful and wrongful uses of freedom. Some civil libertarians will insist that they simply do not trust people in authority to make those distinctions. But what branch of the law, or of moral life, would be tenable if those distinctions could not be understood? And if we begin by ruling out moral grounds of judgment for the law, on what ground could one make any longer the *moral* case for a free press? Apart from everything else, the willingness to soar to rhetorical heights in defense of the *Saturday Press* simply did not accord with the state of facts that was plain to other people who lived in that landscape of Minneapolis in the 1920s, and early 1930s. The people who knew the figures on that landscape, in politics and the press, could explain in an instant just what there was about this supposed newspaper that made it an engine endlessly provocative of violence. Near and Guilford were hardly progenitors of Woodward and Bernstein breaking the Watergate story. There is a danger of falling into a rather warped understanding when commentaries seek to fit Near and Guilford into the familiar categories of respectable journalists pursuing a story that is politically charged. But more than that, as the categories have been converted into clichés, those clichés have misshaped our understanding of other cases. And when it was played out in a dramatic case with the Pentagon Papers, this skewed understanding had the potential effect of doing serious damage to American interests, with a cost in American lives.

I have argued here that something got in the way, for Chief Justice Hughes, something that prevented him from seeing through the distractions, or the allure of concepts, that offered no real hold on the facts of the case in *Near*. I have suggested the analogy of a lens. Whatever produced, in Hughes, this trick-of-the-eye – whatever made him see the urn instead of the woman with the hat – the lens in place would encourage the judges who came after to see, or misperceive, in the same way. It could be that Hughes was distracted by the fact that the controls in this case had to do with the press and political speech, and so the sensitivities of the First Amendment could have come into play. But in that event, the workings of this lens became all the more intriguing, and the results could be seen along two dimensions, which could be set forth here as a puzzle:

(1) In the first place, that lens adopted by the Court would distract us from seeing that the arrangements engaged in Minnesota were not really that

novel. In fact, they were the most familiar of arrangements in many other parts of the law. It was only when they were applied to journalists that they set off alarms, or suddenly took on the aspect of something constitutionally suspect.

(2) In the second place, the lens adopted by the Court focused attention elsewhere. It focused on something that was not at all a "previous restraint" on publication, and in drawing our attention in this way, that lens drew us away from noticing the most notable arrangements in our law that do in fact replicate the features of a "previous restraint." In short, the lens crafted by the Court in the *Near* case induced lawyers and judges to see "prior restraints" where they were not – and not to see them where they really were.

Under the first heading, many examples or similarities may instantly spring to mind if I simply offered a different summary of the arrangements in Minnesota. When cast in abstract terms, which have nothing to do necessarily with publishing, it may become far easier in fact to recognize the examples that have become far more familiar to us. Let us suppose then that we describe the case in these terms:

> A business, a firm, or members of a certain profession, inflict a harm on their clients or their customers, or even members of the general public. They inflict the kind of harm that they are in a position distinctly to inflict because of their professional roles. They may do it through negligence or malice, but either way, they have inflicted harms on people as a result of their professional work. And so a decision is made to remove from them a license to continue in the same business. Or, as a lesser penalty, they are put under a certain probation, where they have to be placed under the supervision of someone in authority.

When cast in these terms, there seems nothing exotic or even remarkable about these arrangements. They would seem to describe the procedures that have become quite familiar in dealing with malpractice in doctors, lawyers, accountants – or anyone else. The owner of a tavern may lose his liquor license if his customers become the source of disorders in the community and cause accidents on the roads. A young reporter working for the *Washington Post* makes up a story, wins a journalistic prize, has the story exposed as a fiction, loses her job – and falls out of the profession. Stockbrokers have lost their licenses, and with the loss of those licenses, lost the chance to earn their livings any longer in this occupation. It is hardly unthinkable then that people engage in malpractice, inflict harms, and then lose the freedom to keep practicing the profession they have abused. Why should it suddenly seem then so portentous if journalists were held to the same standards of responsibility that are routinely enforced on doctors, stockbrokers, and bartenders? Is there any reason that the standards of public responsibility should be lower among journalists than among members of any other occupation?

There may be a conceit that the freedom of the country is willy-nilly more implicated in the work of journalists in a way that it is not implicated in other professions. But people who have made their living in journalism often have a rather more sober view of the motives and shortcomings of the folk who make their livings in this way. Tom Stoppard, the playwright, took up a job on a newspaper rather than going to university, and Stoppard would later offer the prospect of a "reporter doll": "You wind it up and it gets it wrong." Journalists may not always be the most deserving lot. Still, it might be hard to establish precedents for controlling and restraining the press, without venturing into powers of control that could threaten a free press. And yet, the laws of libel have been in place for generations under republican governments. The founders of those governments have not thought that freedom of the press must entail a need to recede from judging the licentiousness of the press. As the late Justice Robert Jackson once observed, no freedom is rendered more secure by teaching that its abuse was inseparable from its proper use.[42] We have long accepted, without strain, that writers and publishers may be punished, or even restrained, for the wrongful hurts they inflict through writing. Those abuses can be punished without disturbing the freedom to write and publish in a domain of fair commentary, and even polemical argument. If that is the case, then we could not be faced with any bar in principle to laws restricting the press. The question then – here, as anywhere else – is whether laws amply justified are applied in a justified way, with a proper discrimination, and with a respect for the freedom to publish legitimate things.

Under this head, Immanuel Kant did us a further service, and offered a teaching running deep, when he observed that for every kind of activity, there is a certain class of those acts that *ought not* be done. To put it another way, there is no activity we can name – whether using a pen or driving a car – that could not be part of a means-end chain leading to the wrongful infliction of a harm. The art of driving could be used to rush a patient to a hospital or to drive a getaway car for the Mafia. A pen could be used to make a generous bequest or to commit fraud. Now, is it possible that, within the universe of experience, the only activity that is never subject to wrongful use would be the activity of writing, especially for a newspaper? But as I

---

[42] "No liberty is made more secure by holding that its abuses are inseparable from its enjoyment." *Terminiello v. Chicago*, 337 U.S. 1, at 37 (1949).

have suggested, democracies ancient and modern have recognized no such detachment from the principles of moral judgment that govern everywhere else, and every other human activity. There is no reason to believe then that every journalistic enterprise is categorically innocent, or somehow worthy of an immunity that runs well beyond anything that the society has been willing to accord to lawyers, beauticians, and chiropractors. And when the matter is cast in those terms, journalists should be the last ones to claim, for themselves, any such detachment from the moral terms that govern and restrain everyone else.

In this case, Near and his colleagues did not suffer the kind of disbarment that has been visited on people in other occupations and barred them from continuing in the business. The argument might be made, though, that there was still something denigrating in being put under a permanent, or at least, a long-running superintendence, administered by a court. Something in that arrangement may well seem incompatible with a newspaper or journal, which needs a certain independence in order to act vigorously in criticizing the government and the politicians of the day.

But once again, have we not seen this arrangement before, and when we have seen it, has it always been regarded as demeaning? This matter of continuing supervision by a judge – have we not seen it employed commonly, in matters small and large? In cases of bankruptcy? Do we not find judges presiding over the distribution of assets, the sales of inventory, and monitoring the progress of things in order to safeguard the interests of the creditors? But apart from the dissolution of businesses, there is, after all, the dissolution of families. Do we not find all about us the melancholy examples of judges presiding, in a continuing way, over the details of management in a family, as spouses divide assets, and as they try to make arrangements for the custody of children? These issues persistently give rise to more vexing quarrels, to claims of evasion and violation, calling for more inquiries, more rules, more intrusions by a judge into the ongoing life of a family. And yet, this experience has become, regrettably, a familiar part of the landscape in America. Less common have been those moments, filled with high portents in the law, when federal judges have taken over whole school systems for the purpose of dismantling racial segregation. From matters, then, of the family to matters of corporations, from matters of small politics to high, judges have wielded their equity powers in a direct, detailed, ongoing way. And so the arrangements devised in Minnesota for the press were hardly innovations. There is almost no area of American life that has not been touched by these equity powers of the courts. The curious question then is why these methods should have occasioned such a crisis when they were applied to the press.

This was the strange effect of the lens that *Near v. Minnesota* helped to fix on judges and on later commentators on the law. They became persuaded that they saw, in this case, a novel, threatening scheme of prior restraint, rather than something far more familiar and common. But then the other side of this strange trick-of-the-eye: by focusing our attention on these spurious versions of prior restraint, the lens of the Court kept distracting us from noticing those parts of our law that did indeed bear the closest resemblance to the schemes of prior restraint. Consider, after all, the ingredients of the problem: An agency of the government needs to extend, explicitly, a permission or "license" to engage in publication. The authority of the government to license constitutes a monopoly of control, or a monopoly of the authority to distribute the licenses. Without that permission or license, there is no right to engage in that publication. The license may also be withdrawn for reasons that are quite vague, without the need of the licensing agency to carry any burden of justification when denying a license. And that shift in presumptions works, with notable effects, on the character of what is written, produced, and disseminated. The picture becomes even clearer, I think, if we remind ourselves that, by "publication," we mean making something public, and widely accessible. We might as aptly speak about "broadcasting" information, disseminating it widely among the public. We do not have a system of licensing for books and magazines, though we have had such systems of censorship and licensing for movies. But we do have, most emphatically, a system of licensing for broadcasting, with the authority concentrated in the federal government. The Federal Communications Commission works under the kind of broad mandate that characterizes those other so-called independent commissions, with powers that are supposed to be "quasi-legislative" or "quasi-judicial." But in practice, it means that the agencies treat, as law, the rules they have promulgated on their own, rules that could rarely be passed in a legislative assembly. At the same time, the commissions are not as constrained as courts in the need to give justifications for what they do.

The FCC has been authorized to confer or withdraw licenses based on its estimates of "meritorious service." These franchises, to operate radio or television stations, may be quite lucrative, and yet the possessors of a license could find the license withdrawn if the FCC decides that the station has been wanting in "meritorious service" because it has caused serious offense or discomfort to a "significant minority" of its audience. Or the license might be withdrawn because the owners of a station have refused to consult with racial minorities who may have an interest in their programming. Or, in the past, because they might have violated the "fairness rule" by not giving a reasonable chance of reply to people who have been attacked in editorials or in commentaries on the air.

In the past, also, broadcasting stations could find themselves in serious trouble if they admitted a stream of obscenities, or lewd language, on the air. I was struck, years ago, by the connection between prior restraint and our own system of licensing for broadcasting, and so out of curiosity I sought to find out whether broadcasters had been sued or prosecuted for the kind of defamation that was found, for example, in *Near v. Minnesota*. In searching, however, I could not find a single case in which charges of defamation had been lodged against the owners of a station. Puzzled, I called a friend, who happened to be settled at that moment as the general counsel at the Federal Communications Commission. I told him that I had not come up with a single case of defamation, and he responded to the effect of, "Are you kidding? What would you expect?" A station that could have its license withdrawn by causing discomfort to a discernible segment of its audience is not likely to have owners bent on staking out strong political views, which may agitate the community or give offense. The managers are more likely to steer a wide course away from material that would offend racial or ethnic groups in the audience, let alone the kind of material so assaulting that it comes close to libel. As my friend summed up his reflections on this enterprise, he had come to the edge of concluding that the whole arrangement could be unconstitutional.

The clients of the FCC behaved precisely in the style one would expect from people who hold a license from the government, with the standards of judgment conspicuously vague. They are not apt to act in the style of buccaneers or crusaders, or stir up the local community with divisive programs. They are likely to act, in other words, with the kind of caution and prudence that was induced by the system of "previous restraints" in England. And yet, this system of licensing does not seem to spark the most impassioned arguments, from civil libertarians, or a campaign to challenge this system pervasively in the name of the First Amendment. In fact, quite the reverse: The main litigation over the First Amendment has come from the same people, by and large, who now favor, quite passionately, what is called "campaign reform." Or from the people who have now become alarmed over the explosive success of conservative "talk radio." The resonance of Rush Limbaugh, or the striking effects of the Swiftboat Vets, in their challenge to John Kerry, seems to have confirmed, for many on the Left, the notion that a robust arena of public discourse may become unwholesomely robust. And so we now seem to be encountering a new wave of nostalgia for the return of the "fairness rules." They were the rules that kept broadcasting under the benign restraints of an official establishment, far more reliable in its political reflexes. With restraints on political campaigning or political advertising, a regulatory body, rather like the FCC, would have the authority to ration speech by rationing, or allocating, the money that may be spent in disseminating that speech and promoting political causes. That is not exactly the system of licensing, or "previous restraints," but it shows, nevertheless, how even "progressive" opinion in politics can settle in with modes of restriction of political speech far more potent – far more likely to suppress political speech – than the restrictions that were involved in *Near v. Minnesota* and the Pentagon Papers case.[43]

And yet, these cases have been given the standing of icons, in marking the dangers to a free press. They have entered now into the orthodoxy of those who have come to regard themselves as the defenders of freedom. There is more than irony, then, in noting that in June 2000, in *Hill v. Colorado*, the Supreme Court took another step in removing, from pro-life demonstrators alone, the doctrines of the First Amendment that have been extended to cover almost all varieties of provocative and assaulting speech.[44] When it comes to the pro-lifers, merely standing in front of abortion clinics, or engaging in silent prayer, the rules typically applied to other cases are virtually suspended or overturned. And all of this is done without the least sense that anything, in the spirit of liberalism, has been impaired or even qualified. It should not bear, then, the least surprise that the defense of *Near* and the Pentagon Papers may summon the deepest passions of people who are otherwise prepared to tolerate the most sweeping restrictions on political speech if it is only attended by the label of "reform" and offered by people who profess the firmest devotion to liberality.

We have then a paradox that persistently brings forth odd, corrosive effects in our public life. On the one hand, the cult devoted to the legend of the Pentagon Papers is quite willing to see political speech suppressed in many quarters, while at the same time, it would withhold injunctions that restrain speech or publication for the sake of protecting lives or averting other, serious

---

[43] For a precise account of the way in which this new regimen of "campaign reform" has been used to silence people of slender means in politics, see Bradley Smith, *Unfree Speech* (Princeton: Princeton University Press, 2001).

[44] See *Hill v. Colorado*, 530 U.S. 703 (2000).

harms. When the Pentagon Papers case is combined with *Near*, the fruits can be seen in cases like *Bartnicki v. Vopper*, decided at the end of 2000. Gloria Bartnicki had been a negotiator acting for teachers in collective bargaining at the Wyoming Valley West High School in Pennsylvania. Anthony Kane had been the president of the local union, a branch of the Pennsylvania State Education Association. In May 1993, Bartnicki used her cellular phone in order to call Kane and have a lengthy conversation about the progress and strategy of the negotiations. As it turned out, that conversation was picked up by someone else and copied on tape. Such eavesdropping and taping was illegal in Pennsylvania and illegal also under federal law.[45] A copy of the tape was put in the mailbox of Jack Yocum, the head of a local organization of taxpayers, a group that had been opposed to the demands of the union during the negotiations with the school board. Yocum, in turn, delivered the tape to Frederick Vopper, the host of a radio talk show. Vopper had been critical of the union and its demands, and he managed to give a prominent, embarrassing playing of the tape on his program. Bartnicki and Kane invoked the federal statute as they sued, seeking damages as punishment for the illegal taping, and for the broadcast of a tape that was made in violation of the laws.

Vopper, the radio host, could claim to be only an innocent receiver of stolen goods. But if the law could be circumvented so easily, one could imagine other, "innocent" third parties suddenly becoming the purveyors of stolen goods, or goods acquired in contravention of the laws. And yet, the Supreme Court, with Justice Stevens writing, thought there was a serious question. Vopper himself had not violated the laws with a surreptitious taping, and he had sought no material gain, apart from furthering the interest in his program on radio. His broadcast of the tape could be laid plausibly to an interest in putting before the public some private conversations that bore directly on a matter of public controversy. The conversations on the tapes were rather pedestrian. But they became newsworthy because they touched on matters of strategy, thought to be sheltered in a domain of privacy.[46]

For Justice Stevens, though, the combination of the Pentagon Papers and *Near* rather entailed the outcome in this case. The tape of the conversation was acquired illegally, but so too were the Pentagon Papers. The publication of the Pentagon Papers was excused or justified by the importance of the issue in the public controversies of the day. By that measure, the conversation of Bartnicki and Kane could fall under the same rule, as a conversation suddenly of interest to the public because it bore on a matter of public controversy. For Justice Stevens, that was good enough. As he pointed out, the case of

---

[45] See the Omnibus Crime Control and Safe Streets Act of 1968, 18 U.S.C.S. 2511(1)(a).
[46] The quoted lines are in *Bartniki et al. v. Vopper*, 532 U.S. 514, at 518–19 (2000).

the Pentagon Papers had not resolved the question of "whether, in cases where information has been acquired unlawfully by a newspaper or by a source, government may ever punish not only the unlawful acquisition, but the ensuing publication as well."[47] There was no attempt here to seek an injunction to restrain the publication of the tapes, and yet Stevens sensed the relevance of the issue. After all, if Bartnicki and Kane were injured in the broadcast of these tapes, they had a plausible case for an injunction to restrain the broadcast before it generated embarrassments and injuries for them. We might only alter the case by just an inch: What if Vopper had found it useful to play the tape in segments, with installments running over two or three days? In other words, what if he had taken his guide from the playbook of the Pentagon Papers? Would there not have been the most understandable move to seek an injunction to stop the playing of this material, illegally gained? And would that move for an injunction not have appeared eminently reasonable?[48]

---

[47] *Ibid.*, at 528, italics in original; and cf. *Landmark Communications, Inc. v. Virginia*, 435 U.S. 829, 837 (1978). It is also worth noting that Justice Stevens wrote for the Court in *Lowe v. SEC* (1985), in which he was sensitive once more to the issue of prior restraint as it bore on a man who had lost his license to act as an "investment adviser." Lowe subsequently published a newsletter, offering advice on investments, but offered impersonally to a public of readers. To the SEC and the federal court of appeals, the difference did not matter: If Lowe had been barred from offering advice to clients on investments, then he could not make his living by doing the same thing in the form of a newsletter. The SEC was willing then to restrain or bar Lowe from publishing. A district court reversed that judgment, but the appellate court sustained it – only to have Justice Stevens and his colleagues reverse once again. Strictly speaking, the Court did not reach the constitutional question, but it was clear that the precedent of *Near* weighed quite importantly for Justice Stevens here. See *Lowe v. SEC*, 472 U.S. 181, at 204–6. Stevens construed the governing statute with the assumption that, of course, Congress would wish to steer around any constitutional problems and avoid any conflict with the First Amendment. And so Stevens offered this construction: "[P]etitioners' publications do not fit within the central purpose of the Act because they do not offer individualized advice attuned to any specific portfolio or to any client's particular needs," *Id.*, at 208. And yet, if we understood that the statute in *Near* was quite defensible, the same reasoning would have covered the case of Christopher Lowe without strain: There was no restraint on publication, based on a prediction of what Lowe *might* say. The restraint was a penalty for an offense that had *already been committed – and adjudicated.* If the government could justly restrain Lowe from offering advice to clients on the stock market, then it was quite plausible for the federal appellate court to conclude that the judgment would not be altered if the investment adviser chose to present his advice "in the guise of traditional newspaper format." See 422 F.2d, at 1377, at 1378 (1984). This case came up again more recently in the federal appellate court for the District of Columbia, and it becomes a matter of interest because it elicited the reflections of Judge John Roberts. See *Taucher v. Brown-Hruska*, 2005 U.S. Appellate Lexis 1402.

[48] This possibility seemed curiously to have been overlooked by Paul Gewirtz in his thoughtful, long essay, mulling over the implications of *Bartniki*. See Paul Gewirtz, *Privacy and Speech*, Supreme Court Review 2001 (Chicago: University of Chicago Press, 2002), pp. 139–99.

In dissent, Chief Justice Rehnquist, joined by Justices Scalia and Thomas, took those injuries as quite real. But that is to say, they took seriously the interests of the government as even Justice Stevens had recorded them: "first, the interest in removing an incentive for parties to intercept private conversations, and second, the interest in minimizing the harm to persons whose conversations have been illegally intercepted."[49] When the law forbade and punished eavesdropping, the law had sought to protect the freedom of people to engage in associations and enjoy a rich freedom of discussion, with people of shared purpose. As the dissenting justices saw the matter, the decision of the Court, in permitting the broadcast of the tape, seriously threatened the critical freedom to engage in those private associations. By withdrawing the restraints of the law, the Court was notably failing to protect that vaunted right of privacy. But it was also endangering the right of association under the First Amendment, and chilling the freedom of speech.[50] And once again, all of this was accomplished through the strange alchemy that came into play when the lens drawn from *Near* was joined with the holding of the Court on the Pentagon Papers.

For some reason, it seemed to elude Professor Paul Gewirtz, in his thoughtful commentary on the case, that the understanding set forth here by Rehnquist (and Scalia and Thomas) offered a far more direct and precise test, with far clearer standards, than the more convoluted approach offered by Justice Breyer. Breyer was willing to conceive, in the Constitution, a larger scheme of interests to be protected apart from freedom of speech. That would have come as no news to the American Founders, who understood from the beginning that some speech was illegitimate, the cause of unjustified juries, and therefore properly subject to restriction. But in Breyer's hands the scheme invests the judges with a license that finally reduces to the artful use of a utilitarian calculus. The judge would gauge the consequences, say, of protecting speech at the cost of certain plausible claims of privacy. Exactly why judges are in a better position than legislators to gauge those consequences and balance those interests is a question never posed or answered. Gewirtz joined Justice Stevens in dismissing the connection to the Pentagon Papers, but as the standards of judgment are focused more precisely, the connection in principle to the Pentagon papers becomes, I think, all the clearer.[51]

---

[49] *Bartniki, supra,* note 48, at 529.
[50] For Rehnquist's argument, see *ibid.,* 541ff.
[51] See Gewirtz, *supra,* note 48, pp. 189, 191, 193–98.

Plainly, the doctrine in *Near* had taken a firm hold in the understanding of judges and lawyers, and in that ascendance of *Near*, we may find the triumph of legal optics: that curious spectacle of people seeing what they wish, selectively, to see, and seeing often in a manner that seems to invert things in the landscape. The true systems of prior restraints go largely unseen and unchallenged. But at the same time, the clichés of prior restraint are employed in situations to prevent the law from seeking means quite moderate to avert the serious harms that may be inflicted through vicious and injurious publications. Still, the sense of the common law prevails everywhere else, and it accounts for why injunctions and restraints have been employed in all other domains of our common life, where harms can be intentionally done, and where the law can still act to avert them.

I have argued here that the judges have produced tricks of perception as they have altered the jural lens, and managed to divert even themselves. But that is not all. Even when they come to discover their mistakes, the same lens may keep them from registering, or incorporating, the correction that they themselves have come to see. And so, nine years after the hurry and pressure of the Pentagon Papers, the Supreme Court was faced with a case of an administrative body, the Central Intelligence Agency, claiming the authority to screen *in advance* any manuscript or book published by former members of the Agency. The Court sustained that system of review and restraint in the face of a serious constitutional challenge. But what seems remarkably unnoticed is that the Court – and Justice White – revisited the arguments that proved decisive in the Pentagon Papers case, and this time *overturned them all*. Yet, more than that: I would argue that the reasoning in *Snepp v. United States* should have been taken not only to overrule the Pentagon Papers case, but *Near v. Minnesota* as well. But wonder of wonders, it has not: The Pentagon Papers and *Near* continue to be regarded as the controlling cases in this part of the First Amendment, as though the reasoning in *Snepp* had never been expressed, or that it had never somehow registered. It may be that the commentators on the law preserve this understanding of the case law because it is the version that happens to be strongly preferred by the class who fills out the media, the law schools, and the judiciary. And yet the confusion may also arise from the fact that the lenses of these earlier cases are still in place, doing what they have ever done. They may shape our vision, and do it in the most decisive way by inducing us to see even what our reason has decisively refuted. In that sense, this system of lenses furthers the project of positivism and modernity, for it teaches, in its own way, that reason may not in the end matter; that it is perception and *will* that finally govern.

That is a stern indictment when taken to its root. Whether that indictment is justified is a matter that can be judged only after we have revisited the case of Frank Snepp and considered, with a close reading, the reasons that finally impressed the judges as compelling – nine years late.

Six

The Saga of Frank Snepp and the New Regime of Previous Restraints

The helicopters were being filled, ready to lift off from the roof of the American embassy in Saigon. It was the spring of 1975, the government of South Vietnam was collapsing, and in these last, desperate moments, Vietnamese who had cast their lot with the Americans – as agents, secretaries, staff of all kinds – were frantically trying to climb walls and break into the American compound. The hope was that they could cling to one of those choppers and be delivered to safety. Frank Snepp, a young intelligence officer, would long remember the scenes of women gripping the bars on the gates, with soldiers clubbing the fingers of these women in an effort to beat them away. For Snepp, it would be a lasting scene of nightmares, marking layers of betrayal. It would also be the source of an enduring outrage that would express itself in a memoir of the American defeat and withdrawal: The story would include an American ambassador so heedless of the intelligence reports that he held back from taking prudent measures to move the files or destroy the records of Vietnamese who had collaborated with the Americans. When Saigon fell quickly, the files would fall nearly as quickly into the hands of the Communists, and for those who had annexed themselves to the side of the Americans the result would be torture and death. All of this would find expression in a memoir called *Decent Interval*, a sardonic reference piled on a cynical construal of Henry Kissinger's diplomatic maneuvers: that the purpose of that diplomacy had been merely to arrange a "decent interval" between the withdrawal of American forces and the collapse of the regime that the Americans had fought to sustain.

Snepp was only thirty-two, a native of North Carolina, but a young man who had found his metier in wartime Vietnam. As an intelligence officer, he became adept at briefing reporters and dignitaries newly arrived. As an interrogator of prisoners he had apparently become quite skilled. That summary description evidently covered many things that it was best not to inquire into too directly. To take again that line from Evelyn Waugh, Snepp's diaries were probably much in need of editing. But he acted with apparent "effect" at all levels because he was a firm believer in the cause, and he had absorbed, thoroughly, the character of the CIA. The memoir he would later write would become the source of a serious controversy with his own government; a controversy that would end his career in the government and nearly make a ruin of his life. And yet, it was the memoir of one still mainly loyal to the cause and to his government. He determined not to be so dishonorable as to reveal secrets touching the security of operations, or anything else, for that matter, that would threaten further harm to those people who had risked their lives by throwing in with the Americans.

Snepp's book offered a density of moral outrage, exploding into charges precisely directed, charges of moral fault, of murderous negligence, of thoughtlessness and betrayal. The moral seriousness was all the more powerful because there was not a touch of sanctimony or moral superiority, and that for the most plausible of reasons: The author shared the guilt and the blame, not in any pro forma way, or in the feigned gestures made famous later by certain politicians in our own day, who would make a minor art of apologizing freely for the wrongs done by their government in the past, though they would find it exceedingly hard to acknowledge, with a comparable conviction, the wrongs they themselves had done. Snepp registered his own, acute sense of self-blame in the most precise, personal, and unnerving way. His memoir was deftly written, but even more deftly and powerfully written was the memoir he would write *of the memoir*: his book, more than twenty years later, on his litigation, his falling out with the CIA, with his family, his lovers, and all threaded through with flashbacks to Vietnam. That memoir of the memoir, *Irreparable Harm,*[1] published in 1999, was not merely a better book but the work of an artful hand that far exceeded the critique he had assembled against his former colleagues in the late 1970s. In the opening pages of that book, he brings back the sense of panic in those last hours, with the dangers suddenly concentrating and swirling around the American embassy. His recollection contains this passage:

> *Memories* – already wheeling through the imagination like unsettled ghosts. . . . Mr. Han, the translator, screaming over his CIA radio for help . . . Loc, the Nung guard, plucking at my sleeve, begging me not to forget him . . . Mai Ly, phoning just hours before the collapse, threatening to kill herself and her child if I didn't find them a way out. . . .

[1] (New York: Random House, 1999).

[Later, he had made it to the *USS Denver*, to which the staff had been ferried for their rescue.] I stared at the *Denver's* wake, trying vainly to put Mai Ly behind me. She'd phoned too late, I kept telling myself. What could she have expected so late? But there was no consolation in that. The first time she'd called, I'd been chained to my typewriter, hammering out another piece of analysis which I was foolish enough to hope would nudge the ambassador toward the choppers. So I'd told her, "Call back in an hour. I'll be glad to help." But in an hour, I'd been down in the ambassador's office, trying to sell him on the analysis, and she'd left a message, "I would have expected better of you," and then had bundled up the baby boy she'd let me believe was my own and had retreated to that dingy room off Tu Do and there had made good her promise.

Mother and child: they might have been sleeping when a friend found them hours later except for the blood on the pallet and my misplaced priorities that day. But no more than the ambassador or any of the others I was now so ready to condemn had I troubled to remember that far more than American prestige was at stake those last moments before midnight.[2]

Was this a sharpened version of *Madame Butterfly*, with Snepp cast as a somewhat more redeemable version of Pinkerton? If so, the difference must appear slender indeed, and that is the sense that Snepp has evidently meant to preserve for the reader – the sense of his own, grievous fault, with only the barest outline of an excuse. I say that Snepp meant to preserve this sense for the reader, this lingering whiff of his unworthiness, because it is not until later in the book that he fills in the story a bit more and introduces an offsetting doubt. It seems that Mai Ly had drifted away for two years, and returned with a child. The reader is left then to draw the inference that the child might not, after all, have been Snepp's, but the child of a former lover, from an interval in which she had been with other men.

For most of the rest of the book, Mai Ly and his neglect of her become important as a story he is shielding from two of his lovers. They were both women who had worked in the CIA; they both had furnished moral support, and more. One was willing to take a lie detector test in order to cover him. Both of them seemed willing to throw their lives and careers away for a man who could not quite commit himself. One of the women, a dark-skinned beauty named Bernie, finally tells Snepp that in the time he has separated himself from her – refusing to let her stay with him during his trial – she has attached herself to a boyfriend, and she shares with Snepp her question:

---

[2] *Ibid.*, p. 4.

Should she marry this new friend? The question, tendered in that way, seemed virtually an invitation to Snepp to concentrate his mind and consider whether he wished to make a trumping offer. Was he, as far as she was concerned, serious? That is a question she never pressed on him before as a condition for their intimacies, but when she pressed it on him now, she apparently found him numb. She drifted into the marriage with that other man, whose child she was already carrying.

With a similar want of commitment, Snepp watched his other lover drift away, too, with time. He then rediscovered a woman, an old acquaintance of striking beauty, who had suffered the ravages of surgery and treatment for cancer. She was the friend, we are told, of his "first wife." After the accounts of lovers, and girlfriends, this bit of news is dropped in passing near the end of the book (p. 293). Only then do we learn that there had been an earlier marriage and divorce. But a "first marriage" implies a second. Yet, nowhere in this memoir of detail and embarrassing candor is there a mention of the woman who would become his second wife. And then, in the closing moments of the book, in the section marked "postscript," Snepp records his own belief that Mai Ly's child was in fact his. He is on a visit to Vietnam in the mid-1980s, part of a crew working on a documentary for television. As he revisits old haunts, he is keenly aware of the fact that his son, had he lived, would now be about eighteen years old. It was, then, his child and the mother of his child whom he had let slip away to their deaths, as he was trying to steady his ambassador and avoid a panic in the embassy.

I raise these points because they are hardly inadvertent. There is, about all parts of Snepp's book, the hand of design. The ingredients in the story were put forth in fragments, altered, taken back, corrected, with a degree and sequence that were hardly an accident. In part, this was Snepp's candor about himself, offered with the evident touches of art – with touches, indeed, that made it hard to miss the art he had cultivated as a writer, faced with deep sadness and misfortune. But with an unmistakable intent, also, he conveyed at the same time that there were many, critical layers in the story that he was holding back.

In other words, Snepp has quite purposely shaped an enigma, and he must surely know that this enigma must play back into the reader's judgment of his story. Snepp has offered feints and ellipses, and tricks of the eye that mislead; and he must stir in the reader the question of just how much one can rely on his account. How far, in the end, can we "trust" Snepp's version? "Trust," after all, is what the case was about, from the beginning to the end, and it might be said that the different layers or meanings of "trust" formed the several layers of the case. When Snepp began with the CIA, as a young analyst out of college, he was inducted, he was told, into a relation of "trust." The confidences of other men and women would hinge on their trust of him, and so too would their lives. On finishing his initiation, he would be asked to sign an agreement pledging that trust. In that covenant, he would commit himself, thereafter, to publish no work arising out of his experience in the CIA without submitting that work first to a board of review. That is an obligation that Snepp seemed to take with a deep seriousness. His fidelity to the different women in his life was unsteady, and he was honest in acknowledging it, even to them. But his fidelity to the cause, or to the code, remained firm. As he himself suggested, he had absorbed thoroughly the "culture" of the agency. Even as he was accused of undermining the CIA and the security of his country, he recoiled from the men who revealed, in their books, classified information, and especially information that could imperil agents in the field. His anger was deepened by the fact that the government and the CIA did not play by the same rules: He thought that Henry Kissinger had leaked information to Bernard and Marvin Kalb; that the former director of the CIA, William Colby, had revealed names and classified information in his own memoir; and in neither case was there a submission of the manuscript to the agency. In neither case, as far as he knew, was permission sought; and in neither one was a prosecution launched, to condemn the breach of security and inflict a punishment. But Snepp *was* targeted for punishment, perhaps to make a point where it seemed least expensive to those in power. For there would be no need to take on the *New York Times* or members highly placed in the establishment. The point could be made by bringing the powers of the government down on younger, less famous men, who were more vulnerable to the penalties that the government could mete out.

"Trust" again: the remedy, or punishment, would take the form of a "constructive trust," an arrangement by which the government could capture all of the royalties and income that Snepp made from his book *Decent Interval.* The dictum arose from a principle of the common law: that wrongdoers should not profit from their wrongdoing. The measure would have had no consequence if it had been applied to a man of independent means, but Frank Snepp lived on the advance for his book when he left his employment in the CIA. When he was put under the order of a court to disgorge $120,000, part of the money had already been spent for his basic expenses in living. The government permitted him to deduct the amount he had paid in federal taxes, though not in state taxes. The burden would then put him in hock to publishers or television stations who were willing to pay for his writing. To his good fortune, he did have real gifts as a writer, and as a person he evidently elicited a sympathy that seemed to be amply deserved. But the constructive trust would have, for him, a real bite as a penalty.

Still, apart from the constructive trust, there was the ongoing, unabating requirement of submitting his work, in advance, for the review and approval of a board in the CIA. That was the system installed when the government won its case against Snepp in 1979–80, and it was the system that remained in effect as he made his career as a writer in television. The same system would still be in place when he submitted his long delayed *memoir of the memoir* in 1997. This latter, compelling book made it through the screening of the CIA – and for all of that, preserved its edge and its force. But consider again: Snepp had been found guilty of wrongdoing in his work as a writer. He had been charged with acting in such a way as to do "irreparable harm" to the security of the United States, even if he himself had revealed no secrets, no classified information. For this offense, duly charged and duly judged in a court – though without a jury – Snepp was placed under compulsion to submit everything he wrote, thereafter, to an official board. That board could then censor and approve, and in failing to approve, bar his freedom to publish. Once we have set in place this description, would we not have described precisely the arrangement that the Supreme Court had denounced, with ringing phrases, in *Near v. Minnesota*? Did the arrangement not in fact describe the conditions of a "prior restraint," as it has come to be known since *Near* – and was that not precisely the arrangement that the judges had bent over backward to avoid in the Pentagon Papers case? Had the government and the Supreme Court now overturned quite dramatically the principle that the Court had installed to its own, grand fanfare in 1931, the principle that the Court had reaffirmed in 1971, with another, suitable round of blaring trumpets and self-congratulation?

Indeed, it curiously reinforces my point to note that this connection was recognized, even at the time, by Snepp's own lawyers. Mark Lynch was assigned to the case by the American Civil Liberties Union, and as a young lawyer, with recent training, he rather assumed that the case against Snepp was likely to be safe in the long run, because the problem of Snepp should have been governed by the precedent in the Pentagon Papers case. As Lynch prepared his brief for the appeal, he recalled the layers of argument in the Pentagon Papers case, and according to Snepp's account he noted that "the Supreme Court had refused to uphold the gags in that case despite the government's claims of grave, impending peril to the national security."[3] After

---

[3] *Ibid.*, at 290–91.

all, the Court had put the burden on the government in showing a direct, immediate danger to the national security before it would uphold an injunction to restrain publication. Was it conceivable that the Constitution would now allow the government simply to declare that the failure of Snepp to submit his manuscript for clearance would constitute, in itself, an irreparable harm to the national security? Was it not reasonable to expect that the standards set forth in the Pentagon Papers case would apply to Snepp quite as well – and make it even harder then to justify a system of "prior restraint"?

Later, as Snepp himself came to study the precedents that bore on his case, he would become aware of *Near v. Minnesota* as the anchoring precedent in this field. He became aware then, with his lawyers, that if the law were ruled, in this domain, by the arguments laid down in *Near* and the Pentagon Papers, he should have been free and clear. And the judgment should not even have been close. But in that event, the implication of Snepp's signal loss in this case should be no less clear. Yet, it seems nowhere recognized in the textbooks, or in the commentaries supplied in the law reviews: namely, that with the decision in *Snepp*, the Court had in effect overruled *both Near v. Minnesota* and the Pentagon Papers case. That announcement would no doubt come as a surprise to most lawyers – and to lawyers dealing with the First Amendment it would seem bizarre. Certainly the Court has never acknowledged any such thing. But that may be another measure of the dissonance that has characterized this problem since the beginning: In this case, the Court pretends that it has a ruling doctrine, forbidding "prior restraints," while at the same time, Frank Snepp continues under that regime of supervision more than twenty-five years after the judgment was entered against him. Beyond that, as we shall see, the counter-precedent established in Snepp has spread rapidly through the government, to many other cases. Regardless of what the judges seem to have discovered yet, or acknowledged, about their own work, and regardless of what is said in the law reviews, *Snepp* has produced a layer of experience in our law quite apart from the storybook version offered in the textbooks. And regardless of the postures struck by the judges – regardless of the high-flown sentiments waved by experts on the First Amendment – the fact of the matter is that the reasons put forth by the Court in the *Snepp* case finally counter and refute every argument that was critical to the judgments in *Near* and the Pentagon Papers.

That sovereign fact about this case might have been concealed by the curious form in which the case was handled and then announced to the world. The Court had initially refused to take certiorari when Snepp had appealed from his loss in the Court of Appeals. But as Snepp himself found years later, when he gained access to the papers of Justice Thurgood Marshall, Justice Lewis Powell had entered a strong dissent on the refusal of certiorari. Powell apparently thought this was a moment in which it was important for the Court to say something more emphatically about the protection of intelligence and American agents. His dissent eventually gained adherents. The accession of four judges made it possible to hear the case, but as Justice White came on board, Powell's faction had the votes not merely to hear the case but to resolve it on their side. But at the same time, there was no oral argument. When the decision was finally issued, it was put forth as an opinion per curiam, a decision *through the court*. No judge then took the responsibility for speaking in the name of the Court. And if the Supreme Court that day was correcting an imbalance arising from other cases, no judge then took the occasion to offer a grand pronouncement, to explain the new course set by the Court.

Those odd circumstances may explain why this opinion of the Supreme Court has not drawn the same notice as *Near* and the Pentagon Papers, or why it has not been recognized as a case that overruled those earlier, landmark decisions. And yet, those circumstances offer a revealing guide to the meaning of the case. Speaking through the Court, speaking per curiam, without any grand opinion attached, by name, to any member of the Court, was a way of making the point sotto voce. The decisions in *Near* and the Pentagon Papers were hailed as grand judgments by the media and the professoriate, even though the Court, in the Pentagon Papers, had spoken per curiam. But when the Court found it necessary, in effect, to back away from those grand gestures – to scale them down, or correct them – the Court would in effect be conceding mistakes made grand. But here the Court chose to speak, sotto voce, in the quietest way, drawing the least attention to its dramatic turnabout.

Nine years earlier, the Republican judges recorded their resentment over a rush to judgment, a press to do things hurriedly, without the kind of "sedate reflection" more fitting a judicial tribunal. Or to put it another way, their aversion was to doing things under conditions in which the judges are not likely to be seen at their best, with their strongest command of the facts, and with the wit that the situation requires. Lewis Powell was not on the Court at the time, but he could still absorb the sense, lingering among the judges appointed by President Nixon, that the Court had been ill-used. The judges had been manipulated, pressed into a willingness to look sophomoric in their offices, for the sake of protecting the interests of the *New York Times*. But now there was a chance to get back at them – at those chattering classes, who make their livings in the press and the media. And yet – most wondrous of

all – one could get back at them without taking on the formidable establishment of the *New York Times*. Nor would there be a need to offend all
of those respectable people who seem to feel vicariously threatened by any
move to treat illiberally the most prestigious of the press. The point could
be made by coming down, with the club of the law, on young Frank Snepp.
Frank Snepp: unattached, isolated, on his own, with the faint look of a rebel,
or a man bearing a grudge. A person then to be discounted, to be treated
as odd, eccentric, perhaps less than respectable, one who might be willing to
embarrass his former superiors. And even at the risk, perhaps, of endangering
some of his former colleagues?

That aspect of things might give the move all the more color of justification, and it was all, strangely enough, more possible now, after the departure
of Nixon. There was a new Democratic administration under Jimmy Carter.
Well before the days of Bill Clinton, Carter and his closest aides were anxious
to show themselves as New Democrats, not liberals in the style of George
McGovern. When it came to matters of defense and intelligence, the administration was determined to show that it could be as tough, as strong in its
postures, as any Republican administration. That interest seemed to be taken
up as an interest of high standing by the new Attorney General, Griffin Bell.
Bell seemed determined to show that Democrats would not be flippant when
it came to issues of defense and intelligence. When the issue of Snepp sur-
faced, then, early in the Carter administration, Bell seemed to pounce upon
it, determined to make a point that would be noticed.

The point would be made, and this quiet but momentous turn in the law
would be allowed to pivot on the case of this young man, detached now
from any party or institution that would have a stake in his defense. He was
cheeky, but scarred. He was apparently given to bravado and a heightened
sense of his own place in the center of foreign intrigue and a zone of war.
He was persistently attractive to women, but curiously impaired or luckless in
preserving his marriage or his romantic alliances. And yet, for all of that, the
outrage that moved him about Vietnam in its last days was an outrage properly
grounded. It proceeded from the sense that the United States was doing an
amply justified thing in risking the lives of its own sons for the sake of resisting
the extended reach of communist power in Southeast Asia and the imposition
of a Communist regime on the people of Vietnam. His passion for the cause
apparently waned as he became all too aware of the flaws, and even the want
of conviction, of those men, high in the government of the day, who were
directing the war. They were directing, with a diminishing conviction, a war in
which they would not be hazarding their own sons. In that respect, there was
a conspicuous contrast, say, between Robert McNamara and Graham Martin,

the last ambassador in South Vietnam, who had lost his own son in the war.[4] But even with all of the souring that one might expect on the part of Snepp, his disaffection at the end came from outrage over the abandonment of allies. And not merely allies in the sense of foreign leaders: What moved him was a vivid awareness of those ordinary Vietnamese who would be targeted for butchery as a result of their involvement with the Americans. He bore his own portion of guilt, as he himself acknowledged quite clearly, and it is hard not to believe that his sorrows were deeply felt.

We might say that, with Snepp, as with the British Order of the Garter, merit had damned little to do with it. In the scales of justice, amply measured, my own reckoning is that this man did not deserve the harshness of the judgment, and the penalties, dished up to him. But that sense of the personal deserts may offer the irony of bringing forth the principles of the case with an ever sharper clarity. That sharpness may lead to a conclusion tinged with melancholy: that the judgment in the case was in fact the right one; that the reasoning of the Court did indeed correct the skewed premises and reasoning of those earlier cases; and that the doctrines put in place now were truer doctrines, more rightly grounded, more rightly aimed. The pity of it all is that, when the judges finally got it right, they brought down the moon and stars, and the most severe of penalties, on young Frank Snepp. With the Pentagon Papers, the judges managed *not* to get it right in a case in which they could have protected the lives of American agents, and taught a notable lesson – namely, that even the Shadow Establishment, the elites formerly in power, were obliged to restrain themselves out of a respect for lawfulness. Instead, when the judges came closer to getting it right, they did it by visiting wreckage on the career of one young man.

The chief figure to have in mind, in tracking the opinion in *Snepp v. United States*, is Justice Byron White. He cannot be watched, his movement in reasoning cannot be followed, because he leaves, in this case, no paw prints. His own voice is not heard, his reasoning not sounded distinctly in an opinion

---

[4] When the Congress had withdrawn support, and the government of South Vietnam was collapsing under the assault of its enemy, Martin was staging a resistance in the embassy that seemed to defy any cool or detached calculation of the odds. Henry Kissinger, looking on with anguish from Washington, could remark to the Secretary of Defense that, after all, Martin had lost his son there. His persisting devotion to the purpose of the war could be explained, at that moment, by a distinctly personal interest, an interest that was taken to cloud his skill, as a diplomat, in reading, with cold realism, the situation before him. See Henry Kissinger, *Years of Renewal* (New York: Simon and Schuster, 1999), p. 543.

presented per curiam. But that makes the presence of White all the more significant in this particular case: White is hidden, and yet what is most striking in this case is that the opinion of the Court addresses, and then overturns, each argument that had been critical to White's own decision in the Pentagon Papers case. The reader may recall that three Republican judges in that case had voted in the minority, to sustain the injunctions. Two judges on the other side, Black and Douglas, were inclined to vote against any injunction, on any terms. White was part of the "swing judges" in the case – troubled, sensing that lives were genuinely at stake, and yet not sure that an injunction could be warranted in this particular case. He sought to explain the reasons for his hesitation, and he suggested alternatives, which a responsible jurist had to consider before resorting to anything as dramatic as an injunction to restrain publication. But now, with the advantage of time and further reflection, White apparently reversed himself on every point that was critical to his argument nine years earlier. And yet, because the opinion of the Court was offered per curiam, White could fold himself in, anonymously. He would not suffer the embarrassment of signing on now to an argument that he had rejected quite explicitly nine years earlier. At the same time, with his name unmentioned, he came under no pressure to offer an account of himself – to explain why he had come to change his mind. As it happens, the reasoning of the Court offers a sufficient explanation of why White would have changed his mind. What is missing then is only an acknowledgment from White that he had indeed changed his mind. But how illuminating it would have been had there been an avowal from White, joined with his own, earnest explanation that the Court had shifted; that the judges were now sustaining a different understanding of "prior restraints," an understanding quite at odds with the doctrines planted in *Near* and sustained in the Pentagon Papers case.

Of course, there was a ground of "plausible deniability" – in this case, a ground on which the judges might persuade themselves that they were not overruling *Near* and the Pentagon Papers case. They could try to persuade themselves that the case of *Snepp* could be entirely separated from those two earlier precedents. And the ground of that deniability could be: contract. It might be portentous to impose, through the law, a regimen of "prior restraints"; but it might be an entirely different matter if that regimen were imposed on people who had already consented to the prospect of having it imposed. That consent might be registered in a "contract" of employment. Or it might be contained in the conditions that people implicitly accept as the terms for entering employment. In the case of Snepp, entering the CIA, there had actually been an agreement, marking the sensitive nature of the work in intelligence. By the explicit terms of that agreement, Snepp pledged that he would "not . . . publish . . . any information or material relating to the Agency, its activities or intelligence activities generally, either during or after the terms of [his] employment . . . without specific prior approval by the Agency."[5] The government would later insist that this was no ordinary "contract" of employment, that it was closer to a "fiduciary" trust, and therefore that it brought obligations far more demanding. Snepp had, after all, the lives of other Americans in his hands. He professed to be deeply aware of that responsibility, and he seemed to have a heightened respect for that material he had in his possession. Indeed, that vaunted sense of the importance of the material seemed to come with the territory. It was the part of the mystique to be absorbed by almost everyone in the agency. There was the sense of possessing privileged information; information that, if casually made public, could be the source of unmentionable disasters.

Snepp amply bore that surety about the importance of the information he harbored, and therefore of the responsibilities he had been obliged to shoulder. But a precise sense of the information also marked, for him, a precise sense of the limits of those obligations: His duty, as he understood it, was to guard, conscientiously, any information that was "classified" and secret. In his commonsense understanding, though, his obligations could not extend to information that was not classified, not regarded by the government as especially dangerous or sensitive. And that seemed especially the case with information that was already part of the public record. For that reason he did not think that his obligations extended to his manuscript for *Decent Interval*, which involved a deep criticism of the American officials in Vietnam. And he thought it rather overdid things – rather touched the problem with hyperbole – to take this agreement he signed quickly, as a young recruit, and treat it so portentously as a "fiduciary" trust, lasting through his lifetime.

Still, the rudimentary sense of the matter was that this agreement was indeed affected by an awareness of the "special" work and dangers of the CIA. There had to be here a serious commitment to be careful, and fastidious, in subjecting oneself to a review and taking extra precautions before running the risk of revealing information that might be prejudicial to the interests of the country. That proposition could be affirmed with conviction by nearly everyone drawn to the CIA, if for no other reason than that it could confirm their own sense of self-importance. As the Court put it, citing from the agreement, there was a promise here by Snepp "not to disclose any classified information relating to the Agency without proper authorization."[6] In the District Court in Virginia, Judge Oren Lewis saw it that way, at least – and

---

[5] Cited in *Snepp v. United States*, 404 U.S. 507, at 507–8 (1980).
[6] *Ibid.*, at 508.

then some. Lewis, a Republican appointed in the last days of Eisenhower, seemed quite hostile to Snepp from the beginning to the end of the trial. Without engaging in any charades of measuring harms, direct or indirect, imminent or distant, Lewis found that Snepp's moves in publishing the book – breaking past the laws, evading any restraint on employees of the CIA – constituted *in itself* an "irreparable harm." For it suggested quite dramatically to the outside world that the American Executive was not in control of its own papers. Lewis found emphatically in favor of the government and brought down upon Snepp both of the penalties that the government had sought. First, there would be an injunction requiring Snepp to submit his writings in the future for "prepublication review." Second, there would be the imposition of a "constructive trust," confiscating all of the profits that Snepp might earn from publishing this book in violation of his "fiduciary obligation."

This decision by Judge Lewis was upheld by the Court of Appeals in its main lines: The judges agreed that Snepp had violated his contract and done "irreparable harm." They thought it quite reasonable to uphold the remarkable requirement of having Snepp submit all of his writings in advance to the CIA, forevermore. But for some reason, after accepting all of these premises, the Court declined to approve the constructive trust, stripping Snepp of his earnings. The judges seemed to think that the penalty went too far, for they thought that Snepp's fiduciary obligation extended only to the point of preserving the confidentiality of classified material. And the government had conceded that Snepp's book divulged no such classified material. The Court of Appeals thought that the judgment could be settled then in this way: The Court would confirm the government's charges against Snepp, but then limit the government to nominal damages – or perhaps punitive damages, if the government could actually prove to a jury that Snepp had been the cause of real injuries. In a dissenting view, Judge Hoffman argued that it was eminently reasonable to impose the constructive trust, because Snepp's contract "gave life to a fiduciary relationship and invested in Snepp the trust of the CIA." But then, too, in an argument that would resonate with the Court – and run back to Justice White's opinion in the Pentagon Papers case – Judge Hoffman insisted that even punitive damages would be both a speculative and inapt remedy for the wrongs charged to Snepp.

The Supreme Court came behind Judge Hoffman now, and sustained the complete array of penalties that Judge Lewis had imposed on Snepp in the District Court. But in sustaining the penalties, the Court also weighed in, responding to the objections of Justice Stevens in dissent. As it did that, the Court managed to fill in the reasons that were never formulated in the Pentagon Papers case. Stevens could not accept the main indictment leveled against Snepp, that he had breached his trust, for Snepp had never disclosed any confidential information. That is, Stevens did not see how the agreement with Snepp could possibly have covered material that was not confidential or classified, and so to impose a requirement of "clearance," or "prepublication review" was to impose a regime of censorship on an American citizen. Even if the Agency could argue that the material published by Snepp was "detrimental to vital national interests" or "identified as harmful," Stevens still did not think that the Agency had any authority to censor its employees, especially after they left the Agency, and especially when they were not dealing with classified material.[7]

Perhaps it was the curious style that came along with an opinion per curiam, but it seems strange, nevertheless, that the majority should have chosen to counter such an important argument in a footnote – and yet address that argument, I think, in a thoroughly compelling way: The Court observed that if it were simply a matter of publishing unclassified material, the Agency would not be that much concerned, for this kind of material is published about the Agency all the time. The more critical point lay elsewhere – as Justice Stevens's colleagues took care now to remind him:

> The problem is to ensure *in advance,* and by proper procedures, that information detrimental to the national interest is not published. Without a dependable prepublication review procedure, no intelligence agency or responsible Government official could be assured that an employee privy to sensitive information might not conclude on his own – innocently or otherwise – that it should be disclosed to the world.[8]

Even if it were entirely clear – and a matter beyond dispute – that Snepp had not revealed sensitive material, there was still something portentous in having an employee of the CIA now assert, in effect, nothing less than a right to make his own decision in "clearing" his own manuscript. Stating the point another way, let us assume that there was no dispute about the standards that should govern the decision to publish and to release information. Let us say that the writer and the Agency agree that no classified or sensitive material should be released. But we might apply those standards under two different regimes or arrangements:

1. The writer should withhold classified material from his book – but he himself should be the judge. He should scan the book himself and pledge that he will be fastidious in withholding, or excising, material that would be better kept secret.

---

[7] *Ibid.,* at 522.
[8] *Ibid.,* at 513, n.8; italics in the original.

2. The writer should withhold classified material from his book – but people should not act as judges in their own cause. They should not have the authority to make the final decision, when their interests, as writers, could tilt them to the side of revealing information previously held secret. Here, as elsewhere, the notion of checks and balances comes properly into play. There should be an institutional mechanism, something to suggest that the restraints of lawfulness are engaged. When the law assigns that authority to institutions, like the CIA, it is a way of recognizing that the interests of the writer are not the sole interests involved in the case; that there may indeed be a larger interest, of the community, at stake here as well.

That kind of distinction seemed to make eminent sense to the Court, and for that reason apparently the Court was willing to sustain the case for "prepublication review," regardless of whether Snepp happened to reveal classified information. One could have come down on this side, that is, even without attributing any malevolence or thoughtlessness to Snepp. The novelist Robertson Davies dealt, in one of his books, with the intriguing problem of forgeries in art, and he pointed out that forgers often reveal themselves by incorporating in their pictures, utterly without the awareness of the painter, styles and artifacts more redolent of their own times. And so, in one case, a painting was passed off as the work of the Flemish painter van Eck, whose life and work carried over from the end of the fourteenth century, on into the fifteenth. The picture in question contained a chained monkey, a figure often used as a symbol of fallen mankind, before the coming of Christ. Davies has one of his characters point out, though, that the monkey in the picture was hanging by his tail. The observation made little impression on the other connoisseurs gathered around the painting. One of them remarked that monkeys usually do hang by their tails. To which Davies's protagonist, a young painter, responded:

> They did not do so in Ghent in van Eck's day. That monkey is a *Cebus capucinus*, a New World monkey. The chained monkey of iconography is the *Macacus rhesus*, the Old World monkey. Such a monkey as that, with a prehensile tail, was unknown in Europe until the sixteenth century, and . . . Hubertus van Eyck died in 1426.[9]

Even the most acute and observant among us might not be aware of just how he has absorbed an assumption of the artifacts and conventions that envelop him. In a similar way, a writer like Snepp, who had been deeply

---

[9] Robertson Davies, *What's Bred in the Bone* (New York: Viking, 1985), pp. 351–52.

immersed in Vietnam and the life of intelligence there, might not have realized just what he was revealing, about Vietnam, or the workaday world of intelligence, as he set about the task of writing a memoir. He too might have profited from having had a second set of eyes looking over the manuscript. That was especially the case if that second editor could have been one tutored in the subject, and attentive then to the scene in Vietnam. He might have been alert, as others were not, to details in the narrative that were telling. They could have been references to places, persons, or things; they could have revealed a knowledge of settings, where meetings might have been held, or events that took place when no Americans were thought to be aware of them.

As it turned out, Snepp's own experience later offered an apt illustration of this very point. In the aftermath of his loss in the Supreme Court, and the seizure of his earnings from the book, he sought to bounce back and find additional sources of income by writing a novel. But the most dramatic source of his own experience, which could be the source of stories "novel" for the larger public, involved once again his work in intelligence in Vietnam. And so he drew once more on that part of his life. When he submitted the manuscript for review, the readers discovered that he had named someone who was still active as a "CIA operative." That person had been named, he found, in another book. Yet, apparently, that naming had slipped past the Agency, and even Snepp admitted that it was reasonable not to dare the fates by printing the name once again. As a measure of Snepp's own honesty – and his evident concern not to be the cause of injury to agents – he observed that "indignant though I was, I couldn't endanger the operative. I removed the name." He went on to allow that "if the Agency had been careless, so had I."[10] Even the most fastidious among us may make mistakes, or not catch every slip; and when the lives of agents and citizens may be at stake, it would take a rare obtuseness to insist that even the most conscientious employee of the CIA should be exempt from those checks and balances, those restraints of lawfulness, that are useful for us all.

Even if Frank Snepp himself happened to be conscientious, his refusal to submit the manuscript in advance could be taken then, with ample reason, as a breach of security and trust. And with that predicate it became reasonable to conclude that Snepp's fault here could indeed have been the source of an "irreparable injury." The claim did not lend itself just yet to precise, empirical measures, and yet there was testimony that became quite plausible.

[10] Snepp, *Irreparable Harm, supra*, note 1, at 357–58.

Admiral Stansfield Turner, Director of the CIA under Jimmy Carter, came in to testify before the District Court, and he offered the surmise that would be taken seriously. As the Supreme Court reported, in its per curiam opinion, Turner "testified without contradiction that Snepp's book and others like it have seriously impaired the effectiveness of American intelligence operations." Turner himself put it in these terms:

> Over the last six months, we have had a number of sources discontinue work with us. We have had more sources tell us that they are very nervous about continuing work with us. We have had very strong complaints from a number of foreign intelligence services with whom we conduct liaison, who have questioned whether they should continue exchanging information with us, for fear it will not remain secret. I cannot estimate to you how many potential sources or liaison arrangements have never germinated because people were unwilling to enter into business with us.[11]

The Court had said, in a telling phrase, that these effects were attributed to "Snepp's book and others like it." That would suggest that the judges were not entirely sure just how much, if any of the problem, could be attributed to Snepp's book. And so they covered, with a sweeping gesture, other books that had appeared recently, involving exposés of the CIA. There were books written by Phillip Agee and Victor Marchetti, and they were begetting a spate of other books, building on the interest in the embarrassments of the CIA.[12] There were some rumors that Phillip Agee would begin naming or "outing" American agents abroad. All of these revelations could contribute plausibly to an inclination on the part of intelligence services abroad to start backing away and keeping a prudent distance. But casting blame on Agee or Marchetti or Snepp was largely a distraction, which diverted attention from the most dramatic event, which had sent tremors abroad to American allies and their intelligence services. The late Claire Sterling, a seasoned, savvy reporter, had the occasion to deal closely with intelligence services in France, Israel, and other places, as she did her book on the international terrorist network, and on the shooting of the Pope in 1981. Sterling reported that the French in particular had become "markedly reluctant to share [information] with the CIA since Watergate – lest it 'show up in the next day's *New York Times.*'"[13]

---

[11] *Snepp v. United States, supra*, note 5, at 512.

[12] See Philip Agee, *Inside the Company: CIA Diary* (New York: Stonehill, 1975), and Victor Marchetti and John Marks, *The CIA and the Cult of Intelligence* (New York: Knopf, 1974).

[13] Claire Sterling, *Time of the Assassins* (New York: Holt, Rinehart & Winston, 1985), p. 196.

Watergate was bound up with the Pentagon Papers in a manner that was too readily overlooked. What Turner had to say then, in conjecturing about Snepp's book, could have been said just as plausibly in regard to the Pentagon Papers. Still, that testimony depended on conjecture about the reasons that moved intelligence services to back away from collaboration with the CIA. That there was a certain backing away is something that could be confirmed now, asserted and attested, by witnesses. But the reason for that backing away was as evident and accessible at the time of the Pentagon Papers case. Again, as Justice Harlan suggested, those possibilities were simply built into the logic of the Supreme Court taking the case. For in taking the case, the Court had made a show of subordinating the Executive to the authority of the federal courts in this field. To put it another way, there was nothing the Court knew, in the case of Snepp in 1980, that could not have been seen in 1971, with the Pentagon Papers case, by those with the eyes to see. Or they could be seen at least by worldly men who could grasp at once the practical implications that had to spring from the Court's handling of the case.

It becomes hard then to look closely at this case without concluding that the political class, having the benefit of more time and reflection, were now recording, in a backhanded way, that they had made a serious mistake in the case of the Pentagon Papers. The tip-off, or the thing to be noticed here by those who track the Court closely, is the way that the Court, in effect, called back the reasoning that proved pivotal in the case of the Pentagon Papers. During the oral argument in the Pentagon Papers case, Justice White had confessed his own strain: He took seriously the prospect that the lives of American agents would be endangered, and so he was reluctant to lift the legal inhibitions on the publishing of the Papers. But on the other hand, he was reluctant to overturn what he thought was now a deeply anchored principle of the law, and permit a "prior restraint" on publication. Under the press of the case, he arrived at this resolution: He would not have the Court impose a prior restraint on the strength of its equity powers, without the direction and support of a statute; but he would be prepared to uphold a prosecution under the Espionage Act.

And yet, that manner of resolving the case invited the further questions that I raised earlier: What would White, or the Department of Justice, know on the day *after* publication that had not been known on the day before? If there was a concern that agents would be endangered, the government still might not know whether those agents were endangered. Was the government to wait until agents were killed? But in that event, there would still be a need to establish an empirical connection between the death of the agent and the appearance of any particular publication associated with the Pentagon

Papers. The problem was still affected on all sides by speculation and conjecture. And on the basis of that conjecture, the government would actually be seeking now to punish someone. In contrast, there was something immanently more defensible in saying: (1) The publication, under these circumstances, is freighted with serious danger, and as a matter of prudence – and concern for your fellow citizens – we enjoin you not to publish. (2) We do not seek your punishment; we seek only to restrain you from doing a harm.

Without quite drawing the strands of the rationale together in this way, the Court now managed to incorporate the reasoning that finally informs this position. The Court of Appeals had sustained the judgment against Snepp in the District Court, but removed the "constructive trust" as a penalty. The District Court would have had the government content itself with nominal damages, or seek punitive damages, if it could prove the harm wrought by Snepp's publication. But in the view of the Supreme Court, this jural compromise rather missed the main points in principle. For the Supreme Court, the penalty of the "constructive trust" was tied in directly with the main offense: Snepp's willingness to publish on his own, without institutional restraints. The constructive trust bore a connection to that wrong in principle – a more apt connection than anything offered in the alternatives of nominal or punitive damages. In the first place, there was no affectation about engaging in the measurement of harms, or producing some false formula, or fiction, which pretends that a material harm has been done. The Court put it this way: "If the agent publishes unreviewed material in violation of his fiduciary and contractual obligation, the trust remedy simply requires him to disgorge the benefits of his faithlessness."[14] Again, putting aside the question of whether this language was not too harsh in relation to Frank Snepp, the Court was simply relying here on a deep moral axiom of the law: namely, that people should not benefit from their wrongdoing. On the basis of this axiom, in recent years, the law has denied to serial killers the right to make a windfall by collecting royalties from their memoirs.

In contrast, the arguments for nominal or punitive damages were in different ways rather inapt. If a serious wrong had been done, why would "nominal" damages offer a response that was plausible in any way? As the Court put it, "Nominal damages are a hollow alternative, certain to deter no one."[15] They would hardly be compensation for the families of agents or soldiers who were killed. Nor would they exactly compensate for the injury to the national interest in projects that were ruined. On the other hand, "the punitive damages

---

[14] *Snepp v. United States, supra,* note 5, at 515.
[15] *Ibid.,* at 514.

recoverable after a jury trial are *speculative* and unusual."[16] Speculative: One word, but it told all. It marked the recognition that, even after publication, the measurement of harm still involved conjecture and speculation. I take this passage to mark nothing less than Justice White's recognition that the assumption on which his argument hinged in the Pentagon Papers case was decisively mistaken: The task of proving the harm might not be in any degree more manageable on the day *after* publication than it had been on the day before. As brief as it was, this passage in the text stood in opposition to the argument White had made, with such strain, in the earlier case, and White offered no separate note of explanation. I take the implication of the passage to be then that, if White had it to do all over again in the Pentagon Papers case, he would have been more likely to come down on a different side and voted with Burger, Blackmun, and Harlan.

That sense of the matter seemed to be confirmed as the Court elaborated on this argument. If the government took up the task, say, of seeking punitive damages, it would have to produce evidence of "tortious conduct." What that meant, in the case of the government, was bringing forth evidence to show the injury done to agents abroad, or to operations of a "clandestine" nature. That was, to put it mildly, an awkwardness for a government that was out to shield the identity of its agents and the character of its operations. The awkwardness promised to deepen into a graver liability if the government were to be open then, in turn, to cross-examination and the demand, on the part of the defense, to more and more documents. As the Court put it:

> Proof of the tortious conduct necessary to sustain an award of punitive damages might force the Government to disclose some of the very confidences that Snepp promised to protect. The trial of such a suit, before a jury if the defendant so elects, would subject the CIA and its officials to probing discovery into the Agency's highly confidential affairs. Rarely would the Government run this risk. In a letter introduced at Snepp's trial, former CIA Director Colby noted the analogous problem in criminal cases. Existing law, he said, "requires the revelation in open court of confirming or additional information of such a nature that the potential damage to the national security preclude prosecution."[17]

That is a course, then, that the government could not practicably take. The prospect brought back again the case of the *Chicago Tribune* during the Second World War, revealing by indirection that the government had broken the Japanese code. If the Japanese had somehow missed that point,

---

[16] *Ibid.*; italics added.
[17] *Ibid.*, at 514–15.

in the story filed in the *Tribune*, the government was hardly willing to call it to their attention by waging an important public trial on that issue. The use of a prosecution had to be the clumsiest and most inapt device for the government under circumstances of this kind, and the Court summed up the matter, quite properly: "When the Government cannot secure its remedy without unacceptable risks, it has no remedy at all."[18]

To this, I'm inclined to say, Amen. But then one is tempted to ask, Why did the Court not see precisely the same, inescapable arguments nine years earlier, in the Pentagon Papers case? And why did it not grasp as well the truth it finally grasped in the case of *Snepp* on the matter of penalties? Writing of the punitive damages, the judges remarked that "even if recovered, they may bear no relation to either the Government's irreparable loss or Snepp's unjust gain."[19] Again, put aside Frank Snepp, and replace him more aptly with the publishers of the *New York Times* and the *Washington Post*. Let us suppose that the government had followed the hints of Justice White and come forth with a prosecution under the Espionage Act. Consider again this ensemble of concerns in the scale: that American agents abroad might be killed; that American operations could be disrupted; that allies throughout the world might find it hazardous to share information with us or engage in joint projects. If these were the harms at stake, how would they have been remedied in any way by (a) a stiff award of damages, against the *Times* and the *Post*, or (b) the jailing of Katharine Graham or Arthur Hays Sulzberger? Would any of these things have compensated families for the losses of life? Would they have repaired the harms done to the interests of the nation in protecting the lives of its people? When we cast the alternative precisely in this way, we might see again that the move of the government for an injunction was in fact the most measured and reasonable thing that a government of law might do in securing its interests, while doing the least damage to other persons and institutions. There would be no attempt to put a newspaper out of business with a knockout award for damages. Nor would there be a pall cast on the freedom of the press through an overhanging threat of putting publishers and editors in jail. There would be a move only to restrain or delay publication. And in the case of the Pentagon Papers, the aim might have been merely to restrain the publication long enough that agents of the government could review the papers and make their entreaties to the publishers.

If the argument I have put in place here is right, the Supreme Court finally made its way to an understanding of the layers of mistakes that the judges had

---

[18] *Ibid.*, at 515.
[19] *Ibid.*, at 514.

fallen into in the Pentagon Papers case. But the judges achieved that clarity now at the expense of young Frank Snepp, hardly a fitting demonstration of doing justice with a sense of proportion. At the same time, the Court allowed the Establishment press and media to keep floating serenely in the assurance that, with the decision on the Pentagon Papers, they had established a landmark guarantee of their freedom – and a notable accretion to the public good. Through the strange muffling of an opinion per curiam, the Court managed to conceal that it had thoroughly rejected every strand of reasoning that was critical both to the Pentagon Papers case and *Near v. Minnesota*.

As I suggested earlier, there has been one colorable ground on which it could be maintained that the decision in Snepp had no bearing on the precedents of *Near* and the Pentagon Papers, and that ground involved the concept of the contract. The defenders of those landmark cases might conceivably try to distinguish them from *Snepp* in this way: The Court, in *Snepp*, had merely permitted a regime of "prior restraint" on publication in cases in which a person had explicitly obligated himself, in a contract of employment, to accept a requirement of official review in advance of publication.

That argument has had an obvious appeal on the surface of things. But one of the ironies in the problem is that this argument is finally embarrassed and undone by Justice Stevens's argument in dissent. Stevens had insisted, after all, that Snepp had engaged, on his side, the core principles of the First Amendment, which he took to be at one with the core principles of the Constitution itself. And yet, if that were indeed the case, then – as Stevens argued – Snepp could not have been free to waive these fundamental rights even through the instrument of a contract. In taking on that argument, Stevens ran back first to the common law and its enforcement of "covenants." Because those covenants usually restricted an individual's "freedom of trade," they were enforceable only if they could survive a "rule of reason." And what did that regimen of reason entail? As Stevens recalled, the restraint in the covenant had to be "reasonably necessary to protect a legitimate interest of the employer (such as an interest in confidentiality)"; that the restraint not be any wider in scope than those interests required; and "that the employer's interest not be outweighed by the public interest."[20] Stevens then annexed the rights of the First Amendment to that "public interest." He feared that this "drastic new remedy," fashioned for *Snepp*, would impair "a citizen's right to criticize his government." And "inherent in this prior restraint is the risk that the reviewing agency will misuse its authority to delay the publication of a critical work or to persuade an author to modify the contents of his

---

[20] *Ibid.*, at 519.

work beyond the demands of secrecy."[21] All very plausible. But then again, there is no legitimate power of the government that may not be misused. And correlatively, it must stand as an axiom that the possibility of misuse cannot supply a ground for denying a power that is otherwise legitimate. Still, Stevens had evidently persuaded himself that all of this was in fact too much to give up, that it could not be given up without creating a deep flaw in the very structure of the First Amendment. For it would allow now a system of restraint, virtually at odds with the principles that the Court had articulated in *Near v. Minnesota* and other cases. In that event, he was prepared to say that, even if Snepp had accepted these conditions as part of a contract, that contract was unenforceable, because it was incompatible with the First Amendment.

But it seems to me that Stevens must be saying something even stronger. Even if Snepp accepted that contract here and now, Stevens's argument committed him to the conclusion that the contract was still not enforceable because it was invalid as a contract. We should remind ourselves of some older language, and ancient understandings, that support at least the form of Stevens's argument. Was Stevens not, after all, drawing on the logic of "unalienable rights"? If, for example, it was indeed wrong in principle for some men to rule others as slaves, then human beings may not waive or "alienate" those rights, even in the form of a contract. And so, even libertarians on the order of John Stuart Mill or, more recently, Milton Friedman, have insisted that there are unalienable rights that stand as limits to our claims of personal liberty. Chief then among the restraints on our liberty is the principle that bars us from contracting away our personal freedom. In this manner, the American courts have refused to uphold contracts for peonage, in which free persons, with the competence to make contracts, have contracted themselves into a form of servitude.[22] To put it another way, to say that it is "wrong" to make slaves of human beings is to say that it is wrong to will that arrangement for anyone, for everyone. If that is the case, that person seeking to contract away his freedom counts as an "anyone," and it would be as wrong to will slavery for oneself as for anyone else.

---

[21] *Ibid.*, at 526.

[22] See, for example, *Bailey v. Alabama*, 219 U.S. 219 (1911), and cf. Milton Friedman, *Capitalism and Freedom* (Chicago: University of Chicago Press, 1960), pp. 33–34. In all strictness, though, Friedman's discussion centers on "madmen" and small children. For these people, he was willing to restrict their freedom to make decisions for themselves. His discussion rather points to unalienable rights, but he may nevertheless have left open the question of a personal freedom, for competent adults, to contract themselves into an arrangement of indentured servitude.

To the extent, then, that we have engaged a genuine principle of justice or moral judgment, a proposition that holds true of necessity, we would be dealing with a proposition that could not be coherently denied – or overthrown in a contract. If Smith had not been born at the time of the crime, there are no circumstances under which his punishment could be justified. Nor is there any conceivable set of benefits, or rollicking good consequences, that could make the punishment of Smith anything other than wrong. And for all of these reasons, the punishment of Smith would not suddenly become plausible or coherent if we were told that Smith himself had consented to the punishment as part of a *contract*.

That could conceivably be the groundwork for the claim that Justice Stevens sought to put in place in the case of *Snepp*. But in order to establish the rightness of that claim, Stevens would have had to show that there was a genuine principle of that kind that bars the restraint of publication in advance; that there were no circumstances under which it could possibly be justified to restrain publication in advance. For reasons we have already considered at some length, that is not an argument to which most functional people could accede. And quite plainly, neither could most of Stevens's colleagues. Neither in the case of the Pentagon Papers, nor in the case of Snepp, could that position clearly command the vote of more than one judge. And as we have seen, there have been numerous cases, known and confirmed by the courts, in which a restraint in advance could be seen as quite reasonable and justified. Where Stevens had it compellingly right was in recognizing the logic, and implications, of an "unalienable" right. If it were truly wrong in principle, wrong under all circumstances, to restrain publication in advance, then Stevens would surely have been right about *Snepp*: Even if Snepp had accepted all of these conditions freely as part of a contract, it could not have been justified to subject Snepp to the requirement of reviewing his manuscripts in advance of publication and barring him from publishing.

But I would point out here that something quite emphatic must flow on the other side from the refusal of Stevens's colleagues to follow him. Their refusal makes sense only if they did not think it wrong, under all circumstances, to impose a restraint on publication in advance. Yet that is to say, their decision holds together only if they recognized now, as a matter of common sense, that the rejection of "prior restraint" formed no real principle of justice, or no genuine principle of the Constitution or the First Amendment. But if that is the ground, the only ground, on which their decision in this case becomes intelligible, then I submit the matter again, this time in a form that would resist, I think, any evasion: The Court, in *Snepp*, must truly have rejected, or overturned, the claim that there is a deep "principle" of the law at the heart of both the Pentagon Papers case and *Near v. Minnesota*; a principle that bars a restraint in advance of publication, even if a person accepts that restraint himself.

The sad part, again, is that these moments of clarity were gained at the expense of Frank Snepp, who surely did not deserve to feel, as acutely as he did, the terrible swift sword of the law. Still, the story of Frank Snepp would bring, in time, some further ironies, and some of them might have offset the bitterness of Snepp's loss. For the understanding in the *Snepp* case came to be applied to some of Snepp's own adversaries. In that fuller application of the principle, Snepp might have found a deeper vindication, even though it worked, at the same time, to vindicate the principles that defined the new position of the Court. And so, vindicated in the same measure was the wisdom of moving away from the faux jurisprudence and the clichés of *Near v. Minnesota* and the Pentagon Papers.

The most compelling part of Snepp's own complaints involved the asymmetry in the policy of the government, or the double standard at work: Snepp could be prosecuted, but as he pointed out, nothing would be done to William Colby, who had served as director of the CIA. Colby would have his own stories to tell about Vietnam. Some of them would be screened from publication when his manuscript was submitted for review at headquarters. But the same manuscript would be sent abroad at the same time, and when the French translation appeared, it appeared without the excisions that had been made in Langley, Virginia. The result was that Colby had circumvented the procedures of the CIA, the same procedures that triggered the action against Snepp.

But then, step by step, something like justice began to unfold. Jimmy Carter's second attorney general was Benjamin Civiletti, a man, as Snepp said, "who'd done so much to finish me off," after the prosecution launched by Griffin Bell. In Snepp's reading, Civiletti saw the potential reach of the holding in his case, and he sought to cabin the ruling. Civiletti issued a directive that sought to rule out such lawsuits except in cases of people who had actually signed agreements pledging secrecy, or with publishers who had actually encouraged people to violate the rules on security. But when the political seasons brought in the governance of a new party, the Reagan administration did not see the justification for confining the rule in the *Snepp* case in that way. The new administration insisted, rather, on a more rigorous application of the ruling in *Snepp*. And one of the first people caught in the new regimen of enforcement was William Colby. In the fall of 1981, the Department of Justice charged that Colby had breached his agreement with the CIA when he permitted Simon and Schuster to review his memoir before it had been reviewed by the censors at the Agency. By the end of the year, Colby's lawyers had worked out a settlement with the government: The former Director would pay a fine of $10,000, and he would promise not to renege again on his obligations. Snepp thought the result merely a "slap on the wrist" in comparison with his own punishment, but that was altogether too flippant. Consider, after all, what had taken place: The same rules that were brought into play against Snepp were applied to a former Director of the Agency. He was reproached, and subjected to a penalty in the law; he was treated as a lawbreaker. And as a further consequence, he would be put under the same regimen that applied to Snepp – the requirement that he submit in advance, to the review of the Agency, anything he wrote. He would be governed, that is, by the same law that was brought forth and justified in the case of *Snepp*.

But that was not all, for the laying of charges so publicly against a high official of state had the effect of throwing the fear of the law into many other celebrities, including two who had some role in the afflictions of Snepp. When he heard about the charges filed against Colby, Griffin Bell, the Attorney General who had brought the action against Snepp, now came forward to submit his own memoirs for review. As a result, he saw several sections deleted at the hands of censors serving under the Reagan administration. But then Snepp must have felt that the circle was truly completed when the Reagan administration applied the same rules to snare Admiral Stansfield Turner, the Director who had backed the action against Snepp and testified against him in court. Turner, too, had a memoir, and the censors in the new administration demanded over a hundred deletions, ranging – as Turner complained – "from borderline issues to the ridiculous." If ever there was a poetic case of inducing people to live under the laws they had enforced against others, this surely had to be it. Turner, with his worldliness and his derring-do, threatened to publish his memoir anyway, unexpurgated, and leave the burden to the government to launch a suit to restrain him. But as Snepp reported, the Department of Justice "outfoxed him": Instead of seeking an injunction, they suggested that they would wait for his publication and then sue him, in the same way that the CIA, under Turner, had sued Snepp. Turner, miffed and stymied, called the action "irresponsible": "The threat to take me to court after the fact could not have retrieved the secrets. It could only have exacted retribution."[23] But yes, exactly. With that epiphany the former Director grasped, at once, the rationale for the prosecution of Snepp, and the reason that a review in

[23] See Snepp, *supra*, note 1, p. 360.

advance was a more fitting remedy than sending someone to jail or eliciting an award for damages. Surely, it may be the source of some satisfaction to Frank Snepp that the Director would come finally to appreciate, the hard way – with a direct, personal cost – the reason behind the judgment that he had joined in leveling at Snepp.

In March 1983, the Reagan administration brought forth a directive that would begin with the rule in *Snepp* and apply it more widely in the Executive branch, with more agreements for confidentiality. Snepp thought the measure draconian, as he had no doubt thought it draconian in his own case. But if there were grounds for regarding that judgment in the case of Snepp as reasonable, then there surely must have been a justification for applying the same rule more broadly to many other, comparable situations, where the breach of confidentiality could be quite injurious. And what better way to test the justice of what was done, in relation to Snepp, than by measuring the willingness to apply the same rule across the board, to everyone else – including, as we have seen, the very people who did so much to torment Frank Snepp? In all of this Snepp might see a passion for secrecy run amok. But from another angle, might we not see something far more redeeming, which we have not seen so much in recent years?: the willingness of people highly placed, in the political class, to live under the same laws that they bring forth so freely for others.

As it turned out, President Reagan modified the severity of the new exec-utive order when he encountered resistance on Capitol Hill. But as Snepp noted, Reagan's successor, George Bush, "tightened the vise and by early 1990 over 140,000 employees of forty-eight federal agencies and one million government contractors were bound by some sort of secrecy pact." Beyond that, several congressional committees thought it warranted to adopt similar rules, and Justice Sandra Day O'Connor, as a new appointee to the Court, "required her law clerks to sign *Snepp*-type covenants."[24]

But again, whether the arrangement is draconian or justified depends on the question of whether the judgment in the case of *Snepp* might have been justified. If there is reason to regard it finally as reasonable and defensible, then it should be no cause of concern if an apt rule is applied more widely to other cases, in which it might be defensible in the same measure. It may be indecorous to remind people, but the rules would not have been enforced with such severity had we not had the experience, in dramatic cases, of people in the government overthrowing their obligations. When trust does indeed break down, and serious injuries may be at stake, it should hardly come as a

---

[24] *Ibid.*

surprise that the resort to the law becomes, in turn, ever more explicit and emphatic. And when casting about, looking for objects of censure, it would reveal a curious vision to look only to people in office. With the Pentagon Papers in mind as another, apt model, we would notice also those people outside the government who had posed, in one scale, the potential damage to the interests of the country and, in the other, their own freedom to publish. And then resolved the issue in their own favor.

I have suggested that, if justice was done here, it was, in the case of Frank Snepp, a rough justice. Of all the people who deserved to have the weight of the law brought down upon them, Snepp could not stand high in the ranks of villainy. One friend, highly placed in the Senate Committee on Intelligence in the 1980s, recalled that the sympathies of the staff ran heavily in favor of Snepp. As this veteran of the Hill remarked, "he was a young man who told the truth." The experience might only have confirmed that Justice may not only be blind, but also, occasionally, oafish: When the judges had an access of clear-headedness, when the recognition finally broke through that something had gone wrong with the Pentagon Papers, something that needed to be corrected, it was one of the sad ironies dished up by life that Snepp's case should suddenly appear as the clearest vehicle for clarifying the issues anew and settling the law in a different cast. The changes would find a firmer ground in the deep axioms of the law than the slogans they had replaced, dressed up as jural principles. That they were delivered at the expense of Frank Snepp, rather than a corporation like the *New York Times*, is a misfortune. But the case nevertheless generated some telling lessons, which tended to confirm the new cast of law that it marked. For one thing, Snepp's own experience – and his candor – revealed the way that even a good man could slip inadvertently into the oversights, or lapses, that made a review by a detached and "responsible" body eminently useful. The fact that the rule articulated in his case was then applied more widely across the board, to people high in the government; that it was applied to some of Snepp's most prominent tormentors; that it was applied to conservatives and liberals alike, does suggest dimensions of the case that are powerfully redeeming. The main thing missing, however, is the recognition that the reasoning in the *Snepp* case should have applied quite as forcefully to the *New York Times* and the *Washington Post*.

And yet there is, standing before us, in the case of *Snepp*, an example that continues, even to this day, to yield the deeper lessons that belie the reigning fictions of the law. As in many other instances, the lessons are contained in things so much before us that they are hardly any longer visible. The most striking exhibit in this regard is the very book, or memoir, with which I began this account. Frank Snepp's *Irreparable Harm* was not published until 1999, nearly twenty years after he had lost his case. In that interval, he had to reassemble the ingredients of his life. He showed his resilience by making his living as a writer, by manifesting his gifts once again. And as this memoir shows, he had cultivated his powers to a notably higher pitch. He became reconciled with his father, from whom he had been estranged. He schooled himself in the law of the First Amendment; and he gained access to the papers of Thurgood Marshall, an access he would use adroitly in explaining and shaping his story. In short, many things happened in the interval that altered or deepened his life. And yet, this book too, this book restating his grievances and chronicling his experience, was submitted for review, in advance, to a board at the CIA. In other words, the system of review and restraint, put in place in 1979–80, had continued for nearly twenty years. That a system of that kind could be in place at all, for a year, a week, or a day, has been regarded, since *Near v. Minnesota*, as a prospect virtually unthinkable. But Snepp's own living example should be enough to show that an arrangement precisely of the kind at issue in *Near v. Minnesota* is not only not unthinkable, but evidently, also, quite practicable. It may not be congenial to the parties concerned, but it is well within the state of the art, and while it has been at work, the fabric of freedom under the Constitution has not suffered any notable impairment. The freedom available to the press in the United States would still have to be regarded as far wider than the freedom available under any other regime claiming to be a constitutional order.

But has it worked well, or justly? The argument against its justice must be the same argument that was brought forth in the case of *Near*: namely, that no real newspaper or journal could function under these arrangements, with a kind of censorship, and still have the character of independent journals, free to discuss issues of real consequence. As I have suggested, the argument on the other side, never fully stated, might have been put in this way: The journal would not be put out of business by the law; the editors would not be jailed; but the newspaper would have to function, under the supervision of a court, to assure simply that the pattern of defamation that brought forth the judgment of the court would not be repeated. The laws of defamation presupposed that it was possible to judge the difference between publications that were defamatory and assaulting, and publications that were lively and contentious without being defamatory. If judges and juries could make those kinds of discriminations, then in principle they must have the wit to recognize when they see "more of the same." In theory, then, it should have been possible for Jay Near's *Saturday Press* to work under the ultimate superintendence of a court, while still preserving a vigorous, substantive newspaper.

Purists in the First Amendment may concede reluctantly that these possibilities must be there in principle, but they might argue that the scheme simply cannot work in practice. Yet, to this comeback Snepp's book itself might possibly stand, in turn, as a telling refutation. *Irreparable Harm* is a serious book, written by a serious writer who has evidently become, over twenty years, even more accomplished as a writer. This memoir, succeeding his earlier memoir, is not only a work of maturity, reflecting the strains of his experience; it is the memoir of a man who has come to a resolution. He has, in many places, a firmer ground for his complaints, while at the same time more detachment and candor about his own faults. What comes forth in the book – as a measure of the man and his experience – is the record of a writer grown more deeply artful, and a good man. The book went through the process of review or clearance. It could be, of course, that after twenty years, things have softened. But the book, screened by the CIA, contains sharp, biting criticisms of people high in the government. It is a record of betrayal and corruption, with hard things said against people of importance, and it came through, in that essential character, even with the screening by the government.

Snepp could no doubt offer examples of things even more biting, of charges running even deeper, that he was compelled to excise. And yet, many writers find themselves cutting material of this kind, where the cuts make them wince, and they are often surprised to hear the judgments of their editors that the book does not lose its edge, even with those cuts. In some instances, in fact, the edge of the book is sharpened. It is hard to imagine a book with an edge much sharper, written under conditions of unrestricted freedom. And on the other side, we have evidence every day of books written under freedom that have no comparable edge or force. But apart from the sharpness of the book, or its compelling qualities as a story, Frank Snepp managed to provide the singular example that by itself dissolves the clichés that have been marshaled over the years against censorship, or even against the regime of restraint that was contained in *Near*. Under a system of having his manuscripts reviewed in advance, Frank Snepp did not only produce a vigorous, cutting, substantive argument against the people who prosecuted him. He managed to produce, at the same time, nothing less than a serious work of art.

Seven

And Yet ... A Good Word on Behalf of the Legal Positivists

But then again ... let me say a word on behalf of legal positivism. I say "then again," because I have expended most of my slender arts as a writer over the last thirty years in making the case for natural rights and natural law. I have been part, that is, of a project, joined by some gifted writers in the academy, to restore the tradition of natural law, and work then against the current so dominant in our times. That current has been defined, of course, by moral relativism in forms now so familiar that most people are hardly even aware of them. Historians seem barely conscious of any vice of "historicism," but they seem to fall easily into the assumption, for example, that the American Founders were men of their own age. The sentiments of the Declaration of Independence had stirred the souls of that age, and there is no gainsaying their deep political effect; and yet the historians understand, with a knowing wink, that the "self-evident" truths of the Declaration were merely the sentiments that summoned credence *at the time*. Almost no historian admits to believing, as Lincoln did, that the proposition "all men are created equal" was in fact, as the Founders thought, a self-evident or necessary truth, "applicable to all men and all times." We find about us now, in the academy, students drawn almost entirely from families claiming to be Christian, Jewish, and Muslim, and yet most of these students are apparently persuaded, at the same time, that understandings of right and wrong must always be "relative" to the "culture" in which they are invented and sustained. From this perspective, we would presume that the Ten Commandments were essentially municipal regulations, dealing with the immediate vicinity of Mt. Sinai.

Conservatives in our politics may decorously turn aside from a vulgar relativism, but they too have absorbed the currents of the age. In their case, that absorption takes the form of a polite diffidence, a certain backing away from the claim to know of "moral truths." In most instances, that backing away comes with the aversion to natural law: Some notable conservative jurists have registered a deep dubiety about natural law because they have seen liberal judges soaring off, untethered, conjuring up new, implausible claims of "constitutional rights" once their forensic skills have been liberated from the text of the Constitution. To put it another way, the conservatives find a more prudent and secure ground to the law by fastening on the positive law of the Constitution. But that move, offered in the name of prudence, incorporates layers of other mistakes. Most critically, there is the self-refuting fallacy I have already noted, the fallacy of presuming that the presence of disagreement, on matters of interpretation, marks the absence of truth. In the law, as anywhere else, the fact that any idea has been misused, or used wrongly, does not itself prove that the idea itself is untrue. The array of opinions on "natural right," the proliferation of new, extravagant claims of rights, cannot itself prove that there is no such thing as "natural right." The very notion of a misuse implies its own, apt remedy: For it implies that one can understand, in the first place, the difference between a misuse, or a wrongful use, and a rightful use; between interpretations that are plausible or implausible, true or false. The remedy lies then mainly in sharpening our sense of how we have made those discriminations. But for the conservative lawyer, the prudential backing away from natural law produces, in its momentum, a backing away precisely from that confidence in reason itself as the ground of moral judgment. It becomes a step toward backing into a "soft relativism."

At the same time, the prudential remedy turns out to remedy nothing. We have ample experience by now to have seen that even judges focused on the text of the Constitution may fall into the most intense disagreements on the meaning of such terms as "compelled to be a witness against himself," to say nothing, of course, of "due process of law" or the "equal protection of the laws." There would not seem to be anything cloudy, anything wanting in clarity, in that provision in the Sixth Amendment on the right of a defendant "to be confronted with the witnesses against him." And yet Justice Scalia was astonished to the point of outrage that most of his colleagues were willing to sustain an arrangement, in Maryland, for receiving the accusations of a child over closed-circuit television. The child could still be questioned, her facts and testimony could be challenged, in testing the truth of the accusation. But for Scalia that was not enough. In his judgment, that provision in the Sixth Amendment could be satisfied with nothing other than a "face to face" encounter.[1] Even more recently, Scalia wrote for a divided Court on the question of whether the Confrontation Clause would be violated if a trial

---

[1] See *Maryland v. Craig*, 497 U.S. 836 (1990).

court accepted for the record the words of a dying victim. Those words put the blame on the assailant for acting without provocation, but that testimony could not be "confronted" and tested.[2]

My point, again, is that even some of the clearest passages in the Constitution, touching genuine principles of justice, have not delivered us from deep disagreements about the meaning of these phrases as they come before us in cases. I have argued in another place that, in dealing with these controversies, in applying the Constitution to the cases that arise in our law, it becomes necessary to trace these passages back, beyond the text of the Constitution, to those deeper principles that lie behind them.[3] In effect, then, we are making our way to those axioms or those principles of the natural law that will have to provide, of necessity, the ground of the law. In the generation of the Founding, John Marshall, Alexander Hamilton, and James Wilson showed, in the most luminous way, their awareness of those "first principles" that underlie the positive law. But in our own day the lawyers drawn to a "conservative jurisprudence" tend to cling tightly to the positive law in order to avoid any temptation to be drawn to "first principles" and the seductions of "natural law reasoning." And yet, they curiously fail to notice that their own rules of construction, their commitment to the positive law, cannot find their source or authority in the positive law. Their schemes of prudence make eminent sense. But they make that sense because they find their source and justification in the reasoning supplied over the years by the natural law.[4]

My good friend Robert Bork has defined himself quite sharply over the years as a positivist on matters jural. He has held to that position most strenuously even as he has been a moralist of the most reliable judgment. In an exchange

---

[2] See *Giles v. California* (June 2008). The assailant had argued that he was acting in self-defense. The majority in the Court thought that the Confrontation Clause should finally weigh in the balance to rule out that kind of testimony as decisive. The minority, led by Justice Breyer, seemed to be guided by the principle that people should not profit from their wrongdoing: In this case, the act of killing the woman should not play to the advantage of the killer by ruling out the most damning testimony against him.

[3] See my *Beyond the Constitution* (Princeton: Princeton University Press, 1990).

[4] In that vein, it is quite apt to recall that passage I cited earlier from Alexander Hamilton in the *Federalist* No. 78. Hamilton had noted there the rule that guided the courts in dealing with statutes in conflict: The statute passed later is presumed to have superseded the law enacted earlier. As Hamilton pointed out, the same rule does not come into play, of course, with the Constitution, for a Constitution framed earlier would have to be given a logical precedence over the statute that came later. But these rules of construction, so critical to our legal system, were nowhere mentioned in the Constitution. As Hamilton remarked, they were "not derived from any positive law, but from the nature and reason of the thing." *The Federalist Papers* (New York: Random House, n.d.), p. 507; see *supra*, ch. 1, p. 25.

once in the pages of *First Things*, the journal (as opposed to the distinguished book of the same title), I noted that Bork had taken, as the anchoring principle of his jurisprudence, the proposition that, in a conflict between the natural law and the positive law, the positive law must be given precedence.[5] I remarked that this was a tenable principle of construction, but it had to be noticed also that this anchoring proposition, held by Bork and others, is nowhere to be found in the positive law. Certainly it is not part of the positive law of the Constitution. What, then, would be the ground on which Bork and others would treat it, not only as a truth, but as one of those *primary* truths, which has the function of ordering a host of lesser judgments in the law? Apparently, for Bork, this proposition seems to reveal its validity in itself, as something that could be grasped by any creature of reason who would only reflect for a moment on the problem in a serious way. But that is to say, he regards it, in effect, as one of those propositions that may stand as an axiom or a first principle.

At the same time, the truth somehow passed by in the sweep of this argument is that there is a ground in natural law for this operating rule, this disposition to give primacy to the positive law. In his dissenting opinion in the *Dred Scott* case, Justice Curtis drew on cases from the American South and the Border States to recall this ancient maxim: that slavery was so contrary to the natural law that it could be sustained only by positive law.[6] Blackstone stated the settled understanding when he taught that where the positive law was silent, the natural law would come back into force.[7] The natural law, we might say, was the residual law. And that sense of natural justice would be controlling on those occasions, certain to arise, where the positive law

---

[5] "Natural Law and the Law: An Exchange [with Robert Bork], *First Things* (May 1992), pp. 45–48.

[6] As Curtis wrote:

> Slavery, being contrary to natural right, is created only by municipal law. This is not only plain in itself, and agreed by all writers on the subject, but is inferable from the Constitution, and has been explicitly declared by this court. The Constitution refers to slaves as "persons held to service in one State, under the laws thereof." Nothing can more clearly describe a *status* created by municipal law. In *Prigg v. Pennsylvania*, . . . this court said: "The state of slavery is deemed to be a mere municipal regulation, founded on and limited to the range of territorial laws." In *Rankin v. Lydia*, . . . the Supreme Court of Appeals of Kentucky said: "Slavery is sanctioned by the laws of this State, and the right to hold them under our municipal regulations is unquestionable. But we view this as a right existing by positive law of a municipal character, without foundation in the law of nature or the unwritten common law." I am not acquainted with any case or writer questioning the correctness of this doctrine.

Dred Scott v. Sandford, 339 U.S., at 624 (1857); my italics.

[7] See Blackstone, *Commentaries on the Laws of England* (Oxford: Clarendon Press, 1765), Bk. 1, p. 91.

could not possibly fill in all the details or anticipate every contingency that might arise. In all strictness of course – if it were possible to know a world of law abstracted from political life – the truth of the matter should be just the reverse. Justice Story touched the heart of the matter when he insisted that the natural law was really the matrix or foundation of the positive law, that any propositions that were at odds with those deep axioms could not really have a coherent claim to be regarded as law. And so, for example, a primate trying to be provocative, may cast up the sentiment that "I have a right to believe I don't exist." Playful it may be, but it is, in all strictness, an incoherent rights-claim. Its incoherence is revealed as soon as the question is posed, "Who is the bearer of that right? The one who does not exist?" Even if a pixilated legislature were willing to enact such a "right" in the positive law, it would not cease to be incoherent. And that, I think, is the sense that Story brought to the matter in the case of *La Jeune Eugenie* (1822). He argued there that slavery was contrary to the natural law, and therefore that the slave trade could not be coherently enforced by any bodies calling themselves courts of law, even if the positive law made its accommodation and respected that branch of "commerce."[8]

And yet Story managed to function as a worldly judge in a system of law. Situated where he was, quite aware of the experience and law of his own country, he knew full well that a decision had been made at the highest level to cast the protections of the positive law around the institution of slavery. In *Prigg v. Pennsylvania*, Story would famously deploy his jural arts to overturn the attempts, in northern states, to cast up barriers to the enforcement of the Fugitive Slave laws.[9] Lincoln would later remark that the commitment to return fugitive slaves – the commitment registered in Article IV of the Constitution – had been "nominated in the bond." It was part of the prudential compromise with slavery made at several points in the Constitution, and it was utterly necessary, he knew, to the agreement that preserved the Union and brought forth the Constitution. The Constitution would also bar any attempt to restrict the "Importation of such Persons as any of the States now

---

[8] Story put the matter with a stringent directness:

> [The trade in slaves] is repugnant to the great principles of Christian duty, the dictates of natural religion, the obligations of good faith and morality, and the eternal maxims of social justice. When any trade can be truly said to have these ingredients, *it is impossible that it can be consistent with any system of law,* that purports to rest on the authority of reason or revelation. And it is sufficient to stamp any trade as interdicted by public law, when it can be justly affirmed, that it is repugnant to the general principles of justice and humanity.

See Story in the case of *La Jeune Eugenie,* 2 Mason 809 (1822); my italics.

[9] See 16 Pet. 539. (100 U.S.) 303 (1842).

existing shall think proper to admit" until 1808 – meaning, of course, the import of slaves as part of the international traffic in slavery. It was another instance, as Lincoln said, in which "covert language" was used – language that would make an accommodation with slavery without mentioning the hateful practice by name and incorporating, in the text of the Constitution, a moral endorsement of the institution. That was indeed the formula: a prudential compromise with an existing evil, which was incompatible at the root with a polity founded on the proposition that "all men are created equal." Without that accommodation, the trade in slaves would continue and expand, unrestricted, unabated. And on the other hand, fugitives from slavery, making their way north, would never be returned. There was of course seepage in enforcement. As Lincoln remarked, "the great body of the people abide by the dry legal obligation in both cases," but the laws were "each as well enforced, perhaps, as any law can ever be in a community where the moral sense of the people imperfectly supports the law itself."[10] It was, again, a prudential compromise, and that kind of compromise could be justified only when "prudence" was governed by a sense of rightful ends. What justified the arrangement to Lincoln, and to the Founding generation, was that it was the only practicable way of bringing forth a Union that was committed, in its constituting premises, to "natural equality" and the natural liberty of human beings.

Slavery would be tolerated within a regime that would cast up barriers in principle to the expansion of slavery within the territories of the United States. At the same time, the supply of slaves from abroad would be cut off at its earliest moment under the Constitution by the administration of President Jefferson, himself the owner of slaves. In other words the positive law would become an instrument of prudence and statesmanship: The positive law could deal with circumstances on the ground, with the shape that evils took in the peculiar landscape of America. It could become, that is, an instrument used by practical men of affairs, as they confronted the things that impaired a perfect justice. And it could be used for the highest purposes of prudence: The positive law, rightly crafted, could make an accommodation with certain evils for the sake of compressing them or putting them, as Lincoln said, in "the course of ultimate extinction." But a statecraft of prudence, rightly understood, could plant the rightful lessons in the law and seek to bring about, over time, a better congruence between the principles of justice and

---

[10] See Lincoln in his First Inaugural Address, in *The Collected Works of Abraham Lincoln*, ed. Roy P. Basler (New Brunswick, N.J.: Rutgers University press, 1953), Vol. 4, pp. 262–71, at 269.

the character of life in the country as it was actually lived. Aquinas caught this melancholy sense of the problem when he famously observed that the purpose of the law was to lead people to virtue, not suddenly, but gradually.[11] It may be an unsettling recognition for some of my friends among the positivists, but some of us find common ground with them precisely because we understand that there is a ground in natural law to justify the positive law. That is especially the case when the positive law becomes the vehicle of statesmen, applying the arts of prudence and judgment, in trying to honor the rightful ends of political life.

The deepest ground of support for the positive law comes, of course, in the commitment to government by consent. In the scheme of "natural rights," rights grounded in the nature of human beings, the first inference drawn by the Declaration of Independence was the claim of human beings to governments "that derive their just powers from the consent of the governed." Washington would later remark on the heresy of lawlessness in a government founded on the authority of the people to govern themselves: Of what purpose was it to establish the right of a people to give laws to itself when the laws, made by the people, need not be obeyed?[12] When we take matters back to the root in this way, we may reach the melancholy recognition that even bad positive laws, passed in a regime of consent, have a claim to be respected until they can be changed, in a lawful way, in a process that depends again on the consent of the governed. After all, in a regime of elections, with the courts open, it is possible for laws to be challenged in different forums; and through deliberation – through the exchange of reasons – those laws may be changed.

---

[11] *Summa Theologica* (London: Burnes Oates and Washbourne, 1915), Part II, Vol. 8. pp. 66–67.

[12] See Washington's Sixth Annual Message to Congress (November 19, 1794), where he was addressing the problem of the Whiskey Rebellion in western Pennsylvania. Armed bands of insurgents had invaded the house of an inspector of revenue, wounding some of the persons in the house; others had taken prisoner a federal marshal and chased him from the district under a serious threat to his life. Washington remarked in his Message to Congress that "to yield to the treasonable fury of so small a portion of the United States, would be to violate the fundamental principle of our constitution, which enjoins that the will of the majority shall prevail." See *George Washington: A Collection*, ed. W. B. Allen (Indianapolis: Liberty Classics, 1988), pp. 492–99, at 493. In his Proclamation on the rebellion, in September 1794, Washington suggested that there was something sinful about lawlessness considering that "the people of the United States have been permitted, under the Divine favor, in perfect freedom, after solemn deliberation, in an enlightened age, to elect their own Government." See *ibid.*, pp. 598–600, at 599. On the attacks made on officers of the law, see the Proclamation of August 7, 1794, in *ibid.*, pp. 589–92, at 590–91.

Nowhere did this problem find a sharper, or more majestic, expression than in Lincoln's statecraft in dealing with slavery as a political question that ran to the heart of the regime. To hold black people in slavery – to rule them without consent – was a violation of the same principle that established the right of the American people to govern themselves.[13] The problem then for Lincoln was that any statesman seeking to put slavery in the course of extinction would have to be constrained by the need to seek the consent of the people to his measures. That the people were deeply divided on this question, that they did not assent readily to a dramatic rollback of slavery, formed the deepest predicament for the political man in a democracy. Harry Jaffa has offered the most precise account of Lincoln's steering through this predicament:

> Lincoln was equally dedicated to the principle of equality and the principle of consent. Statesmanship, for him, consisted in finding that common denominator in existing circumstances which was the highest degree of equality for which general consent could be obtained. To insist on more equality than men would consent to have would require turning to force or to the arbitrary rule of the few. But to turn to oligarchy, as a means of enforcing equality, would itself involve a repudiation of equality in the sense of the Declaration [of Independence]. Precisely because all men are created equal, we have an equal duty to work for equality and to seek consent. Lincoln did not believe he had a moral duty to deprecate the opinion of his countrymen which denied political equality to Negroes. To have done so would have meant denying the right of white men to judge the conditions under which the government could best secure their rights. . . . Lincoln never ceased to summon the people to fidelity to the principle of equality. . . . He would not abandon equality, as [Stephen] Douglas had done, when equality proved unpopular or inconvenient. But neither would he abandon equality's other face, reflected in the opinion of the governed who made up the political community of the United States.[14]

For the statesmen anchored in these understandings, it was no strain to explain why the positive law, made with the consent of the people, had the deepest claim to our respect, a claim grounded in the natural law. And yet,

---

[13] Lincoln put it in this way in his speech in Peoria in October 1854:
> [A]ccording to our ancient faith, the just powers of governments are derived from the consent of the governed. Now the relation of master and slaves is, PRO TANTO, a total violation of this principle. The master not only governs the slave without his consent; but he governs him by a set of rules altogether different from those which he prescribes for himself.

See supra, note 10, Vol. 2, p. 266.

[14] Harry Jaffa, *Crisis of the House Divided* (New York: Doubleday, 1959; University of Chicago Press, 1982), p. 377.

it still seems to come as a surprise to some practical men of the law when we point out that there is no necessary tension between the natural law and the positive law: As I had the occasion to point out earlier,[15] any system of natural law would actually require a supporting system of positive law, and at the same time, the positive law, even on the most prosaic matters, would find its justification in the natural law. We may all have, for example, a sense of why certain speeds in a car, on a winding, narrow lane, may be the cause of serious hazards, both to the driver and to others. We may also grasp, quite readily, why the law would be justified in restraining people from driving in that reckless way, in a manner that poses dangers to innocent members of the public. We roughly grasp, in other words, a principle engaged here, and yet it would be a matter of art and experience to convert that principle into a regulation that says, for example, "45 m.p.h., on *this* branch of the road, rather than the 50 m.p.h. that prevails elsewhere on the same road." We know that, in nature, there is no such "principle," prescribing 45 rather than 50 or 55. But with this move, we contrive a regulation of the positive law, which can translate the deeper principle into terms that have a bearing on the landscape before us, or the peculiar circumstances of our lives. And yet, we may not be alert in the same way to the fact that the law becomes comprehensible and justifiable precisely because there is, behind it, that deeper principle, which tells us that it would be justified to protect innocent lives by restraining recklessness. Immanuel Kant once summarized the relation between natural law and positive law in this way:

> In general, those binding laws for which an external legislation is possible are called external laws (*leges externae*). Those external laws whose obligation can be recognized a priori by reason without external legislation are natural laws; those, on the other hand, which without actual external legislation would neither obligate nor be laws are called positive laws. Hence it is possible to conceive of an external legislation which contains only positive laws; but, then, *it would have to be preceded by a natural law providing the ground of the authority of the legislator* (i.e., his authorization to obligate others by his mere choice).[16]

There is, then, a sustaining, necessary relation between the positive law and the natural law. My main object here is to call attention again to the critical points where natural law and positivism are not really at odds, but

---

[15] See supra, ch. 1, p. 36.

[16] Kant, *The Metaphysical Principles of Virtue*, trans. James Ellington (Indianapolis: Bobbs-Merrill, 1964; originally published in 1797), pp. 24–25; pp. 224–25 in the standard edition of the Royal Prussian Academy. Italics added.

tend to be joined in principle in a common discipline of the law. For the sake of reinforcing that point, I would like to recall a case from our recent past that seems to have sustained some enduring caricatures in our law and politics. That case draws a special, mordant interest, because it was persistently muddled in the arguments put before the Supreme Court, and it has been muddled in the same measure in the understandings that have continued to envelop the case.

The case in point was that notable controversy known as *Bob Jones University v. U.S.*, decided in 1983.[17] The case absorbed an extraordinary degree of controversy, for the same reason that makes the very mention of the university a continuing source of acrimony and political labeling in our own day. During the Republican presidential primaries in 2000, Senator John McCain made an issue of the fact that his main opponent, George W. Bush, had been received with much warmth at the Bob Jones University, and that, in speaking at that school in Greenville, South Carolina, Bush had made a clear tender of his respect for the institution. Bush was later reproached because he had not made of his visit an occasion to upbraid the university for views that put it so conspicuously out of the political mainstream.

For one thing, Bob Jones University, as a fundamentalist school, preserved some attitudes toward Catholicism that were less than flattering. But that was not the offense that drew the sharper anger and condemnation of the liberal members of the political class. The real ground of contention came over race. The Bob Jones University was a Christian, fundamentalist school, and among the tenets held firmly by the founders of the school was the conviction that, in the design of the Creator, revealed in the Bible, the races should be distinguished and separated in the economy of nature. In accord with that sense of things, the university had initially held itself apart racially, by opening itself only to whites, and refusing the admission of blacks. But under opposition from the government, and the overhanging threat of litigation, the university backed away from those policies in the 1970s. Black students were admitted now along with whites, but the original tenets of the university were preserved at one, primal level: The university barred dating and marriage across racial lines. The university was open, that is, to black students who were unmarried, but a strict disciplinary rule barred students who would date and marry across racial lines. This lingering form of discrimination became, of course, a source of lingering controversy, with enduring charges of racism. But as one looks more closely into the policy, it becomes evident very quickly

[17] 461 U.S. 574.

that there were complications that made this case quite unlike those other, leading cases on racial discrimination that have been so thoroughly contested and litigated over the past forty years.

The remarkable haze that surrounded this case should have been dispelled by Justice William Rehnquist, in his dissenting opinion in the case. What Rehnquist brought to the case was a mind-clearing dose of positivism. Rehnquist asked the simplest, most elementary questions. But as simple as they were, those questions would have allowed people on all sides to have seen through the haze – to have seen clearly, without affectation, what was before them.

There was actually a brace of cases here, involving two fundamentalist schools in the South. The "companion" case came in an action against the Goldsboro Christian Schools in Goldsboro, North Carolina. Like the Bob Jones University, the Goldsboro schools regarded themselves as Christian fundamentalist in character. The Goldsboro Schools encompassed the grades ranging from kindergarten through high school. The complex of Bob Jones ran far more comprehensively, from kindergarten through college and even graduate school. But apart from those gross differences in structure, there were some notable differences in the policies bearing on race, and those differences should have had a bearing in turn on the way these cases were resolved. The ruling elders of the Goldsboro Schools held that the races had sprung from the three sons of Noah – Ham, Shem, and Japheth. Asians and blacks were Hamitic in this view; the Hebrews were Shemitic, and Caucasions were Japhethitic. Once again, the teaching of the Bible was thought to prescribe a separation of the races. And until 1963, in accord with that understanding, the school had followed a fairly consistent policy of admitting only white students, with one class of exceptions: children of mixed races, where one of the parents was white. In holding to these policies, the ruling elders of the school were showing a certain obduracy, even in the face of a formidable body of federal laws that were turning decidedly against them in the 1970s.

The most notable change, bearing on private schools, came with the litigation in *Runyon v. McCrary*[18] in the 1970s. When that case was finally decided by the Supreme Court in 1976, it became part of a revival of the Thirteenth Amendment.[19] The Fourteenth Amendment had been directed to the action

---

[18] 427 U.S. 160.

[19] In reaching that landmark judgment in the law of Civil Rights the Court was encouragaged and supported in a brief by the Solicitor General at the time, Robert Bork. For an early, notable essay on this revival of the Thirteenth Amendment, see Gerhard Casper,

of states – to the discriminations that were imposed with the force of law, by officers of states and local governments. The Thirteenth Amendment was not addressed distinctly to the states, but in sweeping away slavery, or "involuntary servitude," its principal legal mission was to sweep away the laws that sustained slavery at every point in the states and local communities. Still, the Amendment had not spoken of states, and that reticence opened the way to a novel and extravagant reading in the surge of civil rights in the 1960s: The "new" Thirteenth Amendment would be taken as a powerful ground of authority for the federal government to reach directly to individuals and private entities, in striking at the lingering "badges and incidents" of slavery.[20] The intimidations of private thugs, or the discriminations of private corporations, could now come within the reach of the Civil Rights Acts dating back to the 1860s. In *Runyon v. McCrary* the Supreme Court would accept the argument that the Civil Rights Act of 1866 could plausibly reach a private, secondary school that discriminated on the basis of race in its admissions to the school. But while that case was making its way in the federal courts in the early 1970s, the new doctrines were being sounded in the rulings in the lower courts, and it was becoming clear to the directors of the Bob Jones University that the times, and the laws, were a-changing. That new reading of the old Civil Rights Act had a breakthrough in the federal court of appeals in 1975.[21] The directors of the Bob Jones University were hardly witless, and

---

"*Jones v. Mayer*: Clio, Bemused and Confused Muse," in Philip B. Kurland, ed., *The Supreme Court Review 1968* (Chicago: University of Chicago Press, 1969), pp. 89ff.

[20] And yet perhaps not so novel: Pursuant to the Thirteenth Amendment, Congress passed the act of March 2, 1867, c. 187, 14 Stat. 546, to bar involuntary servitude and peonage. In the course of legislating, the Congress would cast its proscriptions largely in terms of those exercising authority – those officials enforcing laws that would subject people to forced labor or keep them, in effect, in a state of slavery or peonage. For example: "Every person who holds, arrests, returns, or causes to be held, arrested, or returned, or in any manner aids in the arrest or return of any person to a condition of peonage . . . " And yet the statutes evidently swept more broadly, even at the beginning, for there were also references to people who "obstruct" the enforcement of these statutes, protecting people against slavery and peonage. Some who "obstruct" were in official authority, but it was clear that many of them were private persons. They might have been thugs working for employers, or they might have been those people referred to in the early Ku Klux Klan Acts – those people "who go in disguise on the highway." In any event, those passages from an earlier day, indicating a broader sweep of the Amendment, linger in our current statutes – e.g., 18 U.S.C. Sec.1581: "Whoever obstructs, or attempts to obstruct, or in any way interferes with or prevents the enforcement of this section, shall be liable to the penalties . . . " Or 18 U.S.C. Sec. 1590: "Whoever knowingly recruits, harbors, transports, provides, or obtains by any means, any person for labor or services in violation of this chapter shall be fined under this title or imprisoned not more than 20 years, or both."

[21] See *McCrary v. Runyon*, 515 F. 2d 1082 (CA4).

so in 1975 they took a critical step in revising their policies on admissions when they provided for the admission of black students. Still the change was calibrated: The school would admit black students who were unmarried and who posed no problem about dating across racial lines.

These simple, but telling shifts, made a striking difference in the position of these two fundamentalist schools in relation to the federal law. What seems surprising in retrospect was that these differences should have gone so thoroughly unnoticed, and that the judges and commentators had not been alerted to these differences by the very form of the case, or the way in which the case would be presented to a court of law. In both instances, with the Bob Jones University and the Goldsboro Schools, the action came in response to a move by the Internal Revenue Service to strip them of their status as educational institutions exempt from taxation. We would hardly suppose that the IRS simply scanned the landscape, looking for private schools to unsettle or challenge. The move in the IRS apparently came as complaints were registered about schools that were receiving a benefit conferred by the government even while they were engaging in racial discrimination.

But that very way of bringing the case, or posing the challenge, already sent up signals that should have meant something to people who were practiced in the reading of law: The form of the case revealed that there was no complainant, claiming to be injured by the policies of racial discrimination in these schools. Nothing taking place in these private schools was alleged to have violated anything in that formidable body of federal law that barred racial discrimination even in private businesses or private schools. Again, the form of the case had to be regarded as quite telling: For who would have chosen merely to contest the tax exemption given to these schools if he could have contested a case of racial discrimination covered in the federal laws? After all, if the people offended by the schools succeeded in their complaints to the IRS, no ruling of the IRS would have dislodged those policies on racial discrimination. The result of the holding would have been – as indeed it was – that the Bob Jones University, as a private, religious school, could continue to honor its biblical understanding. But it would simply have to pay more for its freedom to respect its own doctrines. The exemption from taxes would be withdrawn, and the University would have to pay back taxes of about $160,000.[22]

In contrast, something far more astounding and decisive would have taken place if the university had been sued, or indicted, under federal law. A

---

[22] *Bob Jones University v. United States, supra*, note 17, at 584.

judgment of guilt, pronounced by a judge or jury, would have had a pronounced moral resonance. And if the case had been litigated under the same statute involved in *Runyon v. McCrary*, the school might have been subject, in a civil suit, to compensatory and punitive damages.[23] The directors of the school then would have come under the most pressing incentive to divest themselves of the policies that had brought down, on the school, the terrible swift sword of the federal authorities.

Plainly, for anyone who was truly offended by the Bob Jones University, and determined to see the school punished, the path of choice was to register a complaint and launch a suit under the Civil Rights Acts. If that path was not taken, the inference must be equally plain: Apparently the groups that litigate over civil rights could not find a person who was turned away from the school on account of race.

But if that were true, it would not have been merely an interesting sidelight. It would have altered the very premises on which the case was argued, and the scheme in which the case was represented and understood. For in the absence of any violation of federal law, the argument was made in the courts that the Bob Jones University was an unworthy recipient of benefits under the tax code because the policies of the school, on the matter of race, ran counter to "the public policy" of the United States. And yet the school was not charged with breaking any federal laws. What would it mean then to say that the school was running counter to the "public policy" of the federal government? Which "public policy," expressed where, if not in the statutes of the United States? Would the explanation be found in the tax code itself? But could the Bob Jones University be at odds with the "public policy" of the United States, even though it was not violating any statute or executive order of the federal government?

Whether or not the question was framed exactly in these terms, there was a problem to be explained, and the puzzle led the judges back into the momentous question of the *disjunctive* or *conjunctive* "or." The "or" in question found its place in marking, in the statutes, the categories of institutions that could claim an exemption from taxes. A list of exemptions had always attended the income tax, running back to the Act of 1894, which had been struck down by the Supreme Court. Every subsequent act made provisions to exempt certain institutions, whose flourishing was thought to be desirable for the public good. Section 501(c)(3) has become rather famous by now as the section covering all kinds of organizations connected with the academy or education

---

[23] 42 U.S.C. Sec. 1981.

or literary enterprises. By the language of Section 501(c)(3), exemptions are provided to "[c]orporations . . . organized and operated exclusively for religious, charitable . . . *or* educational purposes." Italics mine: there is the "or." The question raised by Chief Justice Burger, in his opinion for the majority, was whether that "or" was "disjunctive": Did the statute not mark off "educational" institutions," along with "charitable" and "religious" organizations, as separate, distinct categories of groups? This was the *disjunctive* "or." The categories were separate, and organizations falling into any one of them could claim an exemption. To put it bluntly, not all charities were schools, and strictly speaking, schools were not always charitable. Those of us who have made our vocation in teaching think we have ample reason to hold that a school directed to its rightful ends also serves a public good. But that may not always be the same as undertaking the kind of work that is more intensely and devotedly "charitable." There may be no selfless ministering to the poor and sick, with no interest in recompense.

And yet, the attack on the Bob Jones University required the IRS and the courts to diagram the sentence by insisting that the "or" was not "disjunctive" but conjunctive or appositional. It was more like the "or" in "We will put the accent, in these lectures, on points that are foundational, primary, or elementary." "Elementary" would not stand here in contradistinction to "primary" and "fundamental." It was but another way of explaining what all of the other terms in the series were seeking in part to describe. That is how the IRS and the critics of the Bob Jones University now proposed to read the tax laws. And so when the laws conferred exemptions on corporations "organized and operated exclusively for religious, charitable . . . or educational purposes," it could now be taken to mean that all of these organizations had to be *charitable* in some way. Curiously, the same reasoning did not require that they all be "religious" in some way. Chief Justice Burger was willing to follow here the line of argument welling up from the bureaucracy and the lower courts, that the notion of "charitable" was somehow implicit in the understanding that attached to all groups thought worthy enough to merit an exemption from taxes. As Burger put it, a study of the tax code

> reveals unmistakable evidence that, underlying all relevant parts of the Code, is the intent that entitlement to tax exemption depends on meeting certain common-law standards of charity – namely, that an institution seeking tax-exempt status must serve a public purpose and not be contrary to established public policy.[24]

[24] *Bob Jones University, supra*, note 17, at 586.

But if there really was, over the years, an understanding, settled but unspoken, that all of these organizations had to be charities, it is rather odd that the Congress had never bothered to make that point explicit, since it was not evident instantly that any literary or educational institution also had to be "charitable." A simpler and more plausible construction, it seems to me, is that the list of exemptions had to assume, of course, that the institutions under these categories were benign, wholesome, *legitimate*. At the time that the *Bob Jones* case was decided, I had written a commentary in which I had remarked on the necessary premise that all of the organizations on the list would be legitimate: It seemed to go without saying that the exemption for "educational" institutions would not go to Mr. Fagin's School of Pickpocketry. The point is so fundamental or axiomatic that it hardly needs saying, and yet it is unmistakable. The tax code would not cover a school for thieves.

Quite independent of my own writing, the same argument found expression in the lower federal courts, and one of the judges invoked that example of Fagin's School of Pickpocketry.[25] That argument was recalled by Chief Justice Burger, in his opinion for the Court, along with this further example: that if anything with the appearance of a "school" could qualify for an exemption, then "a band of former military personnel might well set up a school for intensive training of subversives for guerrilla warfare and terrorism in other countries." Justice Rehnquist, in dissent, found the analogy unpersuasive. And yet, regrettably, his explanation was rather less than luminous. "I have little doubt," he wrote, "that neither the 'Fagin School for Pickpockets' nor a school training students for guerrilla warfare and terrorism in other countries would meet the definitions contained in the regulations."[26] In that sense of things, I have not the least doubt that he was right. But so evident did he regard the conclusion that he did not bother to spell out the reasons. And yet, the reasons did matter. Rehnquist seemed to think that the standards of judgment would become suitably manifest if one simply considered the understandings spelled out by the IRS as it sought to explain what was meant by organizations or institutions dedicated to an "educational" purpose:

> The instruction or training of the individual for the purpose of improving or developing his capabilities. . . . The instruction of the public on subjects useful to the individual and beneficial to the community. . . . An organization whose activities consist of presenting public discussion groups, forums,

---

[25] The point was made by Judge Leventhal in *Green* v. *Connally*, 330 F.Supp. 1150, 1160 (DC), summarily aff'd *sub nom. Coit* v. *Green*, 404 U.S. 997 (1971). The argument by Leventhal was recalled by Chief Justice Burger in *ibid.*, at 592.

[26] *Ibid.*, at 619.

panels, lectures, or other similar programs. Such programs may be on radio or television. . . . An organization which presents a course of instruction by means of correspondence or through the utilization of television or radio. . . . Museums, zoos, planetariums, symphony orchestras, and other similar organizations.

A student I knew twenty-five years ago at Amherst performed as a magician, and he would later stage his performances at meetings of corporate boards. As part of his training in the arts of illusion he had studied the art of pickpocketry. And as he intimated, the Masters who would impart the subtleties of that craft had not always used those arts simply to entertain. It was quite conceivable that there could be an academy to instruct in magic, and that the school would incorporate pickpocketry in the curriculum. What guaranteed that the instruction offered in that school would never be used for corrupted ends? How would one be sure that the art of picking pockets would never be used to steal rather than entertain? As we have seen, any activity we could name could be directed to a harmful and wrongful end. A school of driving could instruct students in the art of driving getaway cars, much as the CIA would instruct some of its people in the art of defensive and evasive driving. For Rehnquist and his colleagues, it seemed to go without saying that the inventory of groups marked off in the tax code would be decent, respectable organizations, not enterprises directed to illegitimate ends.

But then how did one understand or define "illegitimate" ends? If we take the matter to the root, we would mark off the illegitimate by understanding the things that were in principle right or wrong. For Rehnquist the problem was serenely free of puzzles, because the answer to the question was rather direct and simple in the understanding of the legal positivist. From the perspective of the positivist, the question here was "What was illegitimate in the eyes of the law?" The question, posed in that way, was answered unequivocally: What was illegitimate were the *things that were explicitly made unlawful; the things that were against the law.* They were the things explicitly forbidden in the positive law. They were not merely the things roughly thought to be unrespectable or shady, but things that were quite precisely spelled out in their defining features, and in the boundaries of their wrongness, by statutes, executive orders, and the rulings of courts. They were marked off, that is, as wrongs by the precision that typically attended the instruments of the positive law.

The difference in the two answers pointed to notably different grounds of judgment. For in the tradition of law, encompassing the natural law, not everything that was wrong or immoral would be made illegal. Again, legislators might be held back by a sense of prudence. With the counsel of Aquinas, they might be cautious in imposing on imperfect people a law that applies, with a stringent exactitude, the full logic of the principle behind it. Or on the other hand, the lawmakers might be held back from a want of imagination or nerve, or by a failure to recognize the wrongs that deserved to be reached and condemned by the law. In either case, the test of legality was a modest, scaled-down test, and that more modest measure of the law would have made the problem in cases like *Bob Jones* far more tractable. Nevertheless, as we have seen, the positive law finds its ground and justification in principles that are antecedent to the positive law, principles that are not always set down, or recorded, in the laws. And if the problem in the *Bob Jones* case were informed by that larger or more comprehensive understanding, the problem would have been dramatically altered.

Consider, for a moment, how the differences would have played out. Let us suppose that the argument had been cast seriously as a question of principle. The argument might be made, in strenuous terms, that racial discrimination is categorically wrong, wrong in principle; and if that were the case, an enterprise that incorporated in its character a commitment to racial discrimination would be as illegitimate as a school that incorporated in its character a commitment to theft. It could be no more legitimate than Fagin's School of Pickpocketry. To say that racial discrimination is wrong in principle is, of course, to do more than utter a piety. In the construction I have put forth already here as elsewhere, the wrong of racial discrimination is rooted in the very logic of law and moral judgment.[27] By that construction, racial discrimination would be wrong of necessity, wrong categorically, in any system that dares call itself a system of "law."

Let us assume, then, for a moment that the Court had staked out this position in principle as the ground of its judgment. What difference would it have made? In the first place, it would go without saying that no institution that forms its character around racial discrimination could possibly be a "legitimate" institution, claiming the exemptions that are offered under the law to legitimate schools or educational enterprises. But then, in the second place, the rejection of that school, as a legitimate school, would have *nothing to do at all with the pattern of public policy.* Even if there were no laws or executive orders on racial discrimination – even if all of those laws were swept from the

---

[27] *Supra*, ch. 2, pp. 53–56. My fuller arguments here can be found in *First Things* (Princeton: Princeton University Press, 1986), pp. 85–89, and *The Philosopher in the City* (Princeton University Press, 1981), ch. 2, and especially pp. 43–48.

books – this school would still be constituted on a "wrongful" basis. It still could not be a legitimate school and receive an exemption.

That would indeed be the statement of the hardest position, the most stringent argument in principle. And yet to state it in that way, with its full force, is to note that it is radically at odds with the opinion that the majority actually rendered in the case of the Bob Jones University. In fact, it becomes even clearer then that neither side on the Court – neither the judges in the majority nor the dissenter – thought that a categorical proposition was engaged here. Neither side rejected racial discrimination in point of principle. I suppose that some people might be tempted to point out that Mr. Rehnquist, when he was in politics, had never supported the Civil Rights Act of 1964, which carried the strongest assertion that racial discrimination was indeed wrong in principle. And yet, Mr. Rehnquist did not really have to reach that issue here, for his own position depended on a reading of the positive law. That law was limited to the matter of tax exemptions, offered to a limited class of organizations, marked off with a clear enough precision.

The most notable contrast with an argument cast in principle came with the argument actually brought forth by the majority in this case. On this point, the evidence was telltale, and it was spread, unmistakably, throughout the opinion by Chief Justice Burger. Within the space of three pages, the Chief Justice gave this account of the wrong of the case five times over (and the italics, in all instances, are mine):

- "But there can no longer be any doubt that *racial discrimination in education* violates deeply and widely accepted views of elementary justice." (592)
- "An unbroken line of cases following *Brown* v. *Board of Education* establishes beyond doubt this Court's view that *racial discrimination in education* violates a most fundamental national public policy, as well as rights of individuals." (593)
- "Congress, in Titles IV and VI of the Civil Rights Act of 1964, Pub. L. 88–352, 78 Stat. 241, 42 U. S. C. §§ 2000c, 2000c-6, 2000d, clearly expressed its agreement that *racial discrimination in education* violates a fundamental public policy." (593)
- "Few social or political issues in our history have been more vigorously debated and more extensively ventilated than the issue of racial discrimination, *particularly in education*." (595)
- "Whatever may be the rationale for such private schools' policies, and however sincere the rationale may be, *racial discrimination in education* is contrary to public policy." (595)

"Racial discrimination in education": The wrong was narrowed, once again, to a "contingent" wrong – a wrong that was contingent upon its effects in certain settings. As in the famously miscast opinion in *Brown v. Board*, the wrong was apparently not a wrong in principle. The wrong inhered, rather, in some injury that was inflicted on black students distinctly *in schools*. However, the embarrassment in *Brown v. Board* was that there was no evidence of any injury of that kind.[28] The Court had cast its decision in that narrow, empirical way, as a device for avoiding a deeper argument cast in principle. But even though the argument was miscast, the Court did confront, in Brown, some genuine cases of racial segregation ordered by the laws. And yet, the point, strangely passed over in this sweep of rhetoric, was that there was, in the case of the Bob Jones University, no instance of racial discrimination that the law had ever condemned or reached. Strictly speaking, there had been no "racial discrimination" in education because no one had been barred from the school on the basis of race. To put it another way, no racial barrier had come into play to restrict admission to the school, and therefore to any educational program within the school. Chief Justice Burger sought neatly to glide around that point of embarrassment by elaborating his case: The Executive branch, he said, had consistently placed the weight of its authority "behind eradication of racial discrimination," and he cited here, most notably, the orders of President Truman barring racial discrimination in federal employment, or the orders of President Kennedy in prohibiting racial discrimination in housing that was supported by federal funds.[29] True enough, but like "the flowers that bloom in the spring," they had nothing to do with the case. There was, in this case, no allegation of racial discrimination in employment or housing – or even in access to the school. Once again, if any of these laws or executive orders had been violated, there would have been plaintiffs alleging injuries, and seeking remedies far more resounding than the removal of exemptions from taxes.

In the full panoply of federal laws, of statutes and executive orders that touched on the matter of race, *nothing* had been violated. That there was, in the policies of the school, a posture of racial discrimination, could hardly be gainsaid. But the sovereign point, curiously and serenely ignored, was that the kind of discrimination involved in this case had never been addressed by the federal laws. Nor did it seem likely that they would be addressed by the laws any time in the foreseeable future. There was, at the university, a

---

[28] For a review, and a critical account, of the "evidence" presented in *Brown v. Board*, see Arkes, *The Philosopher in the City, supra*, note 27, pp. 233–36, 240; and see Arkes, "The Problem of Kenneth Clark," *Commentary* (November 1974), pp. 37–46.

[29] *Bob Jones University v. U.S., supra*, note 17, at 594.

policy of discrimination in dating and marriage across racial lines. But the meaning of that practice was notably altered as soon as one recognized that there had been no racial tests of admission to this *private* school. The school was a private association composed of students of different races, but students who shared the fundamentalist persuasion of the Bob Jones University. Black or white, they apparently accepted the tenets of the school – otherwise they would not have sought admission to the school. Sharing those tenets, it was apparently no strain to accord themselves with the policy of confining their dating and marriage within racial lines. Since it was a private school, no one was compelled by law to attend. That elementary point offered a telling reminder that the policy at issue in this case, the policy of racial discrimination in the private choice of a spouse, or a partner in dating, was never a policy addressed by the laws. It was a matter wholly of private choice, reflecting the code that was shared in this private enclave by the students who had attached themselves, willingly, to the Bob Jones University.

We might imagine, for example, one of those computer dating services, of "singles" looking for partners. The service is private; no one who does not wish to join is compelled to be a member and come under its rules. But let us suppose, further, that the members are asked for their preferences in partners and that, in the range of preferences, it is considered legitimate for them to record a preference for people of their own race. Evidently, a preference of that kind is regarded as legitimate, even on the part of people who regard themselves as the most cosmopolitan of liberals. Even black people quite committed to civil rights have expressed a certain resentment at times for men who could have married a black woman, but married instead outside the race. There seems to be no purging of such cattiness, even in these, the most liberal of times. But there were telling pieces of evidence all around for anyone willing to notice them. It was mainly in the journals of Left-liberal opinion – journals like the *New York Review of Books* – that one was likely to encounter ads in the "personals columns" reading in this way: "SWM seeks SWF." Translation: Single *white* male seeks single *white* female. The *New York Review* would never have run an ad saying, "White landlord seeking white tenants." That kind of ad was against the law (namely, the Fair Housing Act of 1968), but the *New York Review* would not have run an ad of that kind, even before it was against the law. If there was a genuine principle engaged here on the wrong of racial discrimination, that principle should be quite indifferent to the nature of the "good" or service that is being advertised. The comparisons could not help but yield a moral lesson patently clear: Apparently, even the most liberal parts of the political class – and the most fervent supporters of civil rights – did not understand that the principle that barred racial discrimination did indeed apply in a sweeping, categorical way to every instance of racial discrimination. The principle on racial discrimination might reach to private businesses, and even to owners of single-family dwellings who were renting space in their private homes. But evidently the editors of the *New York Review of Books* did not think that this "principle" carried over to the *private choice of a partner for sex and marriage.*

Or to take the matter to another step of refinement, the understanding of the editors might have mirrored the understanding of the political class who formed the government and shaped the laws: They might have understood that the principle on racial discrimination did indeed cover, in its sweep, all instances of racial discrimination, public and private. But in the most ancient tradition of the law, they might also have understood that, on grounds of prudence, the legislators had not chosen to cover, with the laws, this domain of intimate, private lives.

In all strictness, of course, the principle, *as a principle*, did indeed cover even these cases of discrimination: The principle held that it was wrong to draw adverse moral inferences on the basis of race. On the basis of race one could not infer that a potential partner was more or less worthy of that affection, or that enduring respect, that would justify an enduring attachment. My own students, confronting the case, have been inclined to argue that there might, after all, be "aesthetic" reasons for preferring people of a certain color or complexion. But that kind of argument rather backs into the moral case. Imagine a man who informed us that he had chosen his wife of many years wholly on "aesthetic" grounds: he had been drawn to her complexion and blonde coloring – a coloring that beautifully matched the drapes and furnishings in his apartment. But then, he tells us, he decided to do his apartment over in Art Deco – and she no longer "went with the drapes." That hypothetical reliably elicits a laugh, for one realizes, instantly, that this kind of consideration, in the choice of a spouse, is laughably out of scale: It trivializes utterly the character of the choice, and to grasp that it trivializes is to grasp, at the same time, that there is an inescapable moral dimension to love and marriage among creatures who are constituted as moral beings. To speak after all of an attachment lasting through time is to speak of the things that make a partner enduringly worthy of one's love and respect even as looks wither with age. But to speak in those accents is, of course, to speak of nothing less than the *moral* ingredients that must ever be woven into love and marriage among human beings or "moral agents."

Even in the case of ordinary businesses, it was presumably open also to owners of restaurants to claim that they, too, had certain "aesthetic" consid-erations uppermost in their minds when they made a decision, say, to confine their restaurants or nightclubs to white persons in formal wear. They might express the most acute aesthetic preference for white, blonde people, set off in their coloring by tuxedos and black ties for the men. But a claim of that kind would not have stood against the laws that barred racial discrimination in businesses open to transactions with the public. And no more would it become a plausible ground of evasion if the federal laws on civil rights had ever reached these intimate decisions in the choice of a partner for sex or marriage.

In any event, it was clear beyond caviling that nothing of this kind came within the reach of any laws or executive orders of the United States. No federal law sought to reach cases of racial discrimination in the decisions made by private persons in the choice of a partner for sex or marriage. There is a danger of getting carried away here by slogans just a bit too quick or glib, and so there is probably a need to remind ourselves that the very notion of "laws of marriage" implies the most emphatic restriction on the kinds of decisions that private persons make in the choice of partners for sex and marriage. That is exactly what laws of marriage do. They typically impose those restrictions when they bar men and women from marrying their natural children, when they bar people from marrying more than one person they love, and when they confine marriage to a couple, composed of members of opposite sexes. Of that latter point, we need little reminding today, with all of the controversies over "same-sex" marriage. Federal law has had to address that question, with the Defense of Marriage Act of 1996, for the Full Faith and Credit Clause of the Constitution [Art. IV, Sec. 1] offered an engine for extending gay and lesbian marriage to the rest of the country as soon as it was recognized in one of the states. But long before that, the Congress had taken a keen interest in the suppression of polygamy in Utah in the nineteenth century. The point then is not that the laws of marriage may not interfere with the preferences made by private persons in the choice of partners. Nor is it that the federal government may not itself seek to address the question of marriage, with laws that restrict the decisions made by private persons over the choice of partners. The more precise point here is that neither federal nor state law had sought to reach those private decisions in which people turned away from potential partners on the basis of race.

Justice Rehnquist, as a positivist, simply read the laws before him, and it was apparent to him that the laws had no such reach. And as a positivist, too, it did not seem to be his business to strain over the question of whether there was, behind these positive laws, any such principle, with a categorical sweep. But it was equally plain now that no judge, even on the liberal side, saw a principle of that kind engaged in the case. More than that, as the example of the *New York Review of Books* made clear, even people outside the Court, people on the Left in our politics, were emphatically unwilling to take up such a principle. Yet, in that case, what ground of complaint was left any longer in regard to those people at Bob Jones University? They had held to the view apparently held by all members of the Court and most liberals in the country: namely, that it was legitimate to make discriminations based on race in choosing a partner in sex and marriage. The only vice of the people at Bob Jones is that they shared the moral perspective that prevailed at the *New York Review of Books*.

Or they shared, at least, the moral perspective that the *New York Review of Books* had about the kind of racial discrimination that stood *beyond* the reach of the law. But that brings us back to Justice Rehnquist and his simple, persisting positivism. There can hardly be any question that the mind of the later Chief Justice managed to encompass many layers of refinements, many subtle arts of argument, in law and politics. Still, he found a certain advantage in refracting these rich shades of law and argument through the prism of his positivism, where they were tested by a simple question put to legislators, not judges: Whether we are governed by the sweep of a principle, or held back by a sense of prudence, is *this* proposition before us now – this claim, this idea – something we are prepared to *enact* into law? And when faced with a complaint of the kind that arose in the *Bob Jones* case, the first question of the positivist was, Was there in fact a law that reached this matter? When the Court insisted that the policies of the Bob Jones University ran "counter to the public policy of the United States," the positivist raised the simple, but necessary challenge: Where exactly, in the statutes or executive orders of the United States, was there anything that bore on the wrong alleged at Bob Jones University? Is there any instrument, in federal law, that actually claimed to judge the preferences of race that are indulged by private persons in the choice of their own partners in sex and marriage?

The positivist, who insisted on measuring the law precisely, was the one who focused in this case the light that had the precision of a laser. People may have had the sense that there was something wrong with the policies of the Bob Jones University, but there are many things regarded as wrong or sinful that the law does not reach. By asking in the first place whether the law has reached this matter at hand, the positivist implicitly puts the challenge to the complainant: What account would he give of the wrong he sees engaged in the case? Is it something that is wrong only because it is forbidden in statutes (like missing the deadline on the filing of taxes)? Or is the wrong really a wrong in principle, something we are supposed to know even if it had not been written down – for example, that the laws on theft would cover computers and cars, even though those objects are mentioned nowhere in the law. Yet it was apparent that no one, on the Left or the Right, was willing to assert such a principle here, which could have covered both the Bob Jones University and the *New York Review of Books*.

In fact, it should have been plain from the very cast of the argument offered by the Court that the majority was light years away from even recognizing the properties of an argument in principle. For what Chief Justice Burger proceeded to do was to mark off the inventory of statutes and executive orders touching on racial discrimination, as he said, "in education." Consider in contrast the teacher of physics who sought to explain to his students the principle that came into play when a ball rolled down an inclined plane. He wants to explain to them that the rate of acceleration is directly related to the angle of inclination: that as the angle becomes steeper, the ball rolls all the faster. Would he seek to give an account of that principle by giving us an inventory of all of the results that came about when the experiments were tried with blue planes or wooden planes, with balls made of plastic or aluminum? Would he recite a long inventory of the speeds clocked by the balls as the angle of inclination was altered in each trial? Or would he rather show the students an example or two, draw on their commonsense understanding of what happens as angles of hills and roads become steeper – and then simply draw from the examples *the statement of the principle*?

If the Court thought that there was a wrong here that ran to the deepest principles of the law, then Chief Justice Burger and his colleagues should have given an account of that principle. They should not have been distracting themselves and their readers by listing the inventory of statutes and executive orders – all of them quite off the point – and citing them as though they somehow formed, in their mass, a principle that no one yet had bothered to explain.

In this posture, the judges revealed their own disarray. But in a strange twist that adds a dimension to the story, the Chief Justice, in the last paragraph of his opinion, let on that he and his colleagues were quite aware of that disarray. It must stand as the most telling of signs that only at the very end – and with the curtest of paragraphs – did the Court bother to consider the defense that went to the core: namely, the contention of the University that nothing in its arrangements violated any policy on racial discrimination found in the laws of the United States. To this contention the Chief Justice thought it sufficient to reply in one sentence: "[D]ecisions of this Court firmly establish that discrimination on the basis of racial affiliation and association is a form of racial discrimination, see, *e.g.*, *Loving* v. *Virginia*, 388 U.S. 1 (1967); *McLaughlin* v. *Florida*, 379 U.S. 184 (1964); *Tillman* v. *Wheaton-Haven Recreation Assn.*, 410 U.S. 431 (1973)." To that, Burger saw fit to add no word to explain the bearing of the three cases he was citing. But anyone who knew anything of those cases would have seen at once why there was no willingness to linger with an explanation: The cases were radically inapt. *Loving v. Virginia* involved a *statute* that barred marriage across racial lines. *McLaughlin* v. *Florida* involved *laws* that barred mixed racial couples from cohabiting outside of marriage. *Tillman v. Wheaton-Haven Recreation Assn.* involved a private association formed around a swimming pool in Silver Spring, Maryland. The association barred black people as members, and in this case refused to admit a black woman as the guest of a member. The association was nominally private, but for all intents and purposes, it was open to all white persons in the community without any principle of restriction apart from race. The pool functioned then, in effect, as a facility open to the public. The Court, at the time, was reviving the Thirteenth Amendment and expanding then the reach of the old Civil Rights Acts to private schools and housing. And so, in the third case, a private business open to the public had actually barred people on the basis of race and run afoul of the Civil Rights Acts. Nothing in these cases offered the remotest precedent for a policy of condemning the *private* choices made by private persons, in a thoroughly private entity, on matters of sex and marriage that were not regulated by the law.

The fact that the Chief Justice introduced this issue so late, and dealt with it in such a cursory way, with no explanation, was itself a telling sign that he recognized the utter inaptness of the cases he was citing. From another angle, Burger's opinion might have been read as a kind of "wink from the bench": It was the Chief Justice saying, in effect, "I know that this is inapt, that these cases cannot provide any precedent for what we are doing or any explanation of this judgment. But everyone expects us now to do *something*. All of the respectable people, in the media and the law schools, expect us to come down against racial discrimination, and not on the side containing what they see as a bunch of dim bigots. You know, and we know, that we cannot quite supply a rationale here, but we will have said enough to get through the day. And at times that is as much as one can do. If we are lucky, people will see in the case a principle that we never quite explained, and for the rest, the details may fade from memory."

Anyone who followed the work of the Court at the time was quite aware of the political predicament in which the Court had found itself. The Reagan administration had initially come out in favor of its allies, among the religious conservatives. The inclination of the administration was closer to that of Rehnquist, and so it was leaning to the side of the university. But then the political heat seemed to build; respectable people on all sides were condemning the policies of the university. Suddenly, the administration found itself in an awkward position, which would have required in turn explanations too complicated for the public to bear. It fell to the Court then to dispose of what had become a political problem. The Reagan administration could not find the words to make the political case for its allies among the fundamentalists, and so it sought a quiet way of avoiding embarrassment.

But Rehnquist, with his positivism, would have provided both a political and legal argument. That argument, spare as it was, would have left the conservatives on a higher moral ground, looking down on the critics of the Bob Jones University. Rehnquist, or the positivist, would have pointed out that many people in the landscape are seized with an awareness of wrongs that are not carried into the statutes and condemned with the force of law. He could have invoked the argument that has become almost a theme song among liberal professors of jurisprudence: that not everything regarded as morally wrong is made illegal.[30] To have the sense of a wrong is one thing,

---

[30] A while back, Mr. Mark Belnick, the former general counsel at the Tyco Corp., was being accused of complicity in the antics of the former CEO of Tyco, Dennis Kozlowski. In one of many pieces covering this sad, strange story, Belnick was pilloried for his willingness to provide cover for some of Koslowski's extravagant, private expenses by limiting his reporting to the Securities and Exchange Commission. In one notable incident, a lawyer reviewing records at the company reported to Belnick that Koslowski had given a "loan" of $100,000 from the company to a woman described by the staff as his "girlfriend." Koslowski would subsequently marry that woman. The lawyer thought that the document could not rightly be withheld from the SEC in its queries to the company. But Belnick disagreed. The document might be embarrassing, and yet it was not strictly within the guidelines of the questions posed by the SEC. As the saying went, the document was "non-responsive" to the requests of the agency, strictly and narrowly understood. As reporters from the *Wall Street Journal* looked into the story, they found a corroborating opinion from Professor Alan Bromberg at the Southern Methodist University School of Law. As Bromberg observed, "There's no legal obligation to rat out the client. . . . And if the documents aren't responsive, it's OK to withhold them." See Laurie P. Cohen and Mark Maremont, "E-Mails Show Tyco's Lawyers Had Concerns," *Wall Street Journal* (December 27, 2002), pp. C1, C5. Belnick, then, had reported nothing more than the law strictly required. But for that cautious and narrow reading of the law, he was painted as a figure willing to bend the law for his own uses, while being utterly heedless of the spirit, or deeper principles, behind the law. And yet, the double standard did not apparently spring to recognition: Professors of law, making the case for sexual freedom, had argued for years that the law does not reach everything that can be regarded as immoral. When David Richards makes that argument with his usual elan, he could be regarded as stylish and free-spirited. (See David A. J. Richards, *The Moral Criticism of Law* (1977), or *Free Speech and the Politics of Identity* (1999).) When Mark Belnick followed the same understanding, he was treated with a certain disdain. Apparently, when workaday lawyers and conservatives respected a distinction between law and morality, they were not free spirits, advancing the perimeter of human freedom.

but it is quite another matter to state the principle that explains the wrongness and justifies the reach of the law. Fagin's School of Pickpocketry would not receive a tax exemption, because theft is against the law. In applying principles to cases, the administrators at the IRS would find a need to flex their imaginations even in prosaic cases. But the law has been cast in the form of a statute precisely so that administrators would be spared the need to be, every day, inventive and inspired. It may indeed be that the principle that condemns discrimination on the basis of race would cover, in its sweep, even the people who draw away from lovers and potential spouses on account of their race. That may be the case, and yet, strictly speaking, the law has not incorporated that judgment anywhere in its statutes, or in the orders of agencies and courts. By that reckoning, then, the Bob Jones University did not run afoul of anything in the laws or the public policy of the United States. And for that sovereign reason, the Bob Jones University could not be regarded as anything other than a "legitimate" institution. If the institution passes all of the tests of accreditation that are required of schools, it stands as a legitimate educational enterprise, and it properly claims then, as a matter of right, any tax exemption that would flow to an educational enterprise. The strong burden would have to be placed on anyone who claims otherwise. End of story.

But not of the overtones: As I have suggested, this spare application of positivism could have cleared the fog of this case by bringing out quite sharply the point that there was nothing in this case condemned anywhere in the laws or executive orders of the United States. By focusing on that decisive point, the positivist would have forced the question of whether his colleagues were appealing to "the laws" or to a deeper principle of the law, even a principle that had not found expression in any of the laws that bore on the problem at hand. But by bringing that question to the fore, he would have revealed, in a burst of light, that no one – no judge, no litigant, no bureaucrat in the IRS – was making the argument to explain why racial discrimination was in principle wrong, even in cases of sexual privacy that neither liberals nor conservatives had sought to reach with the laws. The argument cast by the positivist would have exposed the moral posturing in the case as just that – posturing without substance. For it was a posturing that could not finally supply an account of the principle underlying the judgment. The positivist would have compelled the jurists to become more fastidious in doing what Chief Justice Burger so fastidiously avoided doing here: paying attention to the precise meaning of the statutes and executive orders. But at the other end of the scale, the positivist as judge might have made lawyers even more aware of how demanding the argument would be if they were pretending to claim for themselves the mantle of a principle here.

In sum, then, the positivist, asking spare, focused questions in this case, would have been the carrier of a genuine discipline of legal and moral judgment. He would not only have reminded his colleagues and readers of the properties of a principle, but he would have recalled to them also that the law is a blending of prudence and statecraft, as well as the craft of reason. That wondrous blending may account for why I have been able to say over the years, without too much irony, that some of my best friends are positivists. For it becomes ever clearer that the best positivists have been speaking prose all their lives: With their attachment to the conventions of lawfulness, they become the agents of an insistent rationality. They appeal at every turn to the "laws of reason" without being aware at all times that they are doing anything remotely "philosophic." They are constantly bringing into view then the natural law, even while they earnestly profess that they are not practicing it. They remain then the best of company, for when we are with them, we can never be far from the natural law.

Eight

Conclusion and Afterword

Almost exactly a year after the Pentagon Papers were released to the public, and generated their litigation, the hapless burglars were caught breaking into the offices of the Democratic National Committee at the Watergate in Washington. Old Washington hands, and people tuned into politics, still recall that the legendary "Plumbers" offered a thread of connection between the two happenings. The "Plumbers" were a clandestine operation, aimed at the task of unearthing information about Daniel Ellsberg, the curious figure who had helped to assemble – and then leak – the Pentagon Papers. Apparently, the plumbers had broken into the office of Ellsberg's psychiatrist, in the hope of finding some information that could illuminate his political connections – or perhaps turn up other evidence, of a personal nature, that might not be exactly edifying. The disclosure revealed the dark underside of operations long carried out beyond the law, as the intelligence services got round the barriers cast up by the procedures of the law. Was there a suspicion that heroin was entering the country through the diplomatic pouches being sent to an embassy in Washington? Then the attempt to use the conventions of law as a screen for wrongdoing would be combated by other methods, pursued in like measure outside the conventional, legal channels. After a while, that style of operating seemed to spill over into political intelligence. Lyndon Johnson's people complained that John Kennedy's campaign was conducting surveillance of his political opponents, and in time the same complaints would be heard from the adversaries of LBJ. I do not recall these things for the sake of excusing them, but to point out that the moral boundaries had become blurred for people on both sides of the political divide. As the events recede in the mists of memory, there seems to be a critical forgetting that there was in fact a connection between Watergate and the Pentagon Papers. And yet, that forgetting may not be attributed to the normal erosion of remembering,

for there has been a logic at work in this screening. The obtuseness, or the forgetting, has worked with the most convenient political results. What has been
screened out is any noticing of the deeper connections in principle between
the two events; connections that would be quite as troubling for liberals as
well as conservatives.

Of course, an awareness of connections in principle is bound up with a sense
of moral imagination: It is not an accident then that the same people who
thought that Mr. Nixon was guilty of an unparalleled wrong in Watergate
could not see, in the same way, how the leaking of the Pentagon Papers could
have been regarded by Nixon as disturbingly, deeply wrong. For Nixon, the
incident of the Pentagon Papers could have been taken as a clear sign that
the members of the liberal Establishment in exile – the *New York Times*,
the leading lights in the academy, the former, high officials in the Johnson
administration – simply did not consider themselves bound any longer by
the legal and moral restraints that had constrained, in the past, the political
class. The experience of the Pentagon Papers seemed to confirm Mr. Nixon's
sense of the character of his adversaries, and hardened his heart in dealing
with them. But again, the moral imagination was not likely to be engaged in
grasping things from this angle if there was not even a tremor of awareness
that there might be anything even slightly wrong, something worrisome in
principle, about the move to break out the Pentagon Papers. And yet, even if
there had been no mild stirring of the moral sense, people might have been
tipped off to the presence of some tangled questions of principle if they had
merely been more alert to the legal ironies that abounded in the comparison
of the Pentagon Papers and Watergate.

Those ironies would spring forth if we began simply by taking at face value
the moral outrage that the break-in at the Watergate elicited in the circles of
respectable opinion. Why did people affect to be so deeply offended? Why
did they seem to think that a serious wrong had taken place? The break-in
seemed to have a sinister quality because its object was to gain access to
information of a confidential or private nature; information that promised to
be embarrassing if it were disclosed to the public. From the reactions, then,
we would gather that some members of the public were deeply offended
at the prospect that burglars with a political commission were penetrating
spheres of privacy, with the purpose of bringing to the light of public day
information held in secrecy. Did it matter if that information disclosed some
possible wrongdoing on the part of Lawrence O'Brien, the chairman of the
Democratic National Committee, or of anyone else, whose transactions were
to be found in these letters tucked away in the files? Would it have been wrong
to expose to public view any evidence of wrongdoing? Those questions were

not asked, to my knowledge, because the break-in was branded as an offense in itself, a violation of spheres of privacy.

But then this thought-experiment suggests itself: Let us suppose that there was indeed information in the files of the Democratic National Committee that would have been quite embarrassing, with political implications. Let us suppose that some of this material was of a distinctly personal nature. Let us suppose, further, that the Watergate burglars had managed to make copies of the documents they had stolen or photographed, and that the material had been delivered to the *New York Times* and the *Washington Post.* Let us imagine that those journals now planned a series of articles unfolding the revelations that were contained in those files, once held in the security of a private office. Question then: Since the papers were wrongly obtained, since the *Times* and the *Post* had no real "right" to be in possession of them, could the potential victims have sought an injunction to stop the publishers from collaborating in the same act of wrongdoing, by publishing those private papers for a larger public to read?

In the aftermath of the Pentagon Papers case, one would have to suppose that the answers would have been an emphatic no: Perhaps a prosecution, or a suit for personal damages, could be launched later, but it would seem out of the question now that any move should have been made to restrain the publication in advance. And this despite the fact that the act of gaining access to those papers, for a handful of burglars, was thought to be not only wrong but despicable.

Something is morally askew here, and we might as well state it directly: The moral outrage that surrounded the episode in the Watergate cannot be squared with the principles that were proclaimed so loudly in public in connection with the Pentagon Papers. If Watergate were truly as portentous or diabolical an event as Mr. Nixon's critics suggested, then there should have been no hesitation about restraining the publication of any material released from the findings of the burglars. But on the other hand, if the holding in the Pentagon Papers case was right, then the crime in the break-in at Watergate could be severed from any sense of a deeper moral wrong. It could be understood, far more narrowly, as the problem of a band of men breaking into a private office. It was simply another burglary.

In short, the combination of moral outrage over Watergate and a defense of the Pentagon Papers makes for an unstable moral mixture. In comparison, it is worth pointing out that a more distinctly moral perspective, applied in both cases, could preserve its coherence across the board. And so, for example, if there were, in that private office, plans for an assassination or a criminal project, the President might indeed have been justified in ordering a break-in into that private office, or securing a court order for the purpose of gaining access. Newspapers might indeed have been justified in publishing the news of wrongdoing unearthed in that way. Or, on the other side, if the project had been animated by a low motive throughout – if the object of the break-in was to discover evidence of personal scandal that could be used merely as the material for blackmail – then the law could well have been warranted in restraining the publication of this material, which the burglars would have no legitimate business in making public. The problem of coherence afflicts mainly those affable people who made of Watergate a premier crime, while trumpeting a victory for freedom in the case of the Pentagon Papers.

If my reading is correct, then a mistake had to come on one side of the problem for them. The clearer moral judgment is that the people shocked by Watergate were rightly shocked, that there had been a serious wrong in the break-in at the Watergate. In that case, their mistake was with the Pentagon Papers. If they had found their way to firm ground on the matter of Watergate – if they had become clear about the moral axioms that anchored their position in that case – they would have realized what was deeply problematic or wrong about the world of law that many of the same commentators and lawyers had willed into being with the Pentagon Papers case. Part of my purpose here has been to show that we cannot find that world of law tenable – not the world of publishing without moral restraints, marked by this curious new axiom: that "it may be wrong to do X," but I may have a "right nevertheless not to be restrained from doing X." As we recoil from a world governed by maxims of this kind, we begin acknowledging, in one place after another, just where it might be legitimate to restrain publications in advance. In his separate opinion in the Pentagon Papers case, Justice White offered a small inventory of such cases. In their precision and variety, they were quite enough, in themselves, to make the point:

- The Federal Trade Comission is empowered to issue "cease and desist" orders for certain forms of competition, regarded as unfair. And "such orders can, and quite often do, restrict what may be spoken or written."
- In a similar vein, the National Labor Relations Board routinely issues such cease-and-desist orders against employers, who may be found to have coerced or threatened their employees. To the extent that the threats are constituted by menacing or portentous words, those orders bar people from engaging any further in a kind of speech that has been judged already

as wrongful. (That is to say, the situation would contain virtually all of the ingredients that marked the character of the case in *Near v. Minnesota*. A series of publications or utterances have been found to be injurious and wrong, and people have been enjoined to stop producing more of the same thing.)

- And of course there was the defense of copyrights. The authority to protect copyrights was clearly granted to Congress and the federal government under the Constitution; and so, quite apart from the First Amendment, Congress was in fact given an authority to make laws that quite directly abridged the freedom to publish. For under federal law, newspapers or publishers could go into court and get an injunction that effectively barred other persons from publishing material that was protected by a copyright.[1]

In these parts of our "practical" experience, common sense suggested that restraints in advance would be quite reasonable. And as we are reminded of these cases, it just might occur to us that there was something wrong, even in "theory" or principle, with the decision in *New York Times v. United States*. But to realize what is wrong in principle with that scheme of laws suggested in *Near* and the Pentagon Papers is to begin freeing ourselves from the seduction of slogans masquerading as principles of justice. It may be a nice question of whether the imagination is guided by a sense of principle, or whether a certain moral sense or the moral imagination is stirred first by a vivid sense of real injuries at stake. For certain defenders of the First Amendment, there did not appear to be even a trace of awareness of how the experience of the Pentagon Papers might have looked to people who did not share their moral perspective. For someone like Richard Nixon, the episode seemed to confirm the weave of experience that enraged him throughout his political life, and confirmed for him this moral lesson: that the liberal Establishment would not be restrained by any sense of lawfulness in seeking its own advantage, or pursuing its own political ends. The Democrats had drawn the country into the war in Vietnam, and men at the highest level in the administration had continued to manage the war even as they were losing their moral conviction of its rightness.[2] But now, the political opposition to the war emanated from

---

[1] See Justice White in *New York Times v. United States*, 403 U.S. 713, at 731 n.1.

[2] That is the rather sad view that comes through Robert McNamara's memoir *In Retrospect: The Tragedy and Lessons of Vietnam* (New York: Times Books, 1995). But that account, written years later, contrasts sharply with the understanding in the air in 1965–66 in Washington. I was at that time nestled in a wing of the Democratic establishment as a Fellow at the Brookings Institution, coming out of the University of Chicago, where most of the senior faculty in political science were in support of the war. We Democrats had defeated Barry Goldwater a year earlier, in a decisive landslide; we were going on now to pass the Voting Rights Act and filling out the liberal agenda; and we were winning

the same set of people who had been tied to the Johnson administration. In pursuing their opposition to the war, they would not be restrained by the common laws of the country, and by the rules that they themselves had put into place. For Nixon, this must have seemed par for the course – but in spades. For he was well aware of the legends of the law used as a political weapon. In one notable case, Franklin Roosevelt had manipulated the IRS for the sake of hounding his opponent, Mo Annenberg, the father of Walter Annenbeg, and eventually getting Annenberg sent to jail. FDR would stir into action one of the largest investigations undertaken by the Treasury Department, with thirty-five investigators in the field. Mo Annenberg had been using his connections in Pennsylvania to threaten criminal prosecutions against the Democratic governor. FDR was prepared to counter that threat – and raise the stakes. As the President instructed his Secretary of the Treasury, "I want Mo Annenberg for dinner."[3] The stories had been widely circulated that John Kennedy and Lyndon Johnson had engaged in tapping the phones of their political opponents. And if Seymour Hersh's sources in the Mafia had spoken the truth, John Kennedy had the aid of the Mafia, in exertions that were not only useful, but possibly even decisive, in Illinois, West Virginia, and other places during the election of 1960.[4]

"our war" in Vietnam. The people most reserved about the war were the conservative Republicans, men like my friend Frank Waldrop, the retired editor of the McCormick-Patterson paper, the *Washington Herald*. Waldrop would say of the Vietnamese, "They want to go Communist, let them. They'll sink even faster." But we liberals were applying with conviction that doctrine that came out of the experience of the Second World War, with the repudiation of appeasement and isolationism. The reigning maxims came from John Donne (the famous Meditation XVII): "No man is an island entire of itself; every man is a piece of the continent, a part of the maine; . . . any man's death diminishes me, for I am involved in mankind; And therefore never send to know for whom the bell tolls; it tolls for thee." The loss of freedom anywhere in the world diminishes us all. We were vindicating the right of an Asian people to a "government by consent"; their right not to have imposed on them, by force of arms, a totalitarian regime. There was then, at least at that time, in liberal circles, a support for the war that ran beyond calculation of national interest, though the national interest was certainly engaged in the determination to resist the extension of Soviet power in Southeast Asia. But more than calculation of interest, the liberal position was touched, beyond anything else, by moral conviction. McNamara's sorry memoir was a reflection of how deeply that moral conviction had receded.

[3] Ted Morgan, *FDR: A Biography* (New York: Simon and Schuster, 1985), 554–55, 559. With investigations precisely focused and threatened in the same way, FDR managed to rid himself of the opposition, on the national airwaves, of that belligerent radio-priest, Fr. Coughlin. The prospect of an investigation, mingled apparently with other threats, apparently had its effect, and Fr. Coughlin was taken off the air.

[4] Seymour Hersh's account might be overdrawn, but the facts confirmed were damning enough. See Hersh, *The Dark Side of Camelot* (Boston: Little, Brown, 1997), pp. 13–34, 131–54.

I record this all now as one who had been, in 1960, a confirmed Nixon-basher, and a partisan of Kennedy. The seamier news about Kennedy would come out more fully in later years, especially in Seymour Hersh's book *The Dark Side of Camelot*. But much of it was known to Nixon at the time; indeed he was in the best position to know. Yet, with the case of the Pentagon Papers, he had no strictly political interests of his own at stake. The embarrassment of the case was focused entirely on the conduct of those "best and brightest" who had filled out the Kennedy and Johnson administrations. But Nixon understood the interest of the Executive in establishing control over the papers of the Executive. He appreciated the deep damage that would be done to American strength and his own bargaining power with leaders abroad if he let this move by the Establishment press go unchallenged. Of course, he might have known better, but even he must have been astonished when the Establishment refused to act in the style of an Establishment. The *Times* once understood that it was not only a newspaper, but the chief paper of record and journalistic leadership in a free republic and a regime of law. With that understanding of its corporate self, it made no sense to pursue its own interests in a way that damaged the interests, or safety, of that republic. But now, members of the Establishment seemed willing to throw over the restraints they had readily accepted in the past, either because they accepted the principle of restraint or because they had an interest in preserving, unimpaired, the institutions they counted on governing again when the seasons changed and the Republicans were cast from office.

In any case, Nixon could hardly be faulted if he professed to see now a liberal Establishment in exile, so inflamed by his presence that it would not abide any longer the usual legal or moral restraints, in pressing its opposition to him. Without excusing anything he would subsequently do, could one be surprised that someone who viewed the situation in that way might detach himself, in turn, from any exaggerated scruples about the restraints of the law? Or to put it even more strongly, why should he alone treat with reverence the rules that other presidents – and his own adversaries – had been so cavalier in disregarding?

But my purpose here is not to make a new defense of Richard Nixon in Watergate. As we say, sufficient unto the day are the evils thereof, and I have already spent this manuscript writing entirely against the current. I have sought to rehabilitate and defend *Lochner v. New York*, which seems to be condemned by commentators Left and Right, and to reject both *Near v. Minnesota* and the Pentagon Papers, where another consensus seems to have formed that the rulings in these cases are quite settled, beyond reproach, and certainly beyond overturning. But in writing and teaching about these cases over the years I've encountered this paradox: If there is anything more controversial than arguing in favor of cases long condemned, or resisting the consensus on cases long favored, it is making the case, seriously, for the institutions that everyone supposedly endorses. More troubling, or unhinging, to people than a defense of *Lochner*, or a criticism of the Pentagon Papers, is a defense of the American Founders and the Declaration of Independence. It must stand as the most curious reflection of our postmodern state of mind, but some of the people who trumpet the First Amendment and the case for rights of privacy, can be quite adamant also in rejecting the moral premises of the Founders, or the very ground on which the First Amendment and the Constitution were founded. As we know, it is quite out of fashion to speak, in the accents of the Founders, of certain self-evident moral "truths," grounded in "nature." In the academy, and in our politics, the faction most committed to "equality" finds itself rejecting the notion of "natural equality" as a moral truth. That is to say, it rejects the proposition that Lincoln called the "father of all moral principle" among us, "all men are created equal." Of course, the sounding of that aphorism may still elicit a glow, as a fuzzy, benign sentiment. But it is now considered rather unseemly to insist on its standing as a "truth." For by this time, the defense of privacy and sexual freedom has been identified with the rejection of moral truths. The impulse is understandable: It becomes easier to fend off restrictions on freedom if people come to accept the notion that there are no grounds for casting judgments on others or legislating over matters of right and wrong. But again, it must be one of the oddities peculiar to our own age; for it is hard to see how any cause of justice could ever be advanced when its votaries proclaim at the same time that nothing they are saying, about the things that are just or unjust, has any claim to be regarded as true.

That issue has been litigated at length elsewhere, and I have had, on that head, more than my say already. I have sought to approach here a different layer of the problem. I have suggested that even principles we seem to be utterly clear upon – such as the principles on "ex post facto laws" or "prior restraints" – may nevertheless be quite problematic. They yield up implications that, even now, may come as a surprise to us. But in that, as I have suggested, there is nothing the least novel: The moral life itself may involve the enduring surprise of confronting novel cases and discovering the further implications of our principles, implications that had previously gone unnoticed. If we open ourselves to these possibilities, and if we treat the matter as a puzzle, I have argued that we would find surprises of that kind lurking even in concepts we had thought long settled and confined in their meanings.

I have sought to unlock some of those implications here, and suggest that they give us some novel angles on matters of consequence in our current politics and law. They may lead us in a direction that was not suspected, and in doing that, they may illuminate parts of our legal landscape that have gone largely unnoticed.

But however we begin, the formula remains essentially the same: The task is to trace matters back to the root, to those first principles that anchor our judgments. Even writers who have been dubious about natural law and "first principles" will find themselves moving along these paths when they encounter novel cases – or cases that appear to them to be novel. I have sought to show here that the same discipline may be applied to doctrines that have become immured by now in conventions long settled, so that we hardly think they can deliver, any more, meanings unexpected. Yet the lesson, in its essential form, runs in this way: Beneath the layers of law, embedded now in custom, is a structure of moral argument and moral understandings. Those anchoring, first principles explain, at the root, the grounds of our judgments on the things that are right or wrong, just or unjust. If we can return to the root, with an inquiry that is distinctly philosophic, we can expect to tap again the deeper principles of the law; and in opening them anew, see again their fuller reach. At the end of the day, and the end of the exercise, we find ourselves, as we often do, confirming an older wisdom. We may merely remind ourselves of what that first generation of Americans managed to grasp when they said, in the Virginia Declaration of Rights, that "no free government, or the blessings of liberty, can be preserved to any people but by a firm adherence to justice, moderation, temperance, frugality, and virtue" – and "a frequent appeal to first principles."

Index

Breinigsville, PA USA
01 December 2010
250378BV00001B/1/P

9 780521 732086